THE COMFORT FOOD COOKBOOK
MACARONI & CHEESE
MEAT & POTATOES

JOAN SCHWARTZ

GRAMERCY BOOKS
NEW YORK

Originally published in two separate volumes by Villard under the titles:

Macaroni & Cheese copyright © 2001 by Joan Schwartz
Meat & Potatoes copyright © 2003 by Joan Schwartz

This edition contains the complete and unabridged texts of the original editions.

This 2006 edition is published by Gramercy Books, an imprint of Random House Value Publishing, by agreement with Villard, divisions of Random House, Inc., New York.

Gramercy Books is a registered trademark and the colophon is a trademark of Random house, Inc.

Random House
New York · Toronto · London · Sydney · Auckland
www.randomhouse.com

Printed and bound in the United States of America.

A catalog record for this title is available from the Library of Congress.

ISBN-13: 978-0-517-22824-1
ISBN-10: 0-517-22824-6

10   9   8   7   6   5   4   3   2   1

For my grandsons,

Aloni Schwartz and

Avery Gabriel Meer.

You light up my life.

Contents

MACARONI & CHEESE

1. INTRODUCING MAC AND CHEESE 1

2. THE CLASSIC DISHES 13

Marcaroni with Wisconsin Asiago MATTHEW KENNEY 15

London Mac and Cheese MITCHEL LONDON 17

Mac and Cheese Soho Grand JOHN DELUCIE 19

City Bakery Macaroni and Cheese ILENE ROSEN 21

Dad Page's Macaroni and Cheese BARBARA SHINN AND DAVID PAGE 23

Fairway Market Mac and Cheese MICHAEL O'NEILL 25

Baked Four-Cheese Pasta KEITH DRESSER 26

Chat n' Chew Macaroni and Cheese JOSÉ ARTURO MOLINA 28

Comfort Diner Mac and Cheese IRA FREEHOF 30

City Hall Mac and Cheese HENRY ARCHER MEER 32

Ten Minute Mac and Cheese WYLIE DUFRESNE 34

Simple Mac and Cheese for Two JOAN SCHWARTZ 35

Tomatoey Mac and Cheese MITCHELL DAVIS 36

Mom's Mac and Cheese with Tomatoes JOYCE WILDER 38

Queens (N.Y.) Mac and Cheese   LESLIE HOLLEY-MCKEN   39
Mac and Cheddar Salad   JOAN SCHWARTZ   41

3. INTERNATIONAL MAC 43

Rigatoni al Forno   ALAN TARDI   45
Orecchiette con Fonduta   MELISSA KELLY   47
Farfalle at Quattro Formaggi   DON PINTABONA   49
Wish Macaroni and Cheese   ANDREA CURTO   51
Mozzarella Mac   JOAN SCHWARTZ   53
Macaroni Gratin Mas Antoine   ANTOINE BOUTERIN   55
Macaroni and Cheese Provençal with Cod   GORDON HAMERSLEY   57
Greek (and Organic) Macaroni and Cheese   NORA POUILLON   59
Pastitsio   JAMES BOTSACOS   61
Macaroni and Feta Salad   JOAN SCHWARTZ   65
Macaroni and Manchego   ALLEN SUSSER   66
Swiss Mac with Potatoes   JOAN SCHWARTZ   67
Sweet Noodle and Cheese Kugel   JOAN SCHWARTZ   68

4. MAC AND CHEESE TODAY 71

Penne with Roquefort   WALDY MALOUF   73
Macaroni and Cheese Croquettes   ROCCO DISPIRITO   74
Farfalle with Fontina, Tasso Ham, and Baby Spinach   DEBRA PONZEK   76
Macaroni with Cantal Cheese and Westphalian Ham   CHARLIE PALMER   78
Macaroni and Cheese with Oysters and Pork Sausage   GORDON HAMERSLEY   80

Terrine of Macaroni, Goat Cheese, and Foie Gras   GORDON HAMERSLEY   82

Today's Macaroni and Cheese   RICK BAYLESS   84

Macaroni with Many Cheeses in a Red Chile-Herb Crust   KATY SPARKS   86

Green Chile Mac and Cheese   STEVEN PICKER   88

Mac and Smoked Cheddar with Ham and Chipotles   SCOTT CAMPBELL   90

Artie's Deli Mac and Cheese   JEFFREY BANK AND CHRIS METZ   92

Baked Macaroni with White Cheddar Cheese and Cremini Mushrooms   KEVIN JOHNSON   93

Macaroni with Duck Prosciutoo, Chanterelles, and Mascarpone   JANOS WILDER   95

Baked Cellentani with Four Cheeses, Prosciutto, Artichoke Hearts, and Portobellos
          LOREN FALSONE AND ERIC MOSHIER   97

Baked Stuffed Pasta Spirals   JODY ADAMS   100

Fontina and White Truffle Macaroni   ANDREW CARMELLINI   102

Pasta with Fonduta and Fresh Truffles   MARK FRANZ   104

ONEc.p.s. Wild Mushrooms and Truffle Macaroni and Cheese   DAVID BURKE   106

Baked Conchiglie with Roasted Garlic—Cheese Sauce, Ricotta Cheese, and White Truffle Oil
          BOBBY FLAY   108

California Truffled Macaroni and Cheese   TIM GOODELL   110

Chunks of Lobster Swimming in Cheesy Macaroni   ALEX PORTER   112

Joseph's Table Mac and Cheese with Dried Cherry Chutney and Roquefort Sauce
          JOSEPH WREDE   114

Sweetened Mascarpone and Noodle Pudding   LOREN FALSONE AND ERIC MOSHIER   117

SOURCES   119

ACKNOWLEDGMENTS   123

1. INTRODUCING MEAT AND POTATOES   124

ABOUT MEAT   127

ABOUT POTATOES   132

SOURCES   135

2. BEEF AND POTATOES

Grilled Rosemary-Marinated New York Strip Steak with Potato Gratin   NORA POUILLON   141

Grilled Filet Mignon with Tarragon Potato Salad, Beefsteak Tomatoes, and

       Mustard Vinaigrette   PHILIP MCGRATH   143

Grilled Shell Steak with Raclette Potato Pancakes   ANITA LO   145

Seared Rib-Eye Steak with Crisp and Creamy Potatoes   MITCHEL LONDON   148

Sliced Steak and Mushroom Salad with Caramelized Onions and Bacon-Rösti Potatoes

      CRAIG CUPANI   150

Bomboa's Braised Short Ribs with Mashed Boniatos and Gingered Baby Bok Choy

      FELINO SAMSON   153

Braised Short Ribs with Pan-Roasted Ruby Crescent Fingerlings

      DAN BARBER AND MICHAEL ANTHONY   156

Moroccan-Spiced Cassoulet   LAURA FRANKEL   158

Short Rib Shepherd's Pies with Borlotti Beans and Chive Potato Crust   HUGH ACHESON   160

Spicy Short Rib–Stuffed Potatoes   ANDREW DICATALDO   163

Beef Short Rib Hash with Sunny Eggs and Balsamic Syrup   DEBORAH STANTON   166

Roasted Beef Shanks with Vegetables and Potatoes   ARTHUR SCHWARTZ   169

Shepherd's Pie of Beef Shank Braised in Zinfandel   HENRY ARCHER MEER   171

Shepherd's Pie of Merlot-Braised Oxtail   JOHN SUNDSTROM   174

Braised Beef Cheeks with Fingerling Potato Purée   CYRIL RENAUD   178

Provençal Bouilli (Boiled Beef and Vegetables)   ANTOINE BOUTERIN   181

Boeuf Bourguignon   LEVANA KIRSCHENBAUM   183

Malaysian Beef Rendang with Sweet Potato–Coconut Purée   PATRICIA YEO   185

Meat Loaf Stuffed with Mashed Potatoes and Cheddar   MATTHEW KENNEY   187

Crispy Meat Loaf with Chanterelle-Buttermilk Gravy and Potato Gratin   RON CRISMON   189

Chiles Rellenos with Warm Mild Tomato Sauce   DIANA BARRIOS TREVIÑO   192

Potato Gnocchi with Ragù Bolognese   KEITH DRESSER   195

3. VEAL, MIXED MEATS, AND POTATOES

Veal Tournedos with Caramelized and Creamy Potatoes and Sautéed Apple Slices
LAURENT GRAS   200

Country-Style Veal Chops with Potatoes and Mushrooms   JOAN SCHWARTZ   203

Celery Seed–Crusted Veal Roast with Red Pepper–Potato Pancakes
ALLEN SUSSER   205

Veal Stew Baked with Gnocchi   WALTER POTENZA   207

Slow-Braised Veal and Vanilla Sweet Potato Shepherd's Pie   GERRY HAYDEN   210

Veal Croquettes with Dilled New Potatoes   JOAN SCHWARTZ   213

Baeckoefe (Alsatian Meat-and-Potato Casserole)   PHILIPPE BERTINEAU   215

La Svizzera (Italian-Style Hamburgers) with Prosciutto Mashed Potatoes
CARLA PELLEGRINO   217

4. LAMB, VENISON, AND POTATOES

Herb-Grilled Lamb Chops with Chanterelle and Potato Hash   JOHN SUNDSTROM   223

Lamb Chops Champvallon   JEAN-LOUIS GERIN   226

Indian-Spiced Rack of Lamb with Potato Tikki and Mint Yogurt   THOMAS JOHN   228

Potato-Crusted Lamb Cakes   DANIEL ANGERER   231

Roasted Leg of Lamb with Grandmother Jeannette's Truffled Mashed Potatoes
SANDRO GAMBA   234

Roasted Greek Leg of Lamb with Rustic Potatoes and Okra, Onion, and Tomato Stew
JIM BOTSACOS   237

Slow-Roasted Lamb Shoulder with Potatoes, Garlic, and Rosemary   MARK FRANZ   240

Chef Frank's Flavorful Lamb Stew   FRANK COE   242

Old-Fashioned Shepherd's Pie   JOAN SCHWARTZ   244

Lamb-Stuffed Potato Kubbeh   JOAN SCHWARTZ   246

Arrows' Leg of Venison with Roasted Yams   MARK GAIER AND CLARK FRASIER   248

5. PORK AND POTATOES

Brine-Marinated Pork Chops with Scallion-Smashed Potatoes and Grilled Granny Smith Apple Slices
        DEBORAH STANTON   253

New Mexican Rubbed Pork Tenderloin with Bourbon-Ancho Sauce and
        Roasted Garlic–Sweet Onion Potato Gratin   BOBBY FLAY   256

Sweet Potato–Stuffed Roulade of Pork   GLENN HARRIS   260

Split Pea, Ham, and Potato Soup   DEBRA PONZEK   263

Chorizo, Potato, and Goat Cheese Quesadillas   SUE TORRES   264

Dutch Stamppot   MAARTEN PINXTEREN   267

Bacon Lovers' Mashed Potatoes   ALEXANDRA GUARNASCHELLI   269

Tartiflette de Cocotte (Potato Gratin with Cheese and Bacon)   WILLIAM SNELL   271

Roasted New Potatoes with Bacon, Chive Flowers, and
        Green Tomato Dressing   ILENE ROSEN   273

CHEFS' BIOGRAPHIES   •   275

INDEX   •   303

MACARONI AND CHEESE

*T*his book began with an inspired suggestion from my agent, Stacey Glick, of Jane Dystel Literary Management. Thanks to Stacey for planting and nurturing the idea and to Jane, as always, for her support and wisdom.

I am grateful to my editor, Pamela Cannon, who fueled the creative process with her enthusiasm and expertise.

A star-studded cast of chefs (whose biographies comprise the last part of the book) contributed inspiration and hard work, along with consistent good cheer. To all, old friends and new, my boundless gratitude.

I am especially indebted to Eve Lindenblatt, who expertly tested the recipes and shared her insights, skill, and delight.

PART 1

Introducing Mac and Cheese

Macaroni and cheese is my kind of dish! For something so simple at heart, it is amazingly receptive to flights of fancy. It's fun to eat and it makes people happy—always. A good Mac is defined by top-quality ingredients far more than by the cook's experience or patience, and serving it will enhance your reputation as a savvy chef, caring spouse or parent, and intuitive host.

You may notice the use of superlatives throughout *Macaroni and Cheese.* The variations I have collected are sensational, awesome, seductive, wild, and, of course, supremely comforting. With Mac and Cheese, there are many world's-best recipes.

And there are very few losers in the genre. I was disappointed by a take-out portion from a food market (albeit a pricey food market) and didn't include the recipe here, but I ate every bit. It was not as good as some and that sent it to the bottom of my list; however, "bad" does not apply.

A savory, creamy, aromatic Mac is welcome as an entrée or side dish at brunch, lunch, or dinner; and sweet, puddinglike versions make great desserts. For the center of your buffet table, you couldn't do better than a gorgeous pastitsio, a multicolored terrine, or a sparkling pasta and cheese salad. Leftovers, if there are any, will rapidly disappear from the kitchen.

In assembling these recipes, I was struck over and over by the way gifted chefs approached the classic dish, respecting and changing it at the same time. All these classics and transformations start with pasta and cheese, but the results are original to each and every one.

We all grew up on macaroni and cheese and it seems that our ancestors may have done so, too, since pasta in some form was known to the ancient Greeks, Romans, and Etruscans. It was cooked in Sicily as early as the twelfth century, and Renaissance Italians enjoyed recipes that called for combining *maccheroni* with pecorino or caciocavallo cheese. Historian Stefano Milioni writes that eighteenth-century Neapolitans could stroll to the local inn and feast on a dish of macaroni with cheese for a tab of about two cents.

Pasta finally arrived in England in the eighteenth century, and from there, it soon made its way to our shores, where the early colonists prepared boiled noodles with a sort of cream and cheese sauce. Thomas Jefferson lent his considerable influence to the cause when he brought a pasta machine home from Italy in 1787 and began serving his guests at Monticello "Macaroni Pie," an early version of our very own beloved dish.

In our time, macaroni and cheese has proved itself an enduring favorite, and when we crave comfort foods, we welcome it as the most comforting of the lot. Moreover, the basic combination of cheese and pasta presents a blank slate for the imaginative cook—it offers both nostalgia and inspiration.

When you cook up this perfect union of contrasting flavors and textures, keep in mind two rules for success:

> Start with the best ingredients. Cheese determines the flavor of the dish, and pasta gives it a satisfying chewiness. Mediocre cheese and flabby pasta are not worth your time.

> Keep the ingredients in proportion so that each stands out. Too much cheese will overwhelm, while too much pasta will give you a heavy, dense concoction. If crumb topping is part of the recipe, sprinkle on just enough to add a touch of crispness to each mouthful; it will beautifully accent the contrasts.

Look for pasta made from durum semolina, a coarse-milled hard wheat that is high in gluten; it will be sturdy enough to hold up to the cooking that Mac and Cheese requires. The best pasta has been slowly dried and has a slightly rough surface to help absorb the sauce. It should taste good on its own, with a noticeable flavor of the fine wheat that it is made from. But poor-quality pastas, or those made from soft wheat, will be bland in flavor and mushy in texture, and they will reveal their inferiority as soon as they hit the boiling water and turn it cloudy. Chef Alan Tardi (Rigatoni al Forno) recommends artisanal pastas, preferably the Martelli, Rustichella, and Lattini brands, available at specialty shops or through the Internet (see Sources), with commercial Italian pastas such as De Cecco and Del Verde acceptable as second choices.

Americans overwhelmingly choose elbow macaroni for their Mac and Cheese, but any other short, tubular dried pasta can be used, as well as imaginative variations such as butterflies, seashells, and "little ears." Chef Jody Adams's Baked Stuffed Pasta Spirals is based upon sheets of fresh pasta, and my traditional Sweet Noodle and Cheese Kugel is made with egg noodles. Each shape and kind will absorb and contrast with the cheese in its own way, lending subtle variations of texture and chewiness.

These magic words describe pasta that is cooked until tender but still slightly "firm to the tooth." Chefs differ in their suggested cooking times, and package directions for each brand may vary a bit more. A good rule of thumb is to test for doneness after the shortest cooking time given: if instructions (from the chef or manufacturer) call for 8 to 10 minutes, pop a noodle in your mouth after 8 minutes—it should be al dente, or close to that state. Chefs Loren Falsone and Eric Moshier (Baked Cellentani with Four Cheeses, Prosciutto, Artichoke Hearts, and Portobellos) suggest that you stop cooking the pasta 1 minute earlier than the package directions require; and Mitchell Davis (Tomatoey Mac and Cheese) opts for 2 or 3 minutes less than the package directions. Ultimately, your own taste rules, and if you prefer pasta on the soft side, by all means go for a longer initial boil. Just remember that there may be more oven or stove-top time to come.

Cook pasta in a large pot of boiling water, about 6 quarts for 1 pound, with 1 tablespoon of salt. Don't cover the pot, and stir occasionally to make sure the pasta does not stick.

The generic "mac" or "macaroni" in the recipe titles refers to a specific shape in each recipe. Start with that shape and then experiment, if you like, using the options below. Four cups, or 1 pound, of dry pasta will yield 8 cups cooked; 1 pound of egg noodles will yield 7 cups cooked.

Bucatini:	long macaroni tubes
Cavatelli:	small, curly-edged shells
Cavatappi or elbow twists:	tubular corkscrew or spiral shapes
Cellentani:	ridged twisted tubes
Conchiglie:	conch shells
Baby shells:	small conchiglie
Ditali, ditalini, "thimbles":	short, smooth tubes
Ditali ligati:	tiny ditali
Egg noodles:	flat, long pasta made with eggs
Elbow macaroni:	short, curved tubes
Short macaroni:	small elbows
Farfalle:	butterflies or bow ties
Farfalline:	tiny farfalle
Fusilli:	corkscrews
Garganelli:	ridged egg pasta, rolled into thin tubes
Mezzani:	tubular, about 1¼ inches long; thicker than elbows
Orecchiette:	little ears
Pastina, "tiny dough":	very small five-pointed stars made with eggs
Penne:	quills, cut diagonally

Penne rigate:	ridged penne
Radiatore, "radiators":	small, ruffled, ridged tubes
Rigatoni:	1½-inch-wide ridged tubes
Mezza rigatoni:	smaller ridged tubes
Rotelle, "wagon wheels":	small wheel shapes
Rotini:	little corkscrews
Ziti, "bridegrooms":	straight-cut narrow tubes

CHEESES

Although the classic Mac and Cheese brings to mind the flavors of American and Cheddar cheeses, there are endless varieties that will melt beautifully to enrobe your pasta. They may be made from cow's, sheep's, or goat's milk; their flavors may be mild, savory, or sharp; and their textures may run the gamut from soft and semisoft to semihard and hard. Your choices are wide, but not limitless: Chef Katy Sparks (Macaroni with Many Cheeses in a Red Chile–Herb Crust) counsels that any overly aromatic type, such as Limburger, is best avoided.

While some chefs emphasize the flavor of one extraordinary cheese, such as Cheddar (John DeLucie, Mac and Cheese Soho Grand), Manchego (Allen Susser, Macaroni and Manchego), American (Wylie DuFresne, Ten-Minute Mac and Cheese), or Roquefort (Waldy Malouf, Penne with Roquefort), others combine a mild and a sharp, such as Gruyère and Cheddar (Ilene Rosen, City Bakery Macaroni and Cheese). Still others build on a variety of flavors, such as robiola, Taleggio, fontina, and Gorgonzola (Don Pintabona, Farfalle al Quattro Formaggi), or Cheddar, Asiago, and fontina (Keith Dresser, Baked Four-Cheese Pasta). Many of the baked dishes are topped with a grated hard cheese such as Parmesan.

A WORD ABOUT PARMESAN: You will find that both the generic cheese and the superior Parmigiano-Reggiano are called for in these recipes. You won't go wrong using the best you can find and grating it fresh.

Determining amounts: Each ¹/₄ pound of hard cheese, such as Cheddar or Parmigiano-Reggiano, will yield about 1 cup grated. Each ¹/₄ pound of softer cheese, such as Swiss, will yield about

1 cup shredded. Each $1/4$ pound of Roquefort will yield about 1 cup crumbled. Each $1/2$ pound of ricotta or cottage cheese equals 1 cup.

The following cheeses may be used in our recipes:

American:	pasteurized processed cow's milk cheese; excellent for melting
Appenzeller:	cow's milk; tangy
Asiago (Italy):	aged, semisoft cow's milk; mild, sweet flavor; loose texture; irregular holes
Asiago (Wisconsin):	cow's milk; hard cheese; mildly tangy flavor
Bel Paese:	cow's milk; mild, semisoft; excellent melting cheese
Blue cheese:	cow's or sheep's milk; aromatic and often strongly flavored; blue or green veins
Brie:	cow's milk; soft-ripened, creamy, tangy; soft, edible rind
Cabrales:	mixed cow's, goat's, and sheep's milk; creamy semisoft blue cheese with peppery, not overly salty flavor
Caciocavallo:	cow's milk; mild, a bit salty; firm texture when young; when aged, stronger flavor and good for grating
Camembert:	cow's milk; mild, rich, creamy, soft-ripened; soft, edible rind
Cantal:	cow's milk; smooth, semifirm texture; mellow flavor
Cheddar:	cow's milk; firm texture; white to pale yellow or yellow-orange; can be mild, sharp, or extra-sharp, depending upon how long it is aged
Chèvre:	goat's milk; soft, flaky; white rind; mild flavor that gets sharper with age
Comté:	cow's milk; hard but creamy; sweet and piquant flavor; similar to Gruyère

Cottage:	cow's milk; creamy, moist curds; mild flavor
Cream cheese:	cow's milk; smooth, spreadable; mild flavor
Dry Jack:	see Monterey Jack
Emmentaler:	cow's milk; mild, nutlike flavor; firm texture; holes
Feta:	sheep's or goat's milk; soft, rindless; white, salty, tangy
Fontina:	semifirm; rich, nutty flavor; pale gold; small holes
Gorgonzola:	cow's milk; rich, savory, pungent; blue-green veins
Gorgonzola Dolce, Dolcelatte:	cow's milk; soft and melting, sweet; blue veins
Gouda:	cow's milk; semihard; smooth and buttery
Grana Padano:	partially skimmed cow's milk; sharp flavor; granular quality; ideal for grating
Gruyère:	cow's milk; hard or semihard Swiss, with small holes; nutlike flavor; classic for cooking and melting
Kashkaval:	sheep's milk; firm, mildly olivelike flavor
Kasseri:	sheep's milk, semihard; mild flavor, salted with brine and aged six months
Kefalotyri:	sheep's milk; pale yellow; hard, mildly salty; good for grating; similar to pecorino
Manchego:	sheep's milk, semifirm; mild, slightly salty, nutlike flavor
Mascarpone:	cow's milk; double cream; rich, buttery, similar to cream cheese
Monterey Jack:	cow's milk; distant relative of Cheddar. Unaged has mild flavor; semisoft texture. Aged, or dry (Dry Jack), has firm texture; sharp flavor; good for grating.
Mozzarella:	cow's milk, made from stretched curds; milky flavor and color; soft, perfect for melting
Parmesan:	cow's milk; hard; perfect for grating

Parmigiano-Reggiano:	cow's milk; complex nutlike flavor; perfect for grating. Strictly controlled, it can be made only from April through November and must be aged for eighteen months.
Pecorino:	sheep's milk; tangy, peppery; hard, granular, perfect for grating
Raclette:	cow's milk; nutlike flavor; semifirm texture with small holes
Ricotta:	sheep's milk; fresh, slightly salty, soft curds; similar in texture to cottage cheese
Robiola:	cow's milk; fresh, mild and creamy; aged, nutlike, pungent
Roquefort:	sheep's milk; rich, pungent; blue veins
Swiss:	cow's milk; nutlike flavor; firm texture; large holes
Taleggio:	cow's milk; pungent, meaty, nutty, slightly salty, soft-ripened, runny, fruit nuances
Velveeta:	pasteurized prepared cheese product, good for melting

A FINAL NOTE: The major cheese manufacturers have come to the aid of Mac and Cheese lovers in a hurry. For spur-of-the-moment Macs, sealed bags of grated Cheddar, Swiss, and mixed cheeses are available in the dairy case of your supermarket or health food store, usually in 2-cup sizes. They can't be beaten for efficiency, and their quality is equal to that of other packaged cheeses.

CRISP TOPPINGS

Crumbs of some sort provide a textural counterpoint in baked Mac and Cheese and round off the dish perfectly. Every mouthful should have a bit of delicious crunch. To enhance browning, you may place the finished Mac under the broiler briefly, but watch carefully—toppings can burn fast.

FRESH BREAD CRUMBS: **Make them in your food processor or blender, using slightly dry or day-old bread. One slice yields about $1/2$ cup of coarse crumbs. If you dry the bread first in a low oven, 1 slice will yield about $1/4$ cup of fine crumbs.**

TOASTED BREAD CRUMBS: **Spread fresh bread crumbs evenly on a baking sheet and toast in a 300°F oven for about 15 minutes.**

SEASONED BREAD CRUMBS: **Toss each cup of bread crumbs with $1/2$ teaspoon salt and a few grindings of pepper. You may purchase Italian seasoned crumbs or add dried oregano and basil to taste to your own toasted crumbs.**

PANKO: **Large, coarse, irregular-size Japanese bread crumbs, available in many supermarkets and Asian markets.**

CORN BREAD CRUMBS: **Make them in your food processor or blender from your favorite homemade or purchased corn bread. Use fresh, or toast as you would regular bread crumbs.**

TORTILLA CRUMBS: **Process tortilla chips in the food processor or blender. Fourteen to 15 tortilla chips will yield about 3 cups of crumbs.**

CRACKER CRUMBS: **Seven to 10 Ritz or similar crackers will yield $1/4$ to $1/3$ cup of crumbs.**

BÉCHAMEL

Although traditional Mac and Cheese depends on just that—macaroni and cheese (see, for example, Wylie DuFresne, Ten-Minute Mac and Cheese; Henry Archer Meer, City Hall Mac and Cheese; Allen Susser, Macaroni and Manchego)—many recipes will have you stir the cheese into a silken béchamel before combining it with the noodles. This smooth white sauce is made quickly by melting butter and whisking in flour and milk, but you will see that each chef provides his or her own spin on both ingredients and method (Kevin Johnson, for example, makes his sauce with canola oil, for Baked Macaroni with White

Cheddar Cheese and Cremini Mushrooms). It's worthwhile to follow their recipes; you will become a béchamel expert in a very short time.

The general rule, of course, is to use a pan or baking dish large enough to hold the macaroni and cheese mixture comfortably; it may be deep or shallow, depending upon the chef's directions or your preference. The sizes I give are approximate. You may also use individual gratin dishes or ramekins, usually six to eight per pound of pasta.

For 1 to $1^1/_2$ pounds of macaroni, use a 9 by 13-inch pan that holds 15 cups; or a 3- to $3^1/_2$-quart deep baking dish.

For $^1/_2$ pound of macaroni, use an 8 by 8-inch pan that holds 8 cups; or a 9 by 9-inch pan that holds 10 cups.

Please remember these rules, which apply to all our recipes.

> Butter is always unsalted.
> Flour is always all-purpose, unless another type (such as Wondra) is specified.
> Eggs are always large.
> Milk is always whole, unless evaporated milk is specified.
> Salt is always kosher or coarse.
> Pepper is always freshly ground or cracked; black unless otherwise specified.

PART 2

The Classic Dish

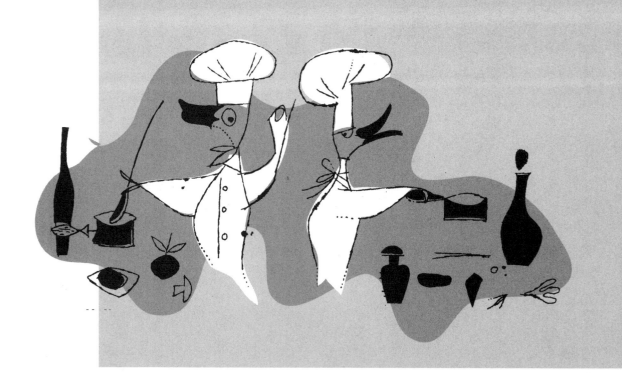

When you find yourself daydreaming about Mac and Cheese, chances are it will be one of the versions offered in this chapter. These are traditional American recipes relying on the primary ingredients: pasta, familiar cheeses, and perhaps tomatoes or onions. This is the place to do your Mac and Cheese research, as it features crisp-crusted baked versions as well as a creamy one quickly made on the stovetop and helps you to master béchamel—the cheese-infused white sauce—or to forgo it entirely.

Here are the versions we know best as pure comfort food, easily put together and guaranteed to satisfy. Creations by Matthew Kenney, Mitchel London, John DeLucie, Ilene Rosen, Barbara Shinn and David Page, Fairway Market's Michael O'Neill, Keith Dresser, José Arturo Molina, and Ira Freehof (of Comfort Diner fame) are luxurious cheese and béchamel combinations that characterize the Macs of our dreams. Think rich, creamy, smooth, cheesy, chewy, savory, and mouthwatering.

They are followed by some kitchen treasures that combine cheese and pasta without the extra step of making a béchamel (some say they are the purest versions). Henry Archer Meer's City Hall Mac and Cheese is simple and sophisticated; Wylie DuFresne's Ten-Minute Mac and Cheese relies on that palate pleaser, American cheese, in a magically quick stovetop dish; and my Simple Mac and Cheese for Two requires minimal time. Memory speaks in Mitchell Davis's Tomatoey Mac and Cheese and Joyce Wilder's Mom's Mac and Cheese with Tomatoes (both come to us courtesy of actual moms); while Leslie Holley-McKen takes us back to the Queens of her childhood, where macaroni and cheese was a special Sunday-night treat.

Mac and Cheddar Salad will help you cool down without forgetting your roots, although it is not quite as traditional as some of the other dishes here. Heaped in a sparkling crystal bowl and glittering with chunks of colorful, crisp vegetables and fresh cheese, it makes a beautiful addition to a summer party. (For a Greek macaroni salad with feta cheese, see Part 3.)

That's the starting lineup, so don't wait any longer—pick a Mac (or several) and dig in!

Macaroni with Wisconsin Asiago

MAKES 6 SERVINGS

Mild, slightly tangy Wisconsin Asiago is a cheese of excellent quality, and it adds special flavor and character to this dish. The creamy combination of Asiago and Cheddar is a favorite at Matthew's ultrastylish yet homey New York restaurant, Canteen.

7 tablespoons butter, plus extra for the gratin dishes	Freshly ground pepper
1 pound cavatelli	2 cups (1/2 pound) grated aged Wisconsin Asiago cheese
1/4 cup plus 2 tablespoons flour	1 cup (1/4 pound) grated sharp white Cheddar cheese
1 quart whole milk	1 1/3 cups (about 5 1/2 ounces) grated Parmigiano-Reggiano cheese
2 teaspoons dry mustard	3/4 cup coarsely chopped flat-leaf parsley
1/8 teaspoon cayenne pepper	1/3 cup minced fresh chives
Dash of Tabasco	1 cup panko (Japanese bread crumbs)
1 tablespoon Worcestershire sauce	
Kosher salt	

1. Preheat the oven to 350°F. Butter six individual gratin dishes.

2. Bring a large pot of salted water to a boil over high heat and cook the pasta until al dente, 10 to 12 minutes. Drain and cool.

3. In a medium saucepan over moderately low heat, melt 6 tablespoons of the butter. Add the flour and cook, stirring, 3 minutes. Whisk in the milk and raise the heat to high. When the milk begins to

boil, reduce the heat to medium and cook, whisking occasionally, until thickened. Add the mustard, cayenne, Tabasco, and Worcestershire and season with salt and pepper.

4. In a large bowl, toss together the pasta, sauce, Asiago, Cheddar, 1 cup of the Parmigiano-Reggiano, the parsley, and chives. Spoon into the buttered gratin dishes. Mix together the bread crumbs and the remaining Parmigiano-Reggiano and sprinkle over the pasta. Dot lightly with the remaining butter and bake on the middle shelf until the crumbs are lightly browned and the sauce is bubbling, 25 to 30 minutes.

London Mac and Cheese

The creations from Mitchel London Foods always have unique richness and depth of flavor. Mitchel is happy to share his macaroni and cheese secrets.

TO MAKE PERFECT BÉCHAMEL: After mixing butter and flour over medium heat to make the roux, remove the pan from the heat and add hot milk all at once, whisking so there are no lumps. Always add hot milk to hot roux.

FOR THE TOMATO TOPPING VARIATION: Never use sun-dried tomatoes—they will be all you can taste. Instead, use fresh plum tomatoes, roasted at a very low temperature to concentrate their flavor but retain their texture and subtlety.

FOR THE BREAD CRUMBS: Use only fresh crumbs for the best texture.

3 cups (³/₄ pound) grated white sharp Cheddar cheese	6 tablespoons flour
1 cup (¹/₄ pound) grated Parmigiano-Reggiano cheese, or substitute Grana Padano or pecorino cheese	¹/₂ teaspoon cayenne pepper
	Small pinch of freshly grated nutmeg
1 pound ziti, penne, or short macaroni	Kosher salt
	Freshly ground white pepper
3³/₄ cups whole milk	¹/₂ cup heavy cream
8 tablespoons butter, plus extra for the baking dish	¹/₂ cup fresh bread crumbs

1. Preheat the oven to 350°F. In a mixing bowl, combine the two cheeses and reserve.

2. Bring a large pot of salted water to a boil over high heat and cook the pasta until al dente, 10 to 12 minutes. Drain and place in a mixing bowl.

3. In a small saucepan over medium-high heat, bring the milk to a simmer.

4. In a large saucepan over medium heat, melt the butter; when it starts to bubble, whisk in the flour. Cook, stirring, for 5 to 6 minutes and then remove from the heat (this is the roux). Whisk in the hot milk all at once. Add the cayenne, nutmeg, and salt and pepper to taste. Return the mixture to high heat and cook, stirring, until it comes to a boil and thickens, 2 to 3 minutes.

5. Reduce the heat to low. Add 2 cups of the combined cheeses to the milk mixture and cook, stirring, until the cheeses have melted completely. Pour the sauce over the pasta in the bowl and mix lightly.

6. Lightly butter a $3^1/_2$-quart deep baking dish and sprinkle $1/_2$ cup of the combined cheeses over the bottom. Cover with one third of the pasta and one third of the remaining cheese. Repeat the layers twice, ending with a layer of cheese. Pour the cream over all, and sprinkle with the bread crumbs. Place on the middle shelf of the oven and bake until the macaroni is bubbling and the crumbs are golden brown, about 30 minutes.

VARIATION: Pour on the cream, top with a layer of oven-roasted tomatoes, and sprinkle with the bread crumbs. Bake as usual.

TO ROAST THE TOMATOES

6 to 8 plum tomatoes, halved
Olive oil for greasing the baking sheet and drizzling over the tomatoes
Kosher salt
Freshly ground pepper

Four to 6 hours before you will use the tomatoes, preheat the oven to 250°F. Arrange the tomatoes cut side up on a lightly oiled baking sheet, sprinkle with salt and pepper, and drizzle with olive oil. Roast until they are dried but still soft, 4 to 6 hours, depending upon their size (smaller tomatoes will take less time).

Mac and Cheese Soho Grand

MAKES 4 SERVINGS

A respected food writer chatting on-line about Mac and Cheese revealed: "The best I've had anywhere is in the restaurant in New York's Soho Grand Hotel." Here is the recipe, tracked down for you!

Chef DeLucie's advice: All ingredients should be the best you can buy—especially the Cheddar.

½ pound cavatappi, or substitute any short, curved pasta	2 teaspoons Dijon mustard
2 cups whole milk	⅛ teaspoon freshly grated nutmeg
2 tablespoons butter, plus extra for the pan	Dash of Tabasco
1 cup (½ to ⅔ pound) finely diced onion	Kosher salt
2 tablespoons flour	Freshly ground pepper
2 cups (½ pound) grated sharp Cheddar cheese, 2 tablespoons reserved	2 tablespoons grated Parmesan cheese

1. Bring a large pot of salted water to a boil over high heat and cook the pasta until al dente, 8 to 10 minutes. Drain and place in a mixing bowl.

2. Preheat the oven to 350°F. In a small saucepan over medium heat, scald the milk.

3. In a sauté pan over medium-high heat, melt the butter and cook the onion until soft and fragrant but not colored, about 3 minutes. Reduce the heat to low, add the flour, and cook, stirring, about 3 minutes. Whisk in the scalded milk, 2 cups of the Cheddar, the mustard, nutmeg, and Tabasco. Keep-

ing it over low heat, simmer, whisking occasionally, until the cheese is melted and smooth. Taste, and season with salt and pepper, if needed. Pour the mixture over the pasta and mix well.

4. Spoon the cavatappi mixture into a lightly buttered 2-quart gratin dish and sprinkle with the reserved 2 tablespoons of Cheddar and the Parmesan. Bake on the middle shelf until bubbling and browned on top, 25 to 30 minutes, and serve immediately.

City Bakery Macaroni and Cheese

MAKES 4 TO 6 SERVINGS

The trick is in the proportions of crisp topping, creamy sauce, and smooth pasta—and Chef Rosen gets it exactly right. She advises that you have some freedom in choosing your pan: just remember that a large, flat pan will give you a greater area of crumb topping than a small, deep one.

6 tablespoons butter, plus extra for the baking dish	Kosher salt
¼ cup corn bread crumbs (or more, depending upon pan size)	Freshly ground pepper
	1¼ cups (5 ounces) grated Gruyère cheese
1 pound elbow macaroni	1¼ cups (5 ounces) grated mild white Cheddar cheese
1 quart whole milk	1¼ cups (5 ounces) grated Grana Padano or Parmesan cheese
6 tablespoons flour	

1. Preheat the oven to 350°F. Lightly butter a 3½-quart deep baking dish or a 9 by 13-inch baking pan.

2. Spread the crumbs in a single layer on a baking sheet and bake until golden brown, 10 to 15 minutes. Set aside.

3. Bring a large pot of salted water to a boil and cook the macaroni until al dente, 8 to 10 minutes. Drain and place in a large bowl. (To prepare up to a day ahead, mix in a small amount of canola oil, cover with plastic wrap, and refrigerate until ready to use.)

4. Bring the milk to a simmer in a small saucepan over medium-high heat.

5. In a medium saucepan over medium-low heat, melt the 6 tablespoons of butter, add the flour, and mix well with a wooden spoon or spatula. Cook, stirring, for 3 minutes. Whisk in the hot milk and

continue whisking until smooth. Raise the heat to medium and cook, stirring continuously, until the mixture thickens enough to coat the spoon. Season with salt and pepper and strain through a fine strainer.

6. Add the sauce to the cooked macaroni. Add 1 cup each of the Gruyère, Cheddar, and Grana Padano and mix well. Taste, and season with salt and pepper if necessary.

7. Pour the macaroni mixture into the baking dish and sprinkle with the remaining cheese. (At this point, the macaroni and cheese may be cooled on the counter, covered, and refrigerated for one day. Before proceeding, preheat the oven to 350°F.)

8. Sprinkle the toasted corn bread crumbs evenly over the casserole and cover with foil. Bake on the middle shelf until heated through, about 20 minutes; remove the foil and continue baking until the top is golden brown, an additional 10 minutes. Allow to stand for 10 minutes before serving.

Food for the Family

Dad Page's Macaroni and Cheese

MAKES 2 TO 4 SERVINGS

Barbara and David, the guiding spirits of Home Restaurant and Shinn Vineyard, like to keep their macaroni and cheese similar to the childhood dish that inspires many happy memories. With the sweet underlying flavors of onion and garlic and the freshness of herbs, this is a true classic.

4 tablespoons butter, plus extra for the pans	1 teaspoon freshly ground pepper
1 pound elbow macaroni	3/4 cup (3 ounces) grated extra-sharp Cheddar cheese
1 large (about 3/4 pound) yellow onion, cut into 1/8-inch dice	3/4 cup (3 ounces) grated Wisconsin Asiago cheese
1 tablespoon minced garlic	3/4 cup (3 ounces) grated Dry Jack cheese
3 tablespoons flour	2 plum tomatoes, sliced
4 cups whole milk	1/2 cup seasoned bread crumbs
1 teaspoon mild paprika	1 tablespoon chopped fresh parsley
1/2 teaspoon freshly grated nutmeg	1 tablespoon chopped fresh thyme
2 teaspoons kosher salt	1 tablespoon chopped fresh chives

1. Preheat the oven to 400°F. Butter two 6-inch cast-iron skillets or one 12-inch skillet.
2. Bring a large pot of salted water to a boil over high heat and cook the macaroni until al dente, 8 to 10 minutes. Drain and place in a large bowl.
3. Melt the 4 tablespoons of butter in a large pot over medium heat. Add the onion and garlic and cook until they are softened, about 2 minutes. Whisk in the flour and cook, stirring constantly, until the mixture turns light brown, about 3 minutes. Gradually whisk in the milk. Add the paprika, nutmeg,

salt, and pepper. Reduce the heat to low and cook, stirring, until the sauce is thickened, about 5 minutes. Add the cheeses and stir until they are melted. Add the macaroni and stir until the noodles are thoroughly coated. Remove from the heat.

4. Transfer the macaroni mixture to the buttered skillets. Top with the sliced tomatoes. Sprinkle the bread crumbs on top.

5. Bake until the cheese is bubbling and golden brown, about 30 minutes. Garnish with the chopped herbs.

Fairway Market Mac and Cheese

MAKES 6 TO 8 SERVINGS

The basic dish matures into upscale comfort food with the addition of Comté, a superlative Gruyère. A favorite of Fairway's cosmopolitan customers, it is creamy and fabulous.

2 tablespoons butter, plus extra for the pan	2 cups (1/2 pound) shredded French Comté cheese
1 pound elbow macaroni (preferably De Cecco)	Kosher salt
2 tablespoons flour	Freshly ground white pepper
3 cups half-and-half	2 tablespoons plain bread crumbs
4 cups (1 pound) shredded extra-sharp Wisconsin Cheddar cheese	

1. Preheat the oven to 350°F. Generously butter a 9 by 13-inch baking pan.

2. Bring a large pot of salted water to a boil over high heat and cook the macaroni until al dente, 8 to 10 minutes. Drain and place in a large bowl.

3. In a large pot over medium heat, melt the 2 tablespoons of butter. Whisk in the flour, mixing well so there are no lumps. Slowly whisk in the half-and-half, raise the heat to medium-high, and bring the mixture to a boil. Add the cheeses, reduce the heat to medium, and whisk well to incorporate. Season with salt and pepper.

4. Add the sauce to the macaroni and mix well to combine.

5. Transfer the macaroni mixture to the baking pan and sprinkle with the bread crumbs. Bake for 20 to 25 minutes, until bubbly and golden.

Baked Four-Cheese Pasta

MAKES 4 TO 6 SERVINGS

Even before your first taste, you can tell just by the creaminess of the sauce how rich and delicious this will be. Keith advises us that this dish will taste best with freshly grated cheeses—especially Vermont Cheddar.

Bake the mixture in a deep casserole because it can easily boil over. If you decide to use a shallow pan, put it on a foil-lined baking sheet.

8 tablespoons butter, plus extra for the baking dish	2 cups ($1/2$ pound) grated sharp Cheddar cheese
1 pound penne	2 cups ($1/2$ pound) grated Asiago cheese
4 cups whole milk	2 cups ($1/2$ pound) grated fontina cheese
6 tablespoons flour	1 cup plain bread crumbs
$1^1/2$ teaspoons kosher salt	$1/2$ cup (2 ounces) grated Parmesan cheese
$1/4$ teaspoon cayenne pepper	2 tablespoons butter, melted
	1 cup heavy cream

1. Preheat the oven to 350°F. Butter a 9 by 13-inch baking dish or $2^1/2$-quart casserole.

2. Bring 6 quarts of salted water to a boil. Add the pasta and cook, stirring occasionally, until al dente, 10 to 12 minutes. Drain the pasta and rinse with cold water. Drain again and place in a large bowl.

3. In a medium saucepan over medium heat, bring the milk to a boil. Remove from the heat.

4. In a medium, heavy-bottomed saucepan over medium-high heat, melt the 8 tablespoons of butter. Reduce the heat to low and whisk in the flour, cooking for 3 to 4 minutes. Be careful not to brown

the mixture. Slowly add the hot milk, whisking constantly (constant whisking will ensure that there are no lumps). Add the salt and cayenne, raise the heat to medium, and simmer, stirring constantly, until the mixture has thickened, 8 to 10 minutes.

5. Remove from the heat and add 1 cup each of the grated Cheddar, Asiago, and fontina, whisking until the cheeses are melted. Pour the cheese sauce over the pasta, tossing to coat the pasta evenly.

6. Place half of the coated pasta in the buttered baking dish and distribute the remaining grated Cheddar, Asiago, and fontina over the top. Cover with the remaining pasta.

7. In a mixing bowl, toss together the bread crumbs, Parmesan, and melted butter. Pour the heavy cream over the pasta and evenly distribute the bread crumb mixture over the top. Bake on the middle shelf until the top is light brown and the mixture is bubbling, 30 to 35 minutes.

JOSÉ ARTURO MOLINA

Chat n' Chew Macaroni and Cheese

MAKES 6 TO 8 SERVINGS

Hearty and a bit spicy, this dish is a warming treat on a cold winter's evening. It is a favorite at Chat n' Chew, the comfortable downtown Manhattan restaurant where Chef Molina presides over the kitchen.

$\frac{1}{2}$ pound butter, plus extra for the baking dish	5 cups ($1\frac{1}{4}$ pounds) shredded sharp Cheddar cheese
$1\frac{1}{4}$ pounds elbow macaroni	8 slices American cheese, broken into small pieces
2 cups heavy cream	
2 cups whole milk	2 cups ($\frac{1}{2}$ pound) grated Parmesan cheese
1 small ($\frac{1}{4}$ to $\frac{1}{3}$ pound) onion, diced small (about $\frac{1}{2}$ cup)	3 tablespoons green Tabasco
	$\frac{1}{4}$ teaspoon ground cumin
4 cloves garlic, minced	Kosher salt
1 cup flour	Freshly ground pepper
	$\frac{1}{2}$ cup seasoned bread crumbs

1. Preheat the oven to 350°F. Lightly butter a 9 by 13 by 4-inch baking dish.
2. Bring a large pot of salted water to a boil over high heat and cook the macaroni until al dente, 8 to 10 minutes. Drain.
3. In a small bowl, combine the cream and milk.
4. In a large saucepan over medium heat, melt the $\frac{1}{2}$ pound of butter and cook the onion and garlic until the onion is translucent, about 6 minutes, stirring occasionally. Add the flour, stirring con-

stantly for 3 minutes. Add the cream mixture in a steady stream and whisk until smooth. Bring to a boil, stirring occasionally, 8 to 10 minutes.

5. Stir in 4 cups of the Cheddar, the American cheese, 1 cup of the grated Parmesan, the Tabasco, and cumin. Stir until all the cheese has melted; the sauce will be very thick and creamy. Season with salt and pepper.

6. Remove the sauce from the heat and stir in the pasta. Pour the mixture into the prepared baking dish. Sprinkle with the remaining Cheddar, then the Parmesan, and finally the bread crumbs.

7. Bake uncovered on the middle shelf for about 20 minutes, until bubbling and brown on top.

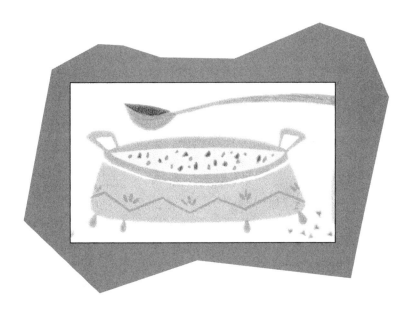

Comfort Diner Mac and Cheese

MAKES 6 SERVINGS

Ira Freehof developed this creamy, crusty Mac for his Comfort Diners in New York, and it has become one of their most popular dishes. At home as well, it offers a lot of contentment to kids and grown-ups alike.

4 tablespoons plus 1 teaspoon butter, plus extra for the baking dish	1 cup (¼ pound) lightly packed grated Italian fontina cheese
1 pound elbow macaroni	Kosher salt
1 tablespoon olive oil or vegetable oil	½ teaspoon freshly ground pepper
3½ cups whole milk	2½ teaspoons Dijon mustard
¼ cup flour	1 cup (¼ pound) shredded Cheddar cheese
1 cup (¼ pound) lightly packed grated American cheese	½ cup fresh bread crumbs

1. Preheat the oven to 375°F. Butter a 9-inch square baking dish.
2. Bring a large pot of salted water to a boil over high heat and cook the macaroni until al dente, 8 to 10 minutes. Drain and rinse with cool water. Place in a large mixing bowl and drizzle with the oil.
3. In a small saucepan over medium-high heat, warm the milk.
4. In a large saucepan over medium-low heat, melt 4 tablespoons of the butter. Sprinkle in the flour and whisk constantly until the flour is absorbed and the mixture is bubbling gently and lightly golden, 2 to 3 minutes. Gradually add the warm milk, whisking continuously. Raise the heat to medium and bring to a simmer, stirring with a wooden spoon until smooth and slightly thickened.

5. Add the American cheese and fontina and remove the pot from the heat. Whisk the mixture until the cheese is almost completely melted; stir in the salt, pepper, and mustard. Pour the sauce over the macaroni and stir to combine. Transfer to the prepared baking dish.

6. In a small bowl, combine the shredded Cheddar and the bread crumbs, and sprinkle evenly over the macaroni. Cut the remaining teaspoon of butter into small bits and dot the casserole. Bake on the middle shelf until bubbling and a crust begins to form, 20 to 25 minutes.

City Hall Mac and Cheese

MAKES 6 TO 8 SERVINGS

American and Monterey Jack cheeses melt beautifully and give a home-style feeling to this elegant dish. The sauce, based on heavy cream and milk, is thick and rich with a hint of spiciness. Try Chef Meer's Mac on its own or as a savory accompaniment to perfectly grilled steaks, as it is served at City Hall, his Manhattan restaurant.

Butter for the pan	1⅓ cups (about ⅓ pound) grated Monterey Jack cheese
1 pound penne rigate	Kosher salt
2 cups heavy cream	Freshly ground pepper
2 cups whole milk	½ cup panko (Japanese bread crumbs)
½ teaspoon cayenne pepper	2 teaspoons chopped fresh parsley
¼ teaspoon freshly grated nutmeg	2 teaspoons grated Parmesan cheese
2 cups (½ pound) grated American cheese	

1. Preheat the oven to 350°F. Butter a 9 by 13-inch baking pan.

2. Bring 6 quarts of salted water to a boil. Add the pasta and cook, stirring occasionally, until al dente, 9 to 10 minutes. Drain.

3. Combine the cream, milk, cayenne, and nutmeg in a large saucepan over medium-high heat and reduce by half, about 15 minutes. (Once the mixture starts to simmer, stir to break the layer of foam so that it will not boil over.) Reduce the heat to medium-low, add the American and Monterey Jack cheeses, and whisk until well blended. Season with salt and pepper.

4. Add the penne and stir vigorously (taking care not to break the pasta)—this will release starch and help to thicken the sauce.

5. Pour or spoon the pasta into the baking dish. Combine the panko, parsley, and Parmesan and sprinkle over the pasta. Bake until bubbly and golden, approximately 15 minutes.

W Y L I E   D u F R E S N E

Ten-Minute Mac and Cheese

MAKES 3 OR 4 SERVINGS

Well, maybe eleven—the time depends entirely upon how long the pasta cooks. Start the cheese sauce when you put the water on to boil and it will be ready by the time the pasta is done; then combine the mezzani and sauce and ladle your creamy Mac into deep bowls. Macaroni and cheese out of a box takes longer!

Chef DuFresne, who is a purist when it comes to Mac and Cheese, prepares this minimalist classic at his downtown New York restaurant, 71 Clinton Fresh Food. He doesn't recommend adding any salt, pepper, or spices, letting the pristine flavor of American cheese carry the dish.

1/2 pound mezzani, or substitute penne or shells	5 teaspoons cornstarch
2 cups whole milk	2 tablespoons warm water
15 slices American cheese, broken into small pieces	1/4 cup toasted bread crumbs

1. Bring 4 quarts of salted water to a boil over high heat. Add the pasta and cook until al dente, 10 to 13 minutes.

2. Meanwhile, in a large saucepan over medium-high heat, bring the milk to a boil. Whisk in the cheese, lower the heat to medium, and cook until completely melted.

3. In a small bowl or cup, dissolve the cornstarch in the water and whisk it into the milk mixture; raise the heat to medium-high and bring the mixture to a boil, whisking occasionally. Remove from the heat and continue whisking until thickened slightly.

4. When the pasta is cooked, drain it well and pour it into the pot with the sauce, stirring to combine. Divide among three or four serving bowls, sprinkle with the toasted bread crumbs, and serve.

Simple Mac and Cheese for Two

MAKES 2 SERVINGS

Easy! Quick! Painless! This is a good basic Mac. Don't expect the cheese to melt before baking—it doesn't have to.

Butter for the ramekins	Kosher salt
1 cup penne	Freshly ground pepper
1 cup half-and-half	2 tablespoons grated Parmigiano-Reggiano cheese
1 cup (¼ pound) grated Cheddar cheese	
Dash of Tabasco	

1. Preheat the oven to 350°F. Butter two 1-cup ovenproof ramekins or small baking dishes.
2. Bring a medium pot of salted water to a boil over high heat and cook the pasta until al dente, 10 to 12 minutes. Drain.
3. In a medium bowl, combine the half-and-half, Cheddar, and penne and season to taste with Tabasco, salt, and pepper. Pour into the prepared ramekins and sprinkle with the Parmigiano-Reggiano. Bake on the middle shelf until set, 15 to 20 minutes. Let rest for 5 minutes before serving.

Tomatoey Mac and Cheese

MAKES 4 TO 6 SERVINGS

This baked macaroni and cheese was a staple in the Davis family while Mitchell, now James Beard Foundation executive editor and publisher, was growing up, and his mother still makes it when he comes home for dinner. Her secret is to use two kinds of Cheddar—extra-sharp and mild—and to cut it into cubes, rather than grate it.

For best results, assemble it the night before and let it sit in the fridge. That way, the noodles will absorb some of the tomato juice and the ingredients will meld together into a delicious whole.

1 pound penne	1 28-ounce can whole tomatoes, roughly chopped, with their juice
4 tablespoons butter, plus extra for the baking dish	2 tablespoons sugar
1/2 pound extra-sharp Cheddar cheese, cut into 1/2-inch cubes	Pinch of kosher salt
1/2 pound mild Cheddar cheese, cut into 1/2-inch cubes	Pinch of freshly ground pepper

1. Bring a large pot of salted water to a boil over high heat and cook the pasta until just al dente, 2 or 3 minutes less than the package directions. Drain in a colander but do not rinse.
2. Return the pasta to the pot and stir in the 4 tablespoons of butter. Add the cheeses, tomatoes, and

sugar, stir to combine, and season with the salt and pepper. Pour into a lightly buttered 2-quart rectangular baking dish (Pyrex works well). Pile high; it will hold. If you are finishing the casserole the following day, cover with plastic wrap and refrigerate overnight.

3. When you are ready to bake, preheat the oven to 375°F. Bake on the middle shelf until the top is brown and crisp and the casserole is bubbling, 40 to 45 minutes (if it has been refrigerated, cook a few minutes longer).

Mom's Mac and Cheese with Tomatoes

MAKES 4 TO 6 SERVINGS

Two recipes from the Wilder family illustrate Mac's wide range. This is the first, and it is perfectly simple and delicious (the second, Macaroni with Duck Prosciutto, Chanterelles, and Mascarpone, page 95, offers an adventurous, creative spin). According to Chef Janos Wilder, his mother Joyce's macaroni and cheese is "the world's best."

Butter for the baking dish	Kosher salt
1 pound elbow macaroni	Freshly ground pepper
1 28-ounce can whole peeled tomatoes, drained, coarsely chopped, and drained again	4 cups (1 pound) coarsely grated sharp Cheddar cheese

1. Preheat the oven to 375°F. Butter a 3-quart deep baking dish.
2. Bring a large pot of salted water to a boil over high heat and cook the pasta until al dente, 8 to 10 minutes. Drain.
3. In the baking dish, make a layer of macaroni, top with a layer of tomatoes, sprinkle lightly with salt and pepper, and top with a layer of Cheddar cheese. Repeat until all the ingredients are used, saving a few pieces of tomato to place on top of the casserole.
4. Bake on the middle shelf until browned, 40 to 45 minutes.

LESLIE HOLLEY-McKEN

Queens (N.Y.) Mac and Cheese

MAKES 4 TO 6 SERVINGS

No Sunday dinner was complete without macaroni and cheese, when New York caterer Leslie Holley-McKen was a child. In this version, based on a family recipe, the cheeses melt into a rich custardy base of evaporated milk, heavy cream, and egg, with mustard and Red Devil Sauce providing a piquant touch.

6 tablespoons butter, plus extra for the baking dish	½ pound Velveeta or American cheese, cut into ½-inch cubes
1 pound elbow macaroni	½ cup heavy cream
3 12-ounce cans evaporated milk	1 egg, lightly beaten
1 tablespoon Dijon mustard	Kosher salt
2 tablespoons Red Devil Sauce	Freshly ground pepper
4 cups (1 pound) coarsely grated sharp Cheddar cheese	1 cup panko (Japanese bread crumbs)

1. Preheat the oven to 350°F. Lightly butter a 3½-quart deep baking dish or a 9 by 13-inch baking pan.
2. Bring a large pot of salted water to a boil over high heat and cook the pasta until al dente, 8 to 10 minutes. Drain, pour into a large mixing bowl, and toss with 4 tablespoons of the butter.
3. In a small saucepan over medium heat, bring the evaporated milk to a scald and add it to the macaroni. Add the mustard, Red Devil Sauce, and Cheddar and stir well (the cheese should start to

melt). Add the Velveeta and cream and stir well. The macaroni and chunks of cheese should be swimming in the sauce. Add the egg and mix well. Season with salt, if needed, and plenty of pepper.

4. Pour into the prepared baking dish that has been placed on a sheet pan to catch spills (the baking dish will be completely full). Sprinkle with the panko and dot with the remaining 2 tablespoons of butter. Bake until golden brown and bubbling, 25 to 30 minutes.

JOAN SCHWARTZ

Mac and Cheddar Salad

MAKES 4 TO 6 SERVINGS

When you crave something cool, pasta salads are a refreshing take on our favorite combination of ingredients. This one is pure farmhouse kitchen.

½ pound elbow macaroni	1 stalk celery, thinly sliced
7 tablespoons olive oil	2 scallions, white and 2 inches of the green, thinly sliced
2 tablespoons fresh lemon juice or white wine vinegar	4 medium radishes, thinly sliced
Kosher salt	1 cup (¼ pound) shredded sharp Cheddar cheese, or substitute American cheese
Freshly ground pepper	
1 small red bell pepper, seeded and julienned	

1. Bring a large pot of salted water to a boil over high heat and cook the pasta until al dente, 8 to 10 minutes. Drain, place in a large salad bowl, and toss with 1 tablespoon of the olive oil. Let cool to room temperature.

2. Combine the lemon juice with a pinch of salt, add pepper to taste, and whisk with the remaining 6 tablespoons of olive oil to make a vinaigrette.

3. Add the bell pepper, celery, scallions, radishes, and cheese to the pasta. Toss with the vinaigrette and season with salt and pepper.

PART 3

International Mac

*L*ike the recipes in Part 2, these are traditional in both ingredients and techniques, but their traditions are global rather than American. Although Italian, Greek, and French influences on pasta dishes are legendary, the international spirit isn't limited to the classics; it inspires the dishes in Part 4, "Mac and Cheese Today," and that often has made recipe placement a very close call. Consider this part a treasury of dishes that would pass muster with an Old World *nonna* or *grandmère*—who happens to be a fantastic cook.

International dishes provide an education in food, and you will see that what is customary in Greece (*ras el hanout,* Aleppo pepper) or Provence (salt cod) can be new and surprising to American macaroni gourmets. The cheeses, especially, are a departure from earlier recipes. In place of Cheddar and American, look for such delights as Manchego, robiola, Taleggio, Gorgonzola, Fontina Val d'Aosta, and kefalotyri.

Italy, the cradle of macaroni, inspires Alan Tardi's Rigatoni al Forno, Melissa Kelly's Orecchiette con Fonduta (with its fascinating sauce method), Don Pintabona's Farfalle al Quattro Formaggi, and Andrea Curto's Wish Macaroni and Cheese, as well my simple Mozzarella Mac.

Antoine Bouterin offers a memory of his Provençal childhood in Macaroni Gratin Mas Antoine, and Gordon Hamersley transports us to France with his charming cod and garlic–enriched Macaroni and Cheese Provençal.

Two Greek pasta dishes share the same spirit but are direct opposites. Nora Pouillon's Greek (and Organic) Macaroni and Cheese couples baked macaroni with an herbal, colorful Greek salad; while

James Botsacos's Pastitsio is a sturdy combination of macaroni, cheese, yogurt, meat, tomatoes, spices, and herbs. And a crisp, refreshing Macaroni and Feta Salad is a showcase of Greek flavors.

Allen Susser's Macaroni and Manchego accents Spanish Manchego cheese with tender shallots and fennel. The Swiss contribute a stick-to-the-ribs winter Swiss Mac with Potatoes; and my favorite Sweet Noodle and Cheese Kugel is an Eastern European Jewish dish passed down from generation to generation, rich with vanilla and creamy cheeses.

Rigatoni al Forno

MAKES 4 SERVINGS

A stellar dish, prepared for a James Beard Awards gala.

Chef Tardi, of Follonico in New York City, suggests that you can be flexible with cheeses: Gorgonzola adds a little funkiness and mozzarella gives chewiness, but feel free to use what you have in the fridge. Most important for flavor and texture, use the best-quality pasta, available at specialty food stores or over the Internet. For his specific suggestions, see page 3.

1 pound rigatoni	½ teaspoon dried oregano or 1 teaspoon chopped fresh oregano
2 cups heavy cream, plus extra if needed	Freshly ground pepper
1 cup whole milk, plus extra if needed	¼ pound unsalted fresh mozzarella cheese, cut into ¼-inch dice
1 small clove garlic, crushed and minced	¼ pound Fontina Val d'Aosta cheese, rind removed, cut into ¼-inch dice
¼ pound Gorgonzola Dolce cheese, broken into small pieces (1 cup)	Olive oil for the baking dish
1 cup (¼ pound) grated Grana Padano or Parmigiano-Reggiano cheese	2 tablespoons plain bread crumbs

1. Preheat the oven to 400°F.

2. Bring a large pot of salted water to a boil over high heat and cook the pasta until al dente, 10 to 12 minutes. Drain and place in a mixing bowl.

3. While the pasta is cooking, in a medium shallow pot or skillet (preferably stainless steel) over medium-high heat, combine the cream and milk and bring to a simmer. Add the garlic; then stir in the Gorgonzola Dolce. When the cheese has melted, add all but 1 tablespoon of the Grana Padano,

reduce the heat to medium, and cook, stirring occasionally, until the sauce is moderately thick and creamy, 10 to 12 minutes. Remove from the heat and add the oregano and pepper.

4. Pour the cream sauce over the pasta. Add the mozzarella and Fontina Val d'Aosta and mix well. The mixture should be moist and creamy; if it is too dry, add a little more milk or cream.

5. Brush the bottom and sides of a 9 by 13-inch baking dish (preferably terra-cotta) with olive oil and pour in the pasta, which should almost entirely fill the baking dish. Sprinkle with the bread crumbs and the remaining Grana Padano. Bake on the middle shelf until the sauce is bubbling and the top is golden brown and crisp, 20 to 25 minutes.

Orecchiette con Fonduta

On a recent visit to Italy, Chef Melissa Kelly discovered Orecchiette con Fonduta, a macaroni and cheese she describes as decadent, luxurious, and *delizioso*! She added her version to the menu of her Maine restaurant, Primo, and loves to serve it when the first spring garlic and ramps (wild leeks) start popping up in the woods and perfuming the air with their wonderful scent. This is Mac and Cheese all grown-up.

½ pound fontina cheese, preferably Italian, rind removed, cut into ¼-inch cubes	Freshly grated nutmeg
2 cups whole milk	Freshly ground white pepper
2 tablespoons butter, plus extra for the pan	Drizzle of white truffle oil (see Sources)
1 loaf Italian or French bread, torn into large pieces	1 pound orecchiette
3 tablespoons extra-virgin olive oil	2 shallots, minced (about ¼ cup)
1 tablespoon minced garlic	4 ounces morels, thinly sliced
Kosher salt	8 ramps (see Sources), greens separated from bulbs, both parts cut into chiffonade (thin ribbons). (If ramps are not available, you may substitute scallions, for a somewhat different flavor.)
Freshly ground black pepper	
5 egg yolks	Summer truffles, optional

1. Place the cheese in a large heat-resistant glass bowl and cover with the milk. Refrigerate, covered, for 1 hour (or up to 4); the milk will soak into the cheese.
2. Preheat the oven to 350°F. Lightly butter a 9 by 13-inch pan.

3. In a food processor, grind the bread into coarse crumbs. Place in a bowl and toss with the olive oil, garlic, and salt and black pepper to taste. Spread on a baking sheet and toast in the oven until crisp and golden brown, about 10 minutes. Reserve.

4. To make the fonduta, place a large pot of salted water over high heat and bring to a boil. Place the bowl of cheese and milk over the pot of boiling water, making sure the water does not touch the bottom of the bowl, and add the egg yolks to the bowl, whisking constantly until the cheese has melted. Season with nutmeg, white pepper, and truffle oil to taste, remove the bowl from the water, and set aside. (This can also be done in a double boiler. In that case, bring another large pot of salted water to a boil over high heat for cooking the pasta.)

5. Add the pasta to the boiling water and cook until al dente, about 10 minutes.

6. While the pasta is cooking, melt the 2 tablespoons of butter in a large saucepan over medium-high heat; when it begins to foam, add the shallots, morels, and ramp bulbs. Season with salt and black pepper and cook, stirring, until tender, 3 to 5 minutes.

7. When the pasta is done, drain and add it to the pan with the sautéed vegetables. Add the ramp tops and the fonduta, combine well, and adjust the seasoning. Pour into the prepared pan, top with the bread crumbs, and bake until the mixture bubbles and turns golden, 20 to 25 minutes. Before serving, shave the truffles over the top (as many as you dare).

Farfalle al Quattro Formaggi

MAKES 4 TO 6 SERVINGS

This mixture of flavorful Italian cheeses—creamy, soft robiola, pungent Taleggio, and rich, nutty fontina—stirred into an oniony béchamel is a winner from the chef of New York's Tribeca Grill. The buttery topping adds an extra kick of Gorgonzola. Absolutely irresistible!

1 pound farfalle, or substitute baby shells, orecchiette, or mezza rigatoni	1/4 pound fontina cheese, broken into small pieces (1 cup)
2 cups whole milk	1/4 pound Taleggio cheese, broken into small pieces (1 cup)
6 tablespoons butter, plus extra for the baking dish	Fresh-cracked black pepper (see Note)
1 medium onion, minced (about 1 1/4 cups)	2 ounces Gorgonzola cheese, crumbled (1/2 cup)
1/4 cup flour	1/3 cup seasoned Italian bread crumbs
2 ounces aged robiola cheese, broken into small pieces (1/2 cup)	

1. Preheat the oven to 350°F.
2. Bring a large pot of salted water to a boil over high heat and cook the pasta until al dente, 10 to 12 minutes. Drain and set aside.
3. In a small saucepan over low heat, bring the milk to a scald.
4. In a large saucepan over medium heat, melt 4 tablespoons of the butter and cook the onion until soft and fragrant, but not colored, 3 to 4 minutes. Reduce the heat to medium-low, add the flour, and cook, stirring, about 3 minutes. Add the scalded milk, raise the heat to medium, and bring to a boil. Simmer, whisking, for 3 to 5 minutes, until thickened and smooth, with chunks of onion.

5. Remove from the heat and gradually stir in the robiola, fontina, and Taleggio, in batches, until the cheeses are incorporated (they need not melt entirely). Add the pasta and stir well to combine. Season with pepper.

6. Butter a 4-quart shallow flameproof baking dish and add the pasta. Sprinkle with the Gorgonzola and the bread crumbs and dot with the remaining 2 tablespoons of butter. Bake on the middle shelf until bubbling, about 25 minutes.

7. Remove from the oven and raise the temperature to broil. Place about 4 inches from the flame, and broil until golden, 1 to 2 minutes.

NOTE: For cracked black pepper, wrap peppercorns in a dish towel and smash them with a heavy pan.

Wish Macaroni and Cheese

MAKES 6 TO 8 SERVINGS

The great Italian flavors in this creamy dish (from the chef of South Beach's popular Wish restaurant) come from savory pancetta, Parmigiano-Reggiano, and buttery fontina.

10 tablespoons butter, plus extra for the baking dishes	1½ cups (6 ounces) grated Parmigiano-Reggiano cheese
1½ cups (almost ⅔ pound) small-diced pancetta	2½ cups (10 ounces) small-diced fontina cheese, cold
½ dry baguette	Kosher salt
1 pound rotelle	Freshly ground pepper
4 cups heavy cream	

1. Preheat the oven to 375°F. Lightly butter six individual baking dishes or a 9 by 13-inch baking pan.

2. Place the pancetta on a baking sheet and bake until just crisp, about 18 minutes. Drain off the fat and reserve the pancetta.

3. Crush the baguette into semifine crumbs (there will be about 1 cup; you may use a food processor). In a large sauté pan over medium heat, melt the 10 tablespoons of butter and toast the crumbs, tossing, until golden brown, 8 to 10 minutes. Set aside.

4. Bring a large pot of salted water to a boil over high heat and cook the macaroni until al dente, 8 to 10 minutes. Drain and place in a large mixing bowl.

5. In a large (4 quarts or more) saucepan over high heat, bring the heavy cream to a boil; lower the heat to medium and simmer until reduced by one third. It will still be pourable and thin. Slowly

whisk in 1¼ cups of the Parmigiano-Reggiano and all the pancetta, and continue reducing until thick.

6. Add the cream mixture and the fontina to the macaroni in the bowl and toss quickly to mix. Season with salt and pepper. Pour the mixture into the prepared baking dishes or large pan and top with the bread crumbs and remaining ¼ cup of Parmigiano-Reggiano. Bake until bubbling and golden, 12 to 15 minutes for the small dishes or 15 to 20 minutes for the large pan.

Mozzarella Mac

MAKES 6 TO 8 SERVINGS

Although the ingredients may bring to mind images of pizza, this is a surprisingly fresh and delicate Mac. The best-quality mozzarella and ripe tomatoes—beefsteak or plum—are key. After a short stay in the oven, the creamy mozzarella sauce infuses the pasta, the tomatoes are barely softened, and the basil ribbons remain bright green and flavorful.

1 pound rigatoni or penne rigate	Kosher salt
Butter for the baking dish	Freshly ground pepper
2 cups half-and-half	2 medium beefsteak tomatoes or 4 large plum tomatoes, juice and seeds squeezed out, cut into medium dice
½ pound mozzarella cheese, cut into small dice (2 cups)	15 basil leaves, cut into thin ribbons
2 cups plus 2 tablespoons (just over ½ pound) grated Parmigiano-Reggiano cheese	

1. Bring a large pot of salted water to a boil over high heat and cook the pasta until al dente, 8 to 10 minutes. Drain and place in a large mixing bowl.

2. Preheat the oven to 375°F. Butter a 9 by 13-inch baking dish.

3. In a medium saucepan over medium-high heat, combine the cream, the mozzarella, and 2 cups of the Parmigiano-Reggiano and bring to a simmer. Reduce the heat to medium and cook, stirring frequently, until the mozzarella has melted and the sauce is slightly thickened. Taste and season with salt (carefully—the Parmigiano-Reggiano may be salty) and pepper. Remove from the heat and stir in the tomatoes and basil. Pour the mixture over the pasta and mix thoroughly.

4. Pour into the prepared dish and sprinkle with the remaining 2 tablespoons of grated Parmigiano-Reggiano. Bake until heated through, 15 to 20 minutes. Allow to sit for 5 minutes before serving.

Macaroni Gratin Mas Antoine

MAKES 6 TO 8 SERVINGS

It's hard to stop eating this gratin from the chef-owner of Bouterin restaurant in Manhattan; his mother, herself a talented cook, prepared this treat in the kitchen of the family's farm in Saint-Rémy-de-Provence. Wild thyme grew just outside the farmhouse (which was called Mas Antoine), along with lavender and other fragrant herbs.

2 tablespoons butter, plus extra for the gratin dish	6 drops of Tabasco or pinch of cayenne pepper
1 pound elbow macaroni	1 teaspoon minced fresh thyme
2 generous tablespoons flour	Pinch of freshly grated nutmeg
2½ cups whole milk	2 cups (½ pound) grated Swiss cheese
Generous pinch of kosher salt	3 tablespoons seasoned bread crumbs

1. Preheat the oven to 400°F. Butter a 9 by 13-inch gratin dish or baking pan.

2. Bring a large pot of salted water to a boil over high heat and cook the pasta until al dente, 8 to 10 minutes. Drain and place in a large bowl.

3. In a large saucepan over medium-high heat, melt the 2 tablespoons of butter. Sprinkle the flour over it and mix well with a spatula or wooden spoon; cook about 2 minutes. Raise the heat to high, slowly whisk in the milk, and bring to a boil, whisking. Add the salt, Tabasco, thyme, nutmeg, and cheese and mix well. Lower the heat to medium and cook, stirring, until the cheese is almost com-

pletely melted and the mixture is thick. Pour the sauce over the macaroni, mix well, and pour into the buttered dish. Sprinkle with the bread crumbs.

4. Bake on the middle shelf until brown and firm, 25 to 30 minutes. If the top has not browned, place under a preheated broiler just until brown and crisp.

GORDON HAMERSLEY

Macaroni and Cheese Provençal with Cod

MAKES 4 TO 6 SERVINGS

The cod is savory and the veggies are crunchy-perfect in this enticing combination of flavors and textures created by the founder and chef of Boston's Hamersley's Bistro. Serve this Mediterranean-inspired dish with a generous ladle, to make sure you get plenty of the delicious sauce.

½ pound penne

½ pound salt cod, soaked and drained (soak for 8 to 24 hours in four changes of cold water, until it feels fresh and tastes barely salty)

4 tablespoons olive oil, plus extra for the baking dish and drizzling

1 medium head fennel (just over 1 pound), cut into medium dice

1 small onion, cut into small dice

5 cloves garlic, finely chopped

1 tablespoon flour

1 red bell pepper, seeded and cut into medium dice

2 cups blanched, peeled, seeded, and chopped fresh tomatoes (4 medium tomatoes), or substitute canned

1 cup white wine

¼ cup (1 ounce) coarsely grated sharp Cheddar cheese

½ cup (4 ounces) pitted and coarsely chopped black calamata olives

1 cup firmly packed shredded basil leaves

Kosher salt

Freshly ground pepper

¼ cup (1 ounce) coarsely grated Asiago cheese

2 tablespoons grated Parmesan cheese

2 tablespoons grated Pecorino Romano cheese

1 shallot, sliced very thin and separated into rings

¼ cup fresh bread crumbs

1. Preheat the oven to 350°F.

2. Bring a large pot of salted water to a boil over high heat and cook the pasta until al dente, 10 to 12 minutes. Drain.

3. Place a pot large enough to hold the cod over high heat and bring 1 quart of water to a boil. Add the cod, lower the heat to medium, and simmer for 10 to 12 minutes. Drain in a colander, reserving 1 cup of the cod liquid. Remove any bones, skin, or fat and flake the cod into bite-size pieces.

4. Heat the 4 tablespoons of olive oil in a large saucepan over medium heat. Add the fennel, onion, garlic, and flour and cook for 2 minutes, stirring occasionally. Add the bell pepper, tomatoes, and wine and continue cooking until the vegetables are cooked through, about 20 minutes. Add the Cheddar and stir until melted. Add the cod, olives, and basil and stir to combine. Stir in some of the reserved cooking water if the mixture seems a bit dry (this will depend upon how much juice the tomatoes release). Season with salt and pepper and remove from the heat.

5. Mix the pasta and the salt cod mixture together so the sauce coats the pasta evenly. Pour into a lightly oiled 9 by 13-inch baking dish.

6. Mix the remaining cheeses with the sliced shallot and bread crumbs. Sprinkle the cheese mixture evenly on top of the pasta. Drizzle with additional olive oil, if desired. Bake on the middle shelf until the pasta is bubbling and the top is crisp and browned, 25 to 30 minutes.

Greek (and Organic) Macaroni and Cheese

MAKES 4 TO 6 SERVINGS

An amazing dish with lively colors and textures, this suggests a Greek salad transformed. Chef Pouillon of Nora and Asia Nora, in Washington, D.C., uses only organic ingredients here and in all the food she cooks, and they are worth seeking out when you shop. Feta contrasts with the sweet, juicy tomatoes and fresh spinach, and the herbs sing of Greece.

1 pound macaroni

1/2 pound spinach, washed and stemmed

1 1/2 pounds crumbled feta cheese (about 6 cups)

2 1/3 cups whole milk

2 tablespoons fresh lemon juice

2/3 cup olive oil

1 teaspoon kosher salt

2 teaspoons freshly ground pepper

3/4 teaspoon minced fresh rosemary

2 teaspoons minced fresh thyme

1 tablespoon finely chopped garlic

1/2 teaspoon red pepper flakes, or to taste

1/2 cup pitted and coarsely chopped black olives, optional

1/2 pound cherry tomatoes, halved

1/2 cup grated Parmesan cheese

1/4 cup mixed chopped fresh herbs, such as parsley, thyme, and rosemary

1. Preheat the oven to 350°F.

2. Bring 6 quarts of salted water to a boil. Add the pasta and cook, stirring occasionally, until al dente, 8 to 10 minutes. Drain and place in a large mixing bowl.

3. Blanch the spinach: Bring 4 quarts of salted water to a simmer over medium-high heat. Have ready a large bowl of ice water and a slotted spoon. Add the spinach to the simmering water (in three or four batches) and submerge it. Let it cook for about 15 seconds, remove with the slotted spoon, and plunge into the ice water. Let the spinach cool completely, drain it, and squeeze out the excess water. If the leaves are large, chop them into bite-size pieces. Reserve.

4. In a blender or food processor, puree the feta cheese with the milk, lemon juice, olive oil, salt, and pepper. Blend in two batches, if necessary. This will not be completely smooth; there will be very small chunks of cheese remaining. Stir the cheese mixture into the cooked pasta, then add the minced rosemary and thyme, the garlic, red pepper flakes, olives, cherry tomatoes, and blanched spinach.

5. Place in a 9 by 13-inch baking pan and sprinkle with the grated Parmesan cheese and the mixed herbs. Bake on the middle shelf until the pasta is heated through and the top is slightly browned, 25 to 30 minutes.

Pastitsio

MAKES 6 TO 8 SERVINGS

The vibrant flavors and textures in this hearty Greek classic from the chef of New York's Molyvos restaurant will bring you back for seconds and thirds. When you set this out on your buffet table, it will disappear in a flash.

Pastitsio is a complex dish with many enticing ingredients in addition to pasta and cheese, so be sure to leave a few hours for preparation. It helps to make the components ahead and refrigerate them separately; you can also complete the dish a day in advance and reheat it before serving. But this one is well worth your time—Pastitsio will make your party.

FOR THE FILLING

- 1/4 cup currants
- 9 tablespoons olive oil
- 1 pound ground beef (90% lean)
- 1 pound ground lamb, or substitute another pound of beef
- Kosher salt
- Freshly ground pepper
- 3 1/2 tablespoons *ras el hanout* (see Note and Sources)
- 2 teaspoons ground Aleppo pepper (see Note and Sources)
- 2 1/2 tablespoons ground cinnamon
- 4 cups finely diced onion (2 large onions, about 1 1/2 pounds)
- 6 cloves garlic, thinly sliced
- 2 cups red wine
- 2 1/2 cups canned whole tomatoes (from a 28-ounce can; keep any extra for another use), crushed by hand, with their juice

1. In a small bowl, cover the currants with warm water and let soak for 30 minutes. Drain and reserve.
2. Heat a large skillet or a 4- to 6-quart pot over medium heat until hot. Add 2 tablespoons of the olive

oil, swirl to coat the pan, and add one quarter of the beef and lamb in small bits. Cook, stirring to break up the meat, until lightly browned. Season with a generous pinch of salt and pepper, 1/4 teaspoon each of *ras el hanout* and Aleppo pepper, and a pinch of cinnamon. Remove from the heat and, with a slotted spatula or spoon, transfer the meat to a bowl. Pour off any excess oil and wipe out the pan with a paper towel; repeat the process until all the meat has been cooked.

3. Return the skillet to the stove over medium heat and heat the remaining tablespoon of olive oil until shimmering. Add the onions and cook until translucent, about 5 minutes. Add the garlic and cook another minute, stirring once to combine. Return the meat to the pan and season with the remaining *ras el hanout,* Aleppo pepper, and cinnamon. Stir to combine well (be careful—the pan will be quite full). Add the wine and reduce the liquid until the mixture is almost dry, 35 to 40 minutes. Stir it occasionally, since the bottom will be drier than the top. Add the tomatoes with their juices, reduce the heat to low, and cook for 5 minutes, stirring once to combine. Add the currants, taste, and adjust the seasoning with salt and pepper. Cook for another 5 minutes. Remove the pan from the heat and transfer the meat to a large bowl to cool.

4. May be refrigerated for up to one day.

FOR THE TOMATO SAUCE	Kosher salt
1/4 cup olive oil	Freshly ground pepper
4 cloves garlic, thinly sliced	1 28-ounce can crushed tomatoes, with juice
1 teaspoon dried Greek oregano	

In a medium saucepan over medium heat, heat the oil until shimmering and sauté the garlic for 2 to 3 minutes. Add the oregano and season with salt and pepper. Sauté for 1 minute more, add the crushed tomatoes, stir once to combine (most of the oil will float to the top), and bring to a boil. Reduce the heat to low and simmer for 25 minutes, stirring occasionally and skimming the surface if necessary. Can be refrigerated, covered, for up to five days, or frozen.

FOR THE YOGURT-BÉCHAMEL TOPPING	Scant 1/2 cup flour
1 1/2 cups whole milk	Kosher salt
1 1/2 cups heavy cream	Freshly ground pepper
1 bay leaf	Freshly grated nutmeg
1/2 medium onion	1/2 cup goat's milk yogurt (available at specialty and health food stores and some greenmarkets) or cow's milk yogurt, drained in a cheesecloth-lined strainer until thick
2 whole cloves	
2 tablespoons butter, softened	

1. Combine the milk and cream in a large, heavy pot, place over medium heat, and bring the milk mixture to a simmer.

2. Meanwhile, lay the bay leaf over the cut side of the onion and pierce it with the cloves; the bay leaf will adhere. Set aside.

3. In a large pot over medium heat, melt the butter and stir in the flour. Blend until smooth and thick (the mixture will resemble thick mashed potatoes). Cook the mixture over low heat for 10 minutes; remove from the heat and whisk in the milk mixture in a steady stream. Place the pot over medium heat, add the clove-studded onion, and cook for 10 minutes, whisking occasionally to make it smooth. Season with salt, pepper, and nutmeg and set aside to cool.

4. When the béchamel comes to room temperature, remove the onion, fold in the yogurt, and combine well. If it isn't smooth, whisk again.

FOR THE PASTA

1 pound penne

2 tablespoons olive oil

Bring a large pot of salted water to a boil over high heat and cook the pasta until al dente (approximately 12 minutes), stirring occasionally to keep it moving freely in the water. Drain in a colander and transfer to a pot of cold water with ice, to stop the cooking process. When the pasta has cooled, drain well and place in a mixing bowl. Toss with the olive oil, to keep it from sticking.

TO ASSEMBLE

1/4 cup (about 1 ounce) grated kefalotyri cheese,
or substitute grated Parmesan cheese

---

1. Preheat the oven to 450°F.
2. Spread 3/4 cup of the tomato sauce in a 9 by 13 by 4-inch baking dish (or use two smaller, shallower baking dishes), covering the bottom thoroughly. Add 1/4 to 1/2 cup of the tomato sauce to the reserved penne and toss to coat. Spread the pasta evenly in the baking dish and spread the meat mixture over the pasta. Pour the yogurt mixture over the meat and sprinkle with the kefalotyri cheese.
3. Put the baking dish on a sheet pan and bake on the middle shelf for 25 minutes. Turn the oven setting to broil and finish the Pastitsio under the broiler until browned, 3 to 5 minutes. Serve hot (use a slotted spoon).

NOTE: *Ras el hanout* (literally "head of the shop"), a Middle Eastern spice blend, contains cinnamon, nutmeg, cloves, turmeric, ginger, and cardamom, among other flavors. Aleppo pepper is made from dried, lightly salted Turkish chiles.

JOAN SCHWARTZ

Macaroni and Feta Salad

MAKES 4 TO 6 SERVINGS

Here, again, are the appealing flavors and textures of a tangy, fresh Greek salad. Macaroni is the mellowing influence, and it fits right in.

½ pound elbow macaroni	1 small red onion, thinly sliced and slices halved
7 tablespoons olive oil	12 black Greek olives, pitted and halved
2 tablespoons fresh lemon juice or white wine vinegar	10 small radishes, thinly sliced
1 teaspoon dried Greek oregano	½ pound cherry tomatoes, halved
Kosher salt	1 cup (¼ pound) crumbled feta cheese
Freshly ground pepper	2 tablespoons minced flat-leaf parsley

1. Bring a large pot of salted water to a boil over high heat and cook the pasta until al dente, 8 to 10 minutes. Drain, place in a large salad bowl, and toss with 1 tablespoon of the olive oil. Let cool to room temperature.

2. For the dressing, combine the lemon juice with the oregano and a pinch of salt and pepper, and whisk in the remaining 6 tablespoons of olive oil.

3. Add the onion, olives, radishes, tomatoes, and feta to the macaroni and toss to combine. Add the dressing, season with salt and pepper, and toss again to combine. Stir in the parsley.

Macaroni and Manchego

MAKES 4 TO 8 SERVINGS

A stovetop version, this is easy to make and subtly flavored, and with its fresh, herbal notes, it is perfect for warmer weather (as we would expect from Chef Allen's restaurant in Miami). Chef Allen tells us that Manchego is one of Spain's most popular cheeses, whose simplicity makes for a comfortable combination with the fennel and macaroni.

3 tablespoons kosher salt	2 tablespoons butter, at room temperature
1 pound elbow macaroni	1 cup (¼ pound) grated Manchego cheese
2 tablespoons olive oil	2 tablespoons chopped fresh basil
3 large shallots, julienned (about ⅓ pound)	2 tablespoons chopped flat-leaf parsley
1 small fennel bulb, julienned (⅔ to ¾ pound)	½ teaspoon red pepper flakes
½ teaspoon minced garlic	

1. In a deep pot, bring to a boil 4 quarts of water with 2 tablespoons of the salt. Add the macaroni and cook until al dente, 8 to 10 minutes. Drain.
2. In a 4-quart pot over medium heat, warm the olive oil and cook the shallots and fennel until softened and aromatic, 8 to 10 minutes. Add the garlic and cook for another minute.
3. Pour the hot macaroni into the shallot mixture. Return to medium heat and add the butter and Manchego cheese, mixing well until melted. Stir in the remaining salt, and the basil, parsley, and red pepper flakes. Transfer to a bowl and serve immediately.

Swiss Mac with Potatoes

MAKES 4 SERVINGS

The Swiss give us a simply prepared, basic Mac and Cheese that is eggy and hearty, with the added texture of potatoes. It will warm you up after a snowy day on the slopes.

Butter for the baking pan	2 cups ($^1/_2$ pound) coarsely grated Swiss cheese
$^1/_2$ pound elbow macaroni	3 eggs, lightly beaten
1 medium potato, peeled and sliced $^1/_2$ inch thick, with slices cut into $1^1/_2$-inch strips	2 cups whole milk
	Freshly ground pepper
Kosher salt	

1. Preheat the oven to 350°F. Butter a 9 by 13-inch baking pan.

2. Bring a large pot of salted water to a boil over high heat and cook the pasta until al dente, 8 to 10 minutes. Drain.

3. Place the potato strips in a medium pot and cover with cold water by $^1/_2$ inch. Add 1 tablespoon salt. Place over high heat, bring to a boil, and cook until the potatoes are softened but still firm, 8 to 9 minutes. Drain.

4. Layer the macaroni, potatoes, and cheese in the baking pan, ending with a layer of cheese (there should be two full layers of each ingredient). In a small bowl, mix the eggs, milk, salt, and pepper, and pour over the macaroni and potatoes. Bake on the middle shelf until hot and bubbly, 20 to 25 minutes.

JOAN SCHWARTZ

Sweet Noodle and Cheese Kugel

MAKES 4 TO 8 SERVINGS

A family favorite, this makes a pleasing vanilla-scented luncheon entrée or a satisfying dessert—not to mention an outstanding nosh at any hour. Since noodle puddings can be quite heavy, I prefer to divide the mixture between two pans and get a lighter, thinner result.

Butter for the baking pans	1 cup whole milk
3/4 pound medium egg noodles	1 heaping teaspoon kosher salt
4 eggs, lightly beaten	3/4 cup plus 2 tablespoons sugar
1/2 pound (1 cup) cottage cheese	2 teaspoons vanilla
1/2 pound cream cheese, cut into small bits	1/2 cup dark raisins, optional
1 cup sour cream	2 teaspoons ground cinnamon

1. Preheat the oven to 350°F. Lightly butter two 8 by 8-inch baking pans.

2. Bring a large pot of salted water to a boil over high heat and cook the noodles, stirring occasionally, until al dente, about 8 minutes. Drain.

3. Meanwhile, in a large mixing bowl, combine the eggs, cheeses, sour cream, milk, salt, 3/4 cup of the sugar, the vanilla, and raisins, if desired. Mix well with a wooden spoon or whisk (lumps of both cheeses will remain). Add the noodles and mix until combined. Divide the mixture between the prepared baking pans.

4. In a small bowl or cup, combine the remaining 2 tablespoons of sugar with the cinnamon and sprinkle evenly over the noodles. Bake until firm, 35 to 40 minutes.

PART 4

Mac and Cheese Today

*T*alk about evolution! This section demonstrates how far our homespun dish has come, as skilled chefs with soaring imaginations deconstruct Mac and Cheese in ways both subtle and stunning. Wild mushrooms, chiles, salsa, fresh figs, dried cherries—even truffles and foie gras—now seem destined to meld with the classic dish and transform it.

Trying to organize the "Mac and Cheese Today" recipes by ingredients was no easy task. Just when I thought I had found a mushroom Mac or two, I discovered duck prosciutto and mascarpone, or artichoke hearts and prosciutto, in the same casserole. But there is a loose sort of progression, and here is a basic rundown:

Waldy Malouf's Penne with Roquefort creates a brand-new dish through an imaginative shift in cheeses; and Rocco DiSpirito's playful method recasts traditional ingredients into a novel, fun form in Macaroni and Cheese Croquettes.

Debra Ponzek's Farfalle with Fontina, Tasso Ham, and Baby Spinach displays the subtlety and perfect balance of components for which her recipes are known. Charlie Palmer uses luxurious but available ingredients in his sophisticated Macaroni with Cantal Cheese and Westphalian Ham.

Gordon Hamersley combines tradition and innovation in Macaroni and Cheese with Oysters and Pork Sausage and provides us with a visual (as well as culinary) treat in his beautiful Terrine of Macaroni, Goat Cheese, and Foie Gras.

The spicy kick of chiles electrifies contemporary Macs. Try Today's Macaroni and Cheese, from Rick Bayless; Macaroni with Many Cheeses in a Red Chile–Herb Crust, from Katy Sparks;

Steven Picker's Green Chile Mac and Cheese; and Scott Campbell's Mac and Smoked Cheddar with Ham and Chipotles.

Jeffrey Bank and Chris Metz, in Artie's Deli Mac and Cheese, add a really surprising flavor, one that unites Mac and Cheese with traditional deli fare: spicy pastrami. Who knew?

Kevin Johnson showcases wild mushrooms in Baked Macaroni with White Cheddar Cheese and Cremini Mushrooms. Mushrooms share the billing with savory accents in Janos Wilder's Macaroni with Duck Prosciutto, Chanterelles, and Mascarpone; as they do in Loren Falsone and Eric Moshier's Baked Cellentani with Four Cheeses, Prosciutto, Artichoke Hearts, and Portobellos. In Jody Adams's Baked Stuffed Pasta Spirals, their earthy note is enhanced by fresh figs and walnuts.

The flavor of truffles combined with macaroni and cheese presents a spectacular union of haute and homey, as offered by Andrew Carmellini, Fontina and White Truffle Macaroni; Mark Franz, Pasta with Fonduta and Fresh Truffles; David Burke, ONEc.p.s. Wild Mushroom and Truffle Macaroni and Cheese; Bobby Flay, Baked Conchiglie with Roasted Garlic–Cheese Sauce, Ricotta Cheese, and White Truffle Oil; and Tim Goodell, California Truffled Macaroni and Cheese. (Why hadn't we thought of these incredible combinations before?)

Alex Porter's seductively named Chunks of Lobster Swimming in Cheesy Macaroni is pure luxury; and Joseph Wrede's Joseph's Table Mac and Cheese with Dried Cherry Chutney and Roquefort Sauce is inspired whimsy.

And for dessert, Loren Falsone and Eric Moshier's ethereal Sweetened Mascarpone and Noodle Pudding gives you a whispered hint of noodle puddings past.

Penne with Roquefort

MAKES 6 TO 8 SERVINGS AS A MAIN DISH, 12 AS A SIDE DISH

Macaroni and cheese becomes a different dish entirely when the cheese is a bold, complex Roquefort. For anyone who loves Roquefort, this is pure bliss, courtesy of Waldy Malouf of New York's and Stamford's Beacon restaurants.

6 tablespoons butter, plus extra for the pan	1 teaspoon freshly ground pepper
1 pound penne	1 teaspoon freshly grated nutmeg
3 cups whole milk	4 cups (1 to 1¼ pounds) crumbled Roquefort cheese
6 tablespoons flour	½ cup (2 ounces) grated Parmesan cheese
2 teaspoons kosher salt	

1. Preheat the oven to 350°F. Butter a 9 by 13-inch pan or a 2- to 2½-quart baking dish or casserole.

2. Bring a large pot of salted water to a boil over high heat and cook the penne until al dente, 10 to 12 minutes. Drain and place in a large mixing bowl.

3. In a small saucepan over medium-high heat, bring the milk to a scald.

4. In a large, heavy saucepan over medium heat, melt the 6 tablespoons of butter. Add the flour and cook, stirring, 3 minutes. Stir in the heated milk and continue stirring until the sauce has thickened (3 to 5 minutes). Reduce the heat to low, add the salt, pepper, and nutmeg, and simmer for 4 to 5 minutes to meld the flavors.

5. Add the Roquefort and sauce to the penne and combine well. Pour the mixture into the baking pan and sprinkle with the grated Parmesan. Bake until the top is nicely browned and the sauce is bubbly, about 25 minutes.

Macaroni and Cheese Croquettes

Here is an ingenious new take on macaroni and cheese from the chef of Union Pacific, known for his skill and creativity. These savory, awesomely crisp, cheese-loaded croquettes are a kid's dream come true.

1 pound elbow macaroni

2 cups (½ pound) coarsely grated sharp Cheddar cheese

1 cup (¼ pound) coarsely grated Gruyère cheese

Kosher salt

Freshly ground pepper

¼ cup sour cream

¼ cup mayonnaise

½ teaspoon chopped flat-leaf parsley

1 to 1½ cups flour

5 eggs, lightly beaten

1 cup plain or seasoned bread crumbs

Canola oil for deep-frying

1. Bring a large pot of salted water to a boil over high heat and cook the pasta until al dente, 8 to 10 minutes. Drain and place in a mixing bowl. Add the Cheddar and Gruyère and mix well. Season with salt and pepper and set aside to cool.

2. When the mixture has cooled to room temperature, add the sour cream, mayonnaise, and parsley, mix well, and form into 8 large or 16 small balls. Dip each ball into flour to coat, dip into the beaten egg, and roll in the bread crumbs until well coated. (After each dip, resqueeze the balls back into shape.)

3. In a heavy pan, heat about 3 inches of canola oil to 365°F. Lower the balls into the oil with a slotted spoon and fry until browned on all sides (avoid crowding). If the oil starts to get white and foamy on top, discard and replace with fresh oil. Drain the croquettes on paper towels and serve hot.

Farfalle with Fontina, Tasso Ham, and Baby Spinach

MAKES 6 SERVINGS

Chef Ponzek's subtle Mediterranean touch defines this bright dish (from her two Aux Délices shops in Greenwich, Connecticut). It has superb flavor, just the right amount of cheesiness, the kick of savory ham, and the fresh note of baby spinach. There is no béchamel and preparation is quick and easy—put a pot of water on the fire and prepare your sauce while the pasta cooks.

1 pound farfalle or penne	1½ cups firmly packed, coarsely chopped baby spinach
1 tablespoon olive oil	
2 shallots, finely diced (about 2 tablespoons)	½ pound tasso ham or Black Forest ham, cut into ¼-inch dice
2 cups heavy cream	Kosher salt
2 cups (½ pound) grated fontina cheese	Freshly ground pepper

1. Bring 6 quarts of salted water to a boil. Add the pasta and cook, stirring occasionally, until al dente, 9 to 10 minutes. Drain and reserve.

2. Preheat the broiler. Set out six individual heatproof bowls or a larger heatproof serving bowl.

3. Meanwhile, in a large saucepan, heat the olive oil over medium-high heat until almost smoking. Add the shallots and sauté until translucent (this will take only about a minute). Add the cream and bring to a boil; stir, and reduce until slightly thickened, 3 to 4 minutes. Add the cheese and stir until

smooth. The sauce will be thick. Stir in the spinach and ham and remove from the heat. Add the cooked pasta and toss until lightly coated. Season with salt and pepper.

4. Divide among the smaller bowls or pour into the serving bowl. Place under the broiler until golden brown, 2 to 3 minutes.

Macaroni with Cantal Cheese and Westphalian Ham

MAKES 6 SERVINGS

The finest ingredients will indeed give you the finest dish. Cantal cheese from France lends a smooth, refined flavor, and Westphalian ham, cured and then slowly smoked, adds a light, savory touch. Chef Palmer (with well-known restaurants in New York City, Los Angeles, Las Vegas, and Sonoma, California) refines technique as well, lightening the macaroni and cheese mixture with beaten egg whites, as for a soufflé. This is a transcendent—but never fussy—Mac.

Butter for the casserole	1½ cups (about 6 ounces) finely chopped Cantal cheese
1 pound elbow macaroni, orecchiette, mini rigatoni, or other short, tubular pasta	2 cups (about ½ pound) finely diced Westphalian ham
1½ cups heavy cream	1 tablespoon minced flat-leaf parsley
2 tablespoons canola oil	Tabasco, to taste
2 cups diced onion	Kosher salt
1 tablespoon roasted garlic puree (see Note)	Freshly ground white pepper
2 tablespoons Wondra flour	3 egg whites
¼ cup dry white wine	¾ cup bread crumbs

1. Preheat the oven to 350°F. Generously butter a 2-quart casserole.

2. Bring 6 quarts of salted water to a boil. Add the pasta and cook, stirring occasionally, until al dente, 9 to 10 minutes. Drain and reserve.

3. Heat the cream in a small saucepan over medium heat.

4. Heat the oil in a large nonstick skillet over medium heat, and sauté the onion until nicely browned and slightly crisp, about 15 minutes. Stir in the garlic puree. Reduce the heat to medium-low and stir in the flour until incorporated into the oil and pan juices. Raise the heat to medium; whisk in the hot cream and then the wine. Cook, stirring constantly, until the mixture has begun to thicken.

5. Turn off the heat and stir in the cheese. When the cheese has melted, mix in the ham and half the parsley. Add the drained pasta and stir to combine. Season to taste with Tabasco, salt, and pepper.

6. Beat the egg whites until they hold soft peaks and gently fold them into the pasta mixture until just barely blended. Pour the mixture into the prepared casserole.

7. Combine the bread crumbs with the remaining parsley and sprinkle over the casserole. Bake until the bread crumbs are browned and the edges are bubbling, about 30 minutes. Serve hot.

NOTE: To roast the garlic, preheat the oven to 300°F. Cut off the bud end and rub the head of garlic with olive oil. Wrap loosely in foil, place on a baking pan, and roast until very soft, 45 minutes to 1 hour. Peel, or squeeze out the softened garlic, and mash (can be refrigerated up to one day).

Macaroni and Cheese with Oysters and Pork Sausage

MAKES 4 SERVINGS

Oysters and macaroni are classic New England partners. In his exciting recipe, Chef Hamersley brings the combination into the twenty-first century and adds new layers of flavor, spice, and texture.

¹/₂ pound penne	¹/₂ cup (2 ounces) coarsely grated Asiago cheese
3 tablespoons butter, plus extra for the baking dish	Kosher salt
1 small onion (about ¹/₄ pound), cut into small dice	Freshly ground pepper
¹/₄ teaspoon herbes de Provence	¹/₂ pound sausage meat
2 tablespoons flour	1 to 2 tablespoons Tabasco, or to taste, optional
1 cup whole milk	16 medium oysters, shucked, excess liquid drained
1 cup light cream	1 shallot, sliced very thin and separated into rings
2 cups (¹/₂ pound) coarsely grated Gruyère cheese	¹/₂ cup fresh bread crumbs
¹/₂ cup (2 ounces) coarsely grated sharp white Cheddar cheese, preferably Vermont	

1. Bring a large pot of salted water to a boil over high heat and cook the pasta until al dente, 10 to 12 minutes. Drain.

2. Preheat the oven to 350°F. Butter an 8 by 8-inch (2-quart) baking dish.

3. In a large saucepan over medium heat, melt the 3 tablespoons of butter. Add the onion and herbes

de Provence and cook until the onion has softened, 5 to 6 minutes. Add the flour and cook an additional 8 minutes, stirring occasionally; it will become golden brown. Do not allow the mixture to burn.

4. Reduce the heat to medium-low, whisk in the milk and cream, and cook for 5 minutes, stirring occasionally. Add $1\frac{1}{2}$ cups of the Gruyère, $\frac{1}{4}$ cup of the Cheddar, and $\frac{1}{4}$ cup of the Asiago. Cook slowly, stirring occasionally, until the cheeses are melted and incorporated into the sauce; season with salt and pepper. The sauce will be very thick. Remove from the heat and set aside.

5. In a small sauté pan over medium heat, cook the sausage meat for 10 minutes. Drain off the fat, and add the Tabasco, if desired (with care—Tabasco is very assertive).

6. Add the pasta, sausage, and oysters to the cheese sauce, mixing well so the sauce coats the pasta evenly. Pour the mixture into the prepared baking dish.

7. Mix the remaining cheese with the sliced shallot and the bread crumbs, and sprinkle evenly over the pasta. Bake on the middle shelf until the pasta is bubbling and the top is crisp and brown, about 30 minutes.

Terrine of Macaroni, Goat Cheese, and Foie Gras

MAKES 4 TO 6 SERVINGS

Chef Hamersley's terrine will be the star of your table, with its eye-catching colors and layers of glorious ingredients. It requires careful preparation, but it can be made a day in advance, refrigerated, and then served at room temperature.

1 10-ounce bag fresh spinach, washed and stemmed, to line the mold	3 leeks, white part and a bit of tender green, trimmed, washed, and diced (about 3½ cups)
½ pound penne or ziti	2 tablespoons chopped fresh thyme
½ pound raw foie gras, duck pâté, or cooked foie gras product	2 cups duck stock (available frozen at gourmet or specialty stores), or substitute chicken stock or canned low-sodium chicken broth
Kosher salt	2 envelopes unflavored gelatin
Freshly ground pepper	1½ to 2 cups (⅓ to ½ pound) crumbled goat cheese
3 tablespoons vegetable oil	
½ cup Armagnac (or substitute Cognac)	
1 medium red onion, diced (about 1 cup)	

1. Bring a large pot of salted water to a boil and blanch the spinach until still bright green, about 5 seconds. Remove and place in a bowl of ice water. Once it is cold, drain and pat out some of the liquid. Do not squeeze, or the leaves will lose their shape.

2. Line a 1½-quart mold with plastic wrap, leaving a 4-inch overhang on all sides. Line the mold with the blanched spinach leaves: use the big leaves first and place them shiny side down and vein side

up on the bottom and up the sides, leaving about a $1/2$-inch overhang. Try to keep the lining one layer thick, but you may patch any holes or tears with the smaller leaves. Reserve any remaining spinach leaves for the top.

3. Bring a large pot of salted water to a boil over high heat and cook the pasta until al dente, 8 to 10 minutes. Drain and reserve.

4. Rinse the foie gras and pat dry. Using a small sharp knife, trim away large veins and membranes. Slice approximately $3/4$ inch thick. Season the slices lightly with salt and pepper.

5. In a sauté pan over medium-high heat, heat 1 tablespoon of the oil until hot, add the uncooked foie gras slices, and sear for 15 to 20 seconds on each side; be careful not to overcook and melt the foie gras. Remove and reserve in a bowl. Pour the Armagnac into the pan and reduce by three fourths, scraping up all the bits of cooked foie gras from the bottom, about 10 minutes. Pour the reduced Armagnac over the foie gras slices. (If you use pâté or cooked foie gras, do not cook it. Place the slices in a bowl and pour the reduced Armagnac over them.)

6. In another sauté pan, heat the remaining 2 tablespoons of oil over medium heat until shimmering. Add the onion and leeks and cook, stirring occasionally, until tender, about 15 minutes. Stir in the thyme and remove from the heat. Season with salt and pepper.

7. In a small saucepan over medium heat, warm the duck stock; add the gelatin, and stir to dissolve. Keep warm over low heat.

8. Layer half the ingredients in the mold in this order: pasta, foie gras, onion-leek mixture, and goat cheese. Sprinkle with salt and pepper and a few spoonfuls of stock, pressing down with a spatula so the stock fills up the pasta tubes. Repeat with the remaining ingredients.

9. Fold the overhanging spinach leaves over the top, or cover with a layer of spinach leaves shiny side up, and wrap the whole terrine in plastic wrap. Place on a plate and weight with heavy cans. Refrigerate 8 to 12 hours.

10. Remove the plastic wrap, run the blade of a thin, flexible knife around the inside of the mold, and invert the terrine onto a platter. Cut the terrine into $1/2$-inch slices.

Today's Macaroni and Cheese

MAKES 8 SERVINGS

Rick Bayless, chef and owner of Chicago's Frontera Grill and Topolobampo, confesses that he grew up on the wonderful slow-baked macaroni and cheese served at his parents' restaurant, which he calls "crusty cheese over submissive macaroni." His adult version is creamy and a little "edgy"— with the delicious jolt of salsa.

2 cups milk	3 cups (³⁄₄ pound) shredded Cheddar cheese
4 tablespoons butter	Kosher salt, about 1¹⁄₂ teaspoons
¹⁄₄ cup flour	1 pound dried pasta (elbow macaroni, cavatappi, rotini, or fusilli)
2 cups good-quality salsa (such as Rick Bayless's Frontera brand Roasted Jalapeño Tomato, or Roasted Poblano Tomato)	Chopped fresh cilantro, for garnish

1. Fill a large pot with about 6 quarts of water and set over high heat. Warm the milk in a small saucepan over medium heat, or in a glass measuring cup in a microwave, for about 1 minute. In a medium saucepan, melt the butter over medium heat, then stir in the flour and whisk until the mixture turns a deep golden, about 2 minutes. Add the warmed milk all at once and continue to whisk constantly until the mixture thickens and comes to a full boil, 4 or 5 minutes. (Whisk diligently and there will be no lumps.) Stir in the salsa, remove from the heat, then stir in the cheese, stirring until it melts. Taste and season generously with salt.

2. When the water has come to a boil, add the pasta. Stir well so no pieces stick together and boil until

the pasta is al dente, about 10 minutes. Drain thoroughly and return to the pot. Stir in the cheese sauce, then spoon into a serving dish. Sprinkle with the cilantro.

NOTE: If you want a wonderful contrasting texture, spoon the macaroni and cheese into a buttered baking dish. Top with $1/2$ cup bread crumbs mixed with 1 tablespoon melted butter and bake in a preheated 375°F oven for 10 to 12 minutes, until richly browned and crisp.

Macaroni with Many Cheeses in a Red Chile–Herb Crust

MAKES 4 TO 6 SERVINGS

This is ideal to put together when you find yourself with many small bundles of cheese scraps in your refrigerator, says Chef Sparks, of Quilty's restaurant in Manhattan. And she advises that the pasta should be the best brand available, made from semolina flour and of good, even color.

When you lift this out of the oven, the heady aroma of anchos invites you to dig in. Serve with a salad of baby greens, to refresh the palate.

10 thyme stems (leaves reserved to use in the red chile–herb crust)

2 teaspoons whole coriander seeds

½ teaspoon dried orange peel

1 bay leaf

6 tablespoons butter, plus extra for the gratin dish

2 shallots, minced (about ⅓ cup)

1 cup (about ¼ pound) thinly sliced shiitake mushroom caps

¾ cup dry white wine

3 cups heavy cream

1 cup panko (Japanese bread crumbs)

2 teaspoons ancho chile powder (not commercial chile powder)

1 teaspoon minced fresh tarragon

1 teaspoon minced fresh thyme leaves (reserve thyme stems)

2 teaspoons minced fresh parsley

Kosher salt

Freshly ground pepper

1 pound farfalle

12 ounces mixed cheeses, grated, shredded, or broken into small pieces (best choices: goat cheeses, Camembert, Brie, Parmesan, Cheddar, Gruyère; best to avoid: smoked cheeses, Limburger!)

Freshly grated nutmeg

1. Make an herb sachet: Place the thyme stems, coriander seeds, dried orange peel, and bay leaf on a small square of cheesecloth. Bring the ends of the cheesecloth together and tie with kitchen string.

2. Melt 2 tablespoons of the butter in a large saucepan over medium heat. Add the shallots and sweat until soft, about 3 minutes; add the shiitakes and cook 3 additional minutes. Add the wine and reduce until almost dry, about 20 minutes. Add the cream and the sachet and simmer, stirring occasionally, until the cream has reduced by half, about 30 minutes.

3. Remove the sachet. Remove the pot from the heat and cover loosely.

4. Make the red chile–herb crust: Melt the remaining 4 tablespoons of butter in a sauté pan over medium heat. Add the panko and stir occasionally until the crumbs become golden brown, about 5 minutes. Add the ancho powder, tarragon, thyme leaves, and parsley and stir until well incorporated. Remove from the heat and season lightly with salt and pepper.

5. Preheat the oven to 400°F. Lightly butter a 9 by 13-inch gratin dish.

6. Cook the farfalle in boiling salted water until just al dente, about 8 minutes, and drain. Off the heat, stir the pasta into the still-warm sauce and add the cheeses. Season to taste with freshly grated nutmeg, salt, and pepper. Pour the pasta mixture into the gratin dish and sprinkle the crust mixture evenly over the entire surface.

7. Bake on the middle shelf for about 10 minutes or until the sauce bubbles around the edges. Remove from the heat and let cool 3 to 5 minutes before serving.

Green Chile Mac and Cheese

MAKES 6 SERVINGS

From the chef of Good restaurant in New York, here is a great Mac for chile lovers. Poblanos, the peppers you often see as chiles rellenos, are hot and flavorful; they give the dish exactly the right amount of spice and an exciting southwestern touch. Tortilla crumbs add texture and ripe tomato makes the perfect garnish.

When charring the peppers, be sure to keep the area well ventilated—this can be a smoky job.

1 pound elbow macaroni	2 cups (½ pound) grated Monterey Jack cheese
Butter for the gratin dishes	¾ cup (3 ounces) grated Parmigiano-Reggiano cheese
3 cups heavy cream	3 cups medium corn tortilla crumbs (see Notes)
1 cup roasted poblano puree (see Notes)	1 small ripe tomato, cut into small dice
¼ cup chopped fresh cilantro	Fresh cilantro sprigs, for garnish
2 teaspoons kosher salt	
1 teaspoon freshly ground pepper	

1. Bring a large pot of salted water to a boil over high heat and cook the macaroni until al dente, 8 to 10 minutes. Drain.

2. Preheat the broiler. Lightly butter six individual gratin dishes or shallow ovenproof bowls or a 9 by 13-inch baking dish.

3. In a medium saucepan over medium heat, combine the cream, poblano puree, chopped cilantro, salt, and pepper and bring to a simmer, about 7 minutes; simmer 3 minutes more to meld the flavors. Stir in the macaroni and cook until the cream returns to a simmer, 3 to 5 minutes. Add the

grated cheeses and bring the mixture back to a simmer, stirring constantly until the cheeses are melted.

4. Divide the mixture among the gratin dishes or bowls or pour into the baking dish. Sprinkle with tortilla crumbs to cover completely, and gently flatten with a large spoon. Place under the broiler until the topping is golden brown, about 2 minutes (watch carefully so it doesn't burn). Garnish with diced tomato and cilantro sprigs.

NOTES:

FOR THE ROASTED POBLANO PUREE

6 or 7 poblano chiles (about 1¾ pounds)

1. Turn a stove burner to high, place the poblanos directly on it, and turn, using tongs, until charred on all sides, about 12 minutes. Place in a brown paper bag, and close the bag (making sure that there are no burning embers on the chiles), or in a bowl covered tightly with plastic wrap, until cool enough to handle. Then rub off the skin and remove the stems and seeds. Puree in a blender and reserve. There should be about 1 cup of puree.

2. A good place to peel the peppers is in the sink under running water. This makes it easy to rinse out extra seeds, as well.

FOR THE TORTILLA CRUMBS

About 14 tortilla chips

Pulse in the food processor to medium crumbs.

Mac and Smoked Cheddar with Ham and Chipotles

MAKES 8 SERVINGS

Here is Chef Campbell's (of New York's Avenue restaurant) spicy, upbeat version of an old favorite. It has a great smoky taste that is just zesty enough, plus delicious crusts on both the top and bottom. When you dip your serving spoon into the top, you can hear the crust crackle—a welcoming sound if ever there was one.

4 tablespoons butter, plus extra for the baking pan and topping

1/3 cup panko (Japanese bread crumbs)

3/4 pound elbow macaroni

2 1/2 cups whole milk

1/4 cup flour

2 1/2 cups (10 ounces) grated smoked Cheddar cheese

1/3 cup julienned smoked ham

4 chipotle peppers (smoked jalapeños), or to taste, stemmed, seeded, and julienned (see Note)

Kosher salt

Freshly ground pepper

1/2 cup (2 ounces) grated Parmesan cheese

1. Preheat the oven to 400°F. Butter the bottom of a 9 by 13-inch baking pan and sprinkle lightly with half the crumbs.

2. Bring a large pot of salted water to a boil. Add the pasta and cook, stirring occasionally, until al dente, 8 to 10 minutes. Drain well and transfer to a large bowl.

3. Warm the milk in a small saucepan over medium heat or in the microwave.

4. In a large saucepan over medium-low heat, melt the 4 tablespoons of butter; when it starts to bubble, whisk in the flour. Cook, stirring occasionally, for 3 to 4 minutes and then whisk in the warm milk. Reduce the heat to low and cook, stirring continually, for 15 minutes. Add the Cheddar, ham, and chipotles and stir until the cheese is melted. The mixture will be somewhat thin. Season with salt and pepper. Pour the mixture over the macaroni and mix well.

5. Pour the macaroni and sauce into the prepared pan. Sprinkle with the remaining bread crumbs and the Parmesan cheese and dot with butter. Bake on the middle shelf until bubbling and a rich golden-brown color, with the sides starting to turn brown, 25 to 30 minutes. Let rest for 10 to 15 minutes before serving.

NOTE: Some tips for cutting chipotles: Use a plastic (or other nonwood) work surface so the aroma and flavor don't carry over to other foods. If you have sensitive skin, wear gloves when working with the peppers and wash your hands with soap when you are done. Keep your fingers away from your eyes!

JEFFREY BANK AND CHRIS METZ

Artie's Deli Mac and Cheese

MAKES 4 TO 6 SERVINGS

Pastrami, the highly spiced cured and smoked beef, adds zing to a creamy Mac and Cheese, as well as a bit of true New York taste. This is an unusual combination—but an addictive one.

4 tablespoons butter, plus extra for the baking dish	2 tablespoons grated Parmesan cheese
1/2 pound farfalle	1/4 pound pastrami, diced (scant cup)
1/4 cup flour	1 teaspoon kosher salt
2 cups whole milk	1/8 teaspoon freshly ground pepper
2 cups (1/2 pound) grated sharp Cheddar cheese	6 to 10 Ritz crackers, pulsed in the food processor, about 1/4 to 1/3 cup crumbs

1. Preheat the oven to 350°F. Butter an 8 by 8-inch baking dish.

2. Bring a large pot of salted water to a boil over high heat and cook the farfalle until al dente, 8 to 10 minutes. Drain.

3. In a large saucepan over medium-low heat, melt the 4 tablespoons of butter. Sprinkle in the flour and stir with a wooden spoon until the flour is incorporated, about 1 minute. Gradually add the milk, stirring, and raise the heat to medium. Cook, stirring frequently, until almost boiling and smooth, about 5 minutes. Add the cheeses and stir until melted and incorporated, 2 to 3 minutes. Stir in the pastrami and lower the heat. Add the pasta and season with the salt and pepper.

4. Transfer the pasta to the baking dish and top with the cracker crumbs. Bake until browned and bubbling, 20 to 25 minutes.

Baked Macaroni with White Cheddar Cheese and Cremini Mushrooms

MAKES 4 TO 6 SERVINGS

Smooth and hearty, with the earthy accent of mushrooms, this is a perfect autumn Mac and Cheese from the chef of New York's Grange Hall. It's the one to make when you've found some great creminis at the greenmarket or your local greengrocer.

16 tablespoons canola oil, plus additional for the baking dish

2 slices white bread (fresh or stale)

1/2 cup (2 ounces) grated Grana Padano cheese, or substitute grated Parmigiano-Reggiano cheese

1/2 pound cremini mushrooms, washed, dried, and sliced 1/8 inch thick

1 pound ziti

6 rounded tablespoons flour

2 cups whole milk

1 1/2 cups (6 ounces) shredded sharp white Cheddar cheese

Kosher salt

Freshly ground pepper

1/2 tablespoon dry mustard

1. Preheat the oven to 375°F. Oil a 9 by 13-inch baking dish or ovenproof casserole.

2. Toast the bread in the oven until golden, 4 to 5 minutes, and allow to cool. Break into chunks, chop into crumbs in a food processor, and mix with the Grana Padano; reserve the mixture.

3. In a large sauté pan over medium heat, heat 4 tablespoons of the canola oil until very hot and sauté the mushrooms until fully cooked, about 5 minutes, stirring often. Remove from the heat and place in a strainer to drain and cool.

4. Bring 6 quarts of salted water to a boil with 4 tablespoons of the canola oil. Add the pasta and cook, stirring occasionally to prevent sticking, until al dente, 8 to 10 minutes. Drain and reserve.

5. In a large saucepan over medium heat, heat the remaining 8 tablespoons of canola oil until moderately hot and whisk in the flour. Cook, whisking constantly, until lightly golden brown, about 5 minutes. Raise the heat and slowly whisk in the milk; cook, whisking, until it comes to a boil. Whisk in the Cheddar until well blended. Add the salt, pepper, and mustard and cook, stirring constantly, until the mixture thickens—it will get quite thick (it starts to thicken as soon as you add the milk, so this part takes only a few minutes). Remove from the heat, add the ziti and mushrooms, and stir until well coated.

6. Pour the macaroni mixture into the prepared baking dish and top with the bread crumb mixture. Bake on the middle shelf until bubbling and the top is golden, about 20 minutes.

Macaroni with Duck Prosciutto, Chanterelles, and Mascarpone

MAKES 4 TO 6 SERVINGS

After growing up with his mother's classic Mac and Cheese with Tomatoes (page 38), Tucson's Chef Wilder (of Janos and J Bar) sought new worlds to conquer. His inspired version combines rich mascarpone cheese, duck prosciutto, fresh chanterelles, basil, and "Sweet 100" tomatoes (so tiny that they come 100 to a pint).

Imaginative, restorative, and summery, this is an irresistible dish.

Butter for the baking dish

1 pound elbow macaroni

1 tablespoon olive oil

3 tablespoons chopped garlic

1/4 pound chanterelle mushrooms, thickly sliced

1 cup dry white wine

3 tablespoons chopped shallots

1 cup heavy cream

1/4 pound mascarpone cheese

1 cup (1/4 pound) coarsely grated Parmigiano-Reggiano cheese

About 3 cups firmly packed shredded basil leaves

5 ounces thinly sliced duck prosciutto, coarsely chopped, or substitute regular prosciutto

2 ounces yellow Sweet 100 tomatoes, whole; or substitute slightly larger tomatoes, such as grape, halved

2 ounces red Sweet 100 tomatoes, whole; or substitute slightly larger tomatoes, such as grape, halved

1 cup (1/4 pound) grated sharp New York Cheddar cheese

Kosher salt

Freshly ground pepper

1. Preheat the oven to 375°F. Butter a 9 by 13-inch or a 4-quart deep baking dish.

2. Bring a large pot of salted water to a boil over high heat and cook the pasta until al dente, 8 to 10 minutes. Drain and place in a large mixing bowl.

3. In a small skillet over medium-high heat, heat the olive oil until very hot and add 1 tablespoon of the garlic and the chanterelles. Sauté until the garlic is golden and the mushrooms are softened but not colored, about 4 minutes, and reserve.

4. Combine the wine, the remaining garlic, and the shallots in a medium saucepan over medium-high heat and reduce by about three fourths, 6 to 8 minutes. Add the cream and reduce by half, about 5 minutes. Lower the heat to medium and whisk in the mascarpone and Parmigiano-Reggiano, until the cheese is melted and well blended.

5. Add the basil and immediately transfer the mascarpone sauce to a blender or food processor. Puree the sauce (which will be a delicate green, with small bits of basil), and reserve.

6. In the mixing bowl, combine the macaroni, duck prosciutto, mushrooms, tomatoes, half the Cheddar, and the mascarpone sauce. Adjust the seasonings. Pour into the baking dish and top with the remaining Cheddar. Bake on the middle shelf until browned, 35 to 40 minutes.

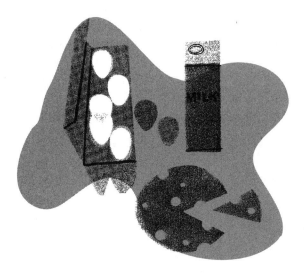

Baked Cellentani with Four Cheeses, Prosciutto, Artichoke Hearts, and Portobellos

MAKES 4 SERVINGS

This modern take on Italian cuisine from the chefs at Empire, in Providence, Rhode Island, is chock-full of welcoming textures and bright contrasts. There are layers of flavor: savory, herbal, earthy, and, especially, pasta-and-cheesy.

2 tablespoons pure olive oil

4 thin slices prosciutto cotto (cooked prosciutto) or good-quality ham

10 tablespoons butter

2 cups whole milk, plus an extra ¼ cup if desired

3 tablespoons flour

1 bay leaf

Kosher salt

¾ pound cellentani or other tubular pasta such as penne, cavatappi, or elbow macaroni

3 tablespoons extra-virgin olive oil

2 medium portobello mushrooms, caps only (about ¼ pound), cleaned well and sliced about ¼ inch wide and 1 inch long

1 cup (¼ pound) finely grated fresh caciocavallo cheese

¼ pound Bel Paese cheese, crumbled (1 cup)

¼ pound fresh mozzarella cheese, cut into ½-inch cubes (1 cup)

4 good-quality Italian artichoke hearts in olive oil, rinsed and sliced thin

¼ pound Italian sweet sausage meat, removed from casing, browned, and cooled, optional

Freshly ground pepper

2 tablespoons dried bread crumbs

2 tablespoons coarsely chopped flat-leaf parsley

1 teaspoon finely chopped fresh rosemary

1 teaspoon finely chopped fresh thyme

Parmigiano-Reggiano cheese, for grating

1. Brush a cookie sheet with 1 tablespoon of the pure olive oil. Lay the prosciutto cotto slices on the sheet and brush with the remaining tablespoon of pure olive oil. Cover and set aside.

2. Smear the inside of a large, ovenproof casserole (about 9 by 13 inches; or 8 inches round, 3 inches deep) with 1 tablespoon of the butter and set aside.

3. Preheat the oven to 400°F.

4. To make the béchamel sauce: In a small saucepan over low heat, bring 2 cups of the milk to a scald and remove from the heat. In another small saucepan, melt 4 tablespoons of the butter over medium-low heat, sprinkle in the flour, and stir with a wooden spoon until the mixture begins to bubble. Continue to cook, stirring constantly, for 1 minute. Slowly pour in the hot milk, whisking constantly. When all the milk has been added, continue to cook, whisking frequently, until the sauce boils. Remove from the heat, add the bay leaf, and season to taste with salt. Pour into a small bowl, cover the surface with plastic wrap (to prevent a skin from forming), and set aside to cool.

5. In a large pot over high heat, bring 3 quarts of salted water to a boil. Add the pasta and cook until al dente, for 1 minute less than the recommended cooking time. Drain and toss with the extra-virgin olive oil. Set aside to cool.

6. In a sauté pan over high heat, melt the remaining 5 tablespoons of butter. Add the sliced mushrooms and sprinkle with a little salt. Reduce the heat to medium and cook, stirring occasionally, until the mushrooms are brown and soft, about 10 minutes. Drain off any excess liquid.

7. In a large bowl, combine the caciocavallo, Bel Paese, mozzarella, artichoke slices, cooked sausage meat (if using), sautéed mushrooms, béchamel (removing the bay leaf), and pasta. If you prefer a thinner sauce, add the additional 1/4 cup milk. Mix gently to combine, season with salt and pepper, and pour into the prepared casserole dish. Sprinkle with the bread crumbs, cover loosely with aluminum foil, and bake on the middle shelf until hot in the center, about 20 minutes.

8. Combine the parsley, rosemary, and thyme.

9. Place the uncovered cookie sheet with the prosciutto in the oven and bake until the slices are hot and beginning to brown at the edges, about 10 minutes. At the same time, uncover the casserole and bake until browned, about 10 minutes.

10. Remove the casserole and the ham from the oven. Divide the macaroni among four warmed pasta bowls and grate the Parmigiano-Reggiano generously over each. Top each serving with a slice of prosciutto and sprinkle with the herbs.

Add macaroni alternately with sauce.   Use a fork to distribute cheese sauce thoroughly.

Baked Stuffed Pasta Spirals

Fresh figs add sweetness to this lush blend of flavors and textures, mushrooms lend their rich flavor and aroma, and nuts provide a bit of crunch. A very light cheese sauce brings together all these good things, in an outstanding dish from Chef Jody Adams of the Boston area's Red Clay and Rialto.

Fresh pasta sheets are available at many specialty grocery and pasta shops, but the frozen variety you find in your local supermarket makes an acceptable substitute. Both types come sprinkled with cornmeal to prevent their sticking together in the package; brush off as much as you can before cooking.

6 tablespoons olive oil	1/4 pound fresh spinach, stemmed, washed, and dried
1 shallot, minced (about 1 tablespoon)	
1 clove garlic, minced (about 1 teaspoon)	6 fresh Turkish (brown) figs, stems removed, cut into 1/4-inch slices
3 large portobello mushroom caps (about 2/3 pound without stems), cut into 1/4-inch-wide, 1-inch-long slices	6 tablespoons grated Parmesan cheese
	2 tablespoons finely chopped toasted walnuts (see Note)
Kosher salt	1 cup heavy cream
Freshly ground pepper	1/2 cup (2 ounces) crumbled Gorgonzola cheese
1/2 teaspoon chopped fresh thyme	4 to 6 sprigs fresh thyme, for garnish
2 fresh pasta sheets, 8 by 12 inches, or substitute frozen sheets (4 sheets, 8 by 6 inches)	

1. Heat 2 tablespoons of the olive oil in a large sauté pan over medium heat. Add the shallot and garlic and cook for 3 minutes. Raise the heat to high and add the mushrooms. Season with salt and pepper and cook until tender, about 3 minutes. Add the chopped thyme and toss to mix. Set aside to cool.

2. Have ready a large bowl of ice water. Bring a large pot of water to a boil over high heat and add 1 teaspoon salt per quart. Add the pasta sheets and cook, stirring occasionally and taking care not to break the sheets, until just tender, about 2 minutes. Transfer the pasta to the ice water to cool; drain immediately (if you leave them in the water too long, they will stick together). Pat the sheets dry with paper towels.

3. Brush a board with 1 tablespoon of the olive oil (make sure it is evenly covered, so the pasta gets coated).

4. Lay one pasta sheet on the board. If you are using 8 by 12-inch sheets, cover with half the spinach, leaving a 2-inch border along the long side farthest from you. Season with salt and pepper. Distribute half the mushrooms evenly over the spinach. Sprinkle half the figs, Parmesan, and walnuts over the mushrooms. If you are using the smaller frozen sheets, use $1/2$ tablespoon of olive oil and one fourth of each ingredient for each.

5. Starting with the long edge closest to you, roll the sheet tightly, jelly roll–style, and seal with the uncovered edge. Cut into six even slices. Repeat this process with the remaining pasta sheet (start by brushing the board with oil). The uncut rolls may be wrapped tightly in aluminum foil and refrigerated up to one day.

6. Preheat the oven to 400°F. Brush a small baking sheet with the remaining 2 tablespoons of olive oil and arrange the spirals on the sheet. Bake on the middle shelf until the spinach is cooked and the rolls are heated through, 10 to 15 minutes.

7. Meanwhile, place the heavy cream in a small pot over medium heat and reduce by one fourth, skimming the foam from the surface. Whisk in the Gorgonzola, stirring until completely dissolved. Season with salt and pepper and keep warm over low heat. The sauce will be thin.

8. Divide the sauce among four to six warmed plates and arrange the pasta spirals on top. Garnish with the thyme sprigs and serve immediately.

NOTE: To toast walnuts: Preheat the oven to 350°F. Place the walnuts on a baking sheet in a single layer and bake on the middle shelf until slightly brown and aromatic, 8 to 10 minutes.

ANDREW CARMELLINI

Fontina and White Truffle Macaroni

MAKES 6 TO 8 SERVINGS

From a chef known for his creativity and virtuosity comes a sophisticated and exciting dish. When he studied in Italy, Chef Carmellini, of Manhattan's Café Boulud, learned traditional pasta-making techniques, as well as how to determine which truffles were the best quality. His experience and skill are evident here.

1 pound penne	2 tablespoons white truffle oil (see Sources)
6 tablespoons butter, plus extra for the baking dish	Kosher salt
1 quart whole milk	Freshly ground pepper
4 sprigs fresh thyme	1/3 cup (about 1 1/2 ounces) freshly grated Parmigiano-Reggiano cheese
1 fresh bay leaf (you may substitute dry)	3 tablespoons fresh bread crumbs
1 small onion (about 1/2 pound), finely chopped	3 ounces fresh white truffle (1 or 2 small pieces; see Sources)
3 tablespoons flour	
1 pound fontina cheese (preferably from Val d'Aosta, Italy), cut into small dice	

1. Fill a medium bowl halfway with ice and cold water. Bring a large pot of salted water to a boil over high heat and cook the pasta until al dente, 10 to 12 minutes. Drain the pasta and transfer to the bowl of ice water. When cool, drain again.

2. Preheat the oven to 450°F. Lightly butter a 3 1/2-quart ovenproof baking dish.

3. In a medium saucepan, combine the milk with the thyme and bay leaf and bring to a scald over medium heat; remove from the heat.

4. In a medium sauté pan over medium heat, melt the 6 tablespoons of butter and cook the onion, stirring occasionally, until soft and translucent, 5 to 7 minutes. Sprinkle with the flour and cook, stirring, for 5 minutes. Slowly pour in half of the scalded milk, whisking to combine, and then add the remaining milk. Simmer for 5 minutes, whisking occasionally, and strain into a clean saucepan. Remove the thyme sprigs and bay leaf. Return to the stove over medium-low heat.

5. Fold the diced fontina cheese into the milk mixture and stir often until all the cheese is melted. Add the white truffle oil and season with salt and pepper (this is the béchamel sauce).

6. Toss the penne with three fourths of the béchamel sauce and transfer to the prepared baking dish. Drizzle the remaining sauce over the top and sprinkle with the grated Parmigiano-Reggiano and the bread crumbs. Cover loosely with aluminum foil and bake until bubbly, about 20 minutes. Remove from the oven, preheat the broiler, and place the uncovered dish under the broiler until crisp and golden brown, about 2 minutes.

7. Divide the fontina macaroni among six to eight warm dinner plates and shave the truffles generously over each serving.

Pasta with Fonduta and Fresh Truffles

MAKES 8 SERVINGS

Imagine a silken, rich Penne Alfredo with truffles. Yes, you have arrived in paradise—or perhaps Farallon restaurant in San Francisco.

Chef Franz advises you to take care with this gorgeous dish. The fonduta (fontina sauce) needs to be cooked very slowly so the eggs don't curdle—a double boiler helps, although it's not really necessary. Fresh chopped black truffles are preferred, but canned truffle peelings are passable (a 1½-ounce jar of truffle carpaccio, or shaved truffles, is available at many gourmet shops).

Shave fresh black truffles, as much as your budget allows, over the pasta before serving. Fresh white Italian truffles in season are the ultimate luxury, but they should be used only as a garnish—they lose all their flavor and aroma when heated.

1 pound penne, fusilli, or ziti	1 whole fresh black truffle, chopped, or
2 cups heavy cream	2 tablespoons canned truffle peelings, plus
4 egg yolks	1 whole fresh black or white truffle for garnish, optional (see Sources)
4 cups (1 pound) shredded Italian fontina cheese	Freshly ground pepper
4 tablespoons butter	Freshly grated nutmeg

1. Set the oven to 150°F (warm) and put in eight individual rimmed bowls.
2. Bring a large pot of salted water to a boil over high heat and cook the pasta until al dente, 10 to 12 minutes. Drain, reserving 1 or 2 tablespoons of the pasta water. Place the reserved water and the pasta in a large mixing bowl.

3. In a medium, heavy-bottomed saucepan, whisk together the cream and egg yolks. Put the saucepan over low heat and add the cheese and butter. Cook carefully, stirring constantly, until the cheese melts and the mixture has thickened. The sauce can also be made in the top of a double boiler set over, but not touching, simmering water. Some water may boil away; replace with hot tap water. (The sauce can be made up to a day ahead, refrigerated, and then reheated in a low microwave or in a double boiler over simmering water.)

4. Add about 1 cup of the warm sauce and the chopped truffle to the pasta in the bowl and toss to combine. Season with freshly ground pepper.

5. Divide the pasta among the eight warmed bowls and ladle the remaining sauce on top. Sprinkle with nutmeg and, if you wish, shave the remaining truffle over the dish for garnish.

ONEc.p.s. Wild Mushroom and Truffle Macaroni and Cheese

MAKES 6 TO 8 SERVINGS

This dish is based on the macaroni and cheese tart served at Chef Burke's celebrated restaurant on Central Park South in New York City. It is infused with rich mushroom flavor, along with the luxurious notes of truffle butter, truffle oil, and shavings of the earthy diamonds themselves. But it is still Mac and Cheese—an extraordinary blend of haute cuisine and country cooking.

1 pound ditalini	2 cups (½ pound) mascarpone cheese
Butter for the tartlet pans	½ cup (2 ounces) grated Parmigiano-Reggiano cheese
1 pound mixed wild mushrooms, cleaned, stems removed and reserved	2 tablespoons truffle butter (see Sources)
2 cups chicken stock or canned low-sodium broth	1 tablespoon truffle oil (see Sources)
¼ cup chopped dried porcini mushrooms	Kosher salt
1 tablespoon clarified butter (see Note)	Freshly ground white pepper
2 shallots, minced	½ pound raclette cheese, in 1 piece
1 teaspoon minced garlic	¼ cup fresh truffle shavings

1. Bring a large pot of salted water to a boil over high heat and cook the ditalini until al dente, about 11 minutes. Drain and cool.

2. Preheat the broiler. Generously butter six to eight individual tartlet pans and set aside.

3. Coarsely chop the mushroom caps and set aside.

4. Place the chicken stock in a medium saucepan over medium-high heat and add the dried porcini and the mushroom stems. Bring to a simmer; lower the heat and simmer until the stock is nicely infused with mushroom flavor, about 15 minutes. Remove from the heat and drain the liquid through a fine sieve lined with cheesecloth (or a double thickness of paper towels) into a clean bowl, discarding the solids. Set aside.

5. Heat the clarified butter in a large saucepan over medium heat. Add the shallots, garlic, and chopped mushroom caps and sauté until softened, 8 to 10 minutes.

6. Add the reserved mushroom stock, raise the heat to high, and bring to a boil. Immediately add the ditalini and stir to combine. Lower the heat to medium and stir in the mascarpone cheese, Parmigiano-Reggiano, truffle butter, and truffle oil. Stir to incorporate and season to taste with salt and white pepper. Pour an equal portion of the ditalini mixture into each prepared tartlet pan.

7. Using a cheese shaver (or a vegetable peeler, or the large slicing ridge on a box grater), shave a generous helping of raclette cheese over the top of each tartlet. Immediately place under the broiler until the cheese is melting, lightly browned, and bubbly, 3 to 4 minutes. Remove from the heat and sprinkle truffle shavings over the top of each tartlet. Serve very hot.

NOTE: To clarify butter: Melt the butter in a small pot over medium-low heat. Pour off the clear liquid (the clarified butter) and discard the solids that remain.

Baked Conchiglie with Roasted Garlic–Cheese Sauce, Ricotta Cheese, and White Truffle Oil

MAKES 4 TO 6 SERVINGS

The shells provide a great hiding place for cheese or a piece of garlic, so when you bite into each piece of pasta, you may be pleasantly surprised. Because the garlic has been roasted, it is sweet and subtle, and doesn't overwhelm the other flavors in this luscious dish from the chef of New York's Mesa Grill and Bolo.

1 head garlic

Olive oil, for rubbing the garlic

4 tablespoons butter, plus extra for the baking dish

1 pound conchiglie (medium shells)

2½ cups whole milk

1 medium onion (⅓ to ½ pound), finely diced

3 tablespoons flour

1 cup (¼ pound) grated mozzarella or fontina cheese

1 cup (½ pound) whole-milk ricotta cheese, drained

Kosher salt

Freshly ground pepper

½ cup (2 ounces) grated Parmigiano-Reggiano cheese

2 tablespoons white truffle oil (see Sources)

1. Preheat the oven to 300°F. Cut off the bud end and rub the head of garlic with olive oil. Wrap loosely in foil, place on a baking pan, and roast until very soft, 45 minutes to 1 hour. Peel, or squeeze out the softened garlic, and mash (can be refrigerated up to one day).

2. Raise the oven temperature to 375°F. Butter a 9 by 13-inch baking dish.

3. Meanwhile, bring 6 quarts of salted water to a boil. Add the pasta and cook, stirring occasionally, until al dente, about 13 minutes. Drain and reserve.

4. In a small saucepan over medium heat, bring the milk to a scald.

5. In a medium saucepan over medium heat, melt the 4 tablespoons of butter. Add the onion and cook until softened, about 5 minutes. Reduce the heat to low and whisk in the flour; cook, whisking, about 2 minutes, not allowing it to color. Whisk in the hot milk a little at a time. Once all the milk has been added, raise the heat to medium and cook, stirring occasionally, until the sauce thickens slightly. Whisk in the roasted garlic and the grated mozzarella and continue whisking until blended. Remove from the heat.

6. Add the cooked pasta and the ricotta to the roasted garlic–cheese sauce and stir to combine. Season with salt and pepper. Pour or spoon the mixture into the buttered baking dish and sprinkle the Parmigiano-Reggiano evenly over the top. Bake until the top is golden brown, about 25 minutes. Remove from the oven and drizzle with the truffle oil. Let rest for 5 minutes before serving, so the dish can absorb the truffle flavor.

California Truffled Macaroni and Cheese

MAKES 6 SERVINGS

Tim Goodell assures us that when people order generous servings of his Mac and Cheese for lunch at his restaurants, Aubergine, Troquet, and Red Pearl Kitchen, they don't order more food—they have no room for anything else. It is uncomplicated, yet elegant, perfectly spiced, and satisfying.

4 tablespoons butter, plus extra for the baking dish

1 pound elbow macaroni

2 quarts whole milk

1/2 cup flour

1/2 tablespoon minced garlic

1/2 pound sharp Cheddar cheese, cut into 1/4-inch dice

1/4 pound Montgomery Cheddar cheese (or substitute a mild Cheddar), cut into 1/4-inch dice

2 ounces Gorgonzola cheese, crumbled

1/2 teaspoon Tabasco

1 teaspoon black truffle oil (see Sources)

Kosher salt

Freshly ground pepper

1/2 cup (2 ounces) grated Parmigiano-Reggiano cheese

1/4 cup panko (Japanese bread crumbs)

Fresh chives, for garnish

1. Preheat the oven to 350°F. Lightly butter a 9 by 13-inch baking dish and set on a foil-lined sheet pan (to catch any spills).

2. Bring a large pot of salted water to a boil over high heat and cook the pasta until al dente, 8 to 10 minutes. Drain.

3. In a large saucepan over medium-high heat, heat the milk until almost scalding.

4. In a large saucepan over medium-low heat, melt the 4 tablespoons of butter, add the flour, and cook, stirring occasionally, until smooth and straw-colored, about 3 minutes. Raise the heat to medium, whisk the hot milk into the flour mixture, and continue whisking until smooth. Slowly bring to a boil, stirring occasionally to make sure that the milk at the bottom doesn't burn, and remove from the heat. Add the garlic and sharp Cheddar, Montgomery Cheddar, and Gorgonzola cheeses and mix carefully. Add the Tabasco and truffle oil and season with salt and pepper. Stir in the cooked macaroni.

5. Pour into the prepared baking dish. Combine the grated Parmigiano-Reggiano and the panko crumbs and sprinkle over the macaroni mixture. Bake until bubbling and browned, 15 to 20 minutes. Garnish individual servings with chives.

Chunks of Lobster Swimming in Cheesy Macaroni

MAKES 4 TO 6 SERVINGS

The chef of Norma's at New York's Le Parker Meridien Hotel gives us a recipe that is as sumptuous and sublime as it sounds. Think of Alex Porter's luxurious combination of lobster and creamy cheeses when you plan your New Year's Eve menu, or any time you deserve a bit of pampering.

1 pound elbow macaroni	Freshly grated nutmeg
2 cups heavy cream	Dash of Tabasco, optional
1¼ cups (5 ounces) coarsely grated sharp Cheddar cheese	2 tablespoons butter
	1 small onion, finely chopped (about ½ cup)
1 cup (¼ pound) coarsely grated Monterey Jack cheese	5 lobster tails (¼ pound each), shelled and cut into bite-size pieces (see Note)
¾ cup (3 ounces) coarsely grated blue cheese	1 cup white wine
Kosher salt	1¼ cups (5 ounces) coarsely grated Gruyère cheese
Freshly ground pepper	

1. Bring a large pot of salted water to a boil over high heat and cook the pasta until al dente, 8 to 10 minutes. Drain and reserve.

2. Preheat the oven to 350°F.

3. In a large (3½- to 4-quart) saucepan over medium heat, bring the cream to a boil and reduce it by half, watching closely so it doesn't boil over. Reduce the heat to low and stir in the Cheddar, Mon-

terey Jack, and blue cheese and simmer, stirring constantly, until melted. Season with salt, pepper, nutmeg, and Tabasco, if desired. Turn off the heat and let sit, stirring occasionally.

4. In a large skillet over medium heat, melt the butter and sauté the onion until translucent, about 6 minutes. Add the lobster pieces and stir to combine. Add the wine, raise the heat to medium-high, and bring to a boil. Reduce the heat to medium or medium-low and cook, stirring occasionally, until the wine has evaporated (about 30 minutes). Remove from the heat.

5. Add the cooked macaroni and the cheese mixture to the lobster mixture, stir to combine, and divide among four to six shallow, ovenproof bowls, or pour into a 9 by 13-inch baking pan. Top with the Gruyère and bake until the sauce is bubbly and the top is golden and crusty, 15 to 20 minutes.

NOTE: Lobster tails are available frozen. Ask the fishmonger to crack the shell—it will be easier to remove the meat. You can defrost the tails overnight in the fridge or place them in a bowl and run a steady stream of cold water over them until they are completely thawed.

JOSEPH WREDE

Joseph's Table Mac and Cheese with Dried Cherry Chutney and Roquefort Sauce

MAKES 4 TO 6 SERVINGS

Joseph is known for his inspired combinations, as the following dish makes abundantly clear. Creamy Roquefort sauce mellows out the potent flavors of the chutney, but that is only the beginning: endive adds crunch with a hint of bitterness and crumbled bacon provides savory crispness. Add all these to Mac and Cheese and you are soaring.

FOR THE DRIED CHERRY CHUTNEY (Makes about 2 cups)	½ cup chopped onion
1 cup champagne vinegar	½ cup tomato concasse (see page 116)
1 cup sugar	½ cup peeled and finely diced ginger
1 tablespoon ground mustard seeds	½ cup dried cherries

Combine all the ingredients in a medium saucepan over medium-high heat and cook, stirring occasionally, until the liquid has evaporated, 20 to 25 minutes. Be careful not to burn. It will be very thick, like jam. (May be made up to two days ahead and refrigerated, covered.)

FOR THE ROQUEFORT SAUCE
(Makes about 1¹/₂ cups)

3 cups heavy cream

1 cup apple cider

1 cup (¹/₄ pound) crumbled Roquefort cheese

Freshly ground pepper

In a large saucepan over medium-high heat, combine all the ingredients and bring to a boil. Lower the heat to medium and simmer until reduced by half (about 45 minutes).

TO ASSEMBLE THE DISH

1 pound elbow macaroni

Butter or oil for the baking dish

3 heads (about 1 pound) Belgian endive, cleaned and sliced into thin circles

1 pound bacon, cooked until crisp, drained, and crumbled (use your favorite method—stovetop, oven, or microwave)

Kosher salt

Fresh-cracked black pepper (see Note)

---

1. Preheat the oven to 350°F.
2. Bring a large pot of salted water to a boil over high heat and cook the macaroni until al dente, 8 to 10 minutes. Drain.
3. Butter a 3¹/₂-quart deep baking dish or a 9 by 13-inch baking pan and pour the macaroni into it. Distribute the endive, chutney, and bacon evenly over the top and pour the Roquefort sauce over all. Season with salt and pepper. Bake on the middle shelf until golden brown and bubbling, about 25 minutes.

NOTE: For cracked black pepper, wrap peppercorns in a dish towel and smash them with a heavy pan.

TO MAKE 1/2 CUP TOMATO CONCASSE

1 medium ripe tomato, cored, with a small X cut on the bottom

Bring a small pot of lightly salted water to a boil and immerse the tomato for 10 to 15 seconds. Remove from the water and peel—the skin should slip off easily. Cut in half and squeeze gently to remove the seeds and juice. Cut the flesh into 1/4-inch dice.

Sweetened Mascarpone and Noodle Pudding

MAKES 4 SERVINGS

A dreamy spin on Mac and Cheese, this orangy custard dessert uses just a sprinkle of pasta to provide a bit of texture. With both pasta and cheese on the ingredients list, it fits our requirements, but the result is a surprise—sweet, refined, and rarefied.

1/2 teaspoon plus 1 pinch kosher salt	1 tablespoon coarsely chopped lemon zest
2 tablespoons (1 ounce) soup-style pasta, such as ditali ligati, farfalline, pastina, or alphabets	1 tablespoon coarsely chopped orange zest
1 teaspoon granulated sugar	1 vanilla bean
1/4 cup whole milk	1 egg plus 3 egg yolks
1 1/2 cups heavy cream	1/4 cup (2 ounces) mascarpone cheese
1/4 cup plus 2 tablespoons powdered sugar	Fresh seasonal fruits, sliced or cubed, for serving

1. Preheat the oven to 275°F. Have ready an 8-inch round (or square), 3-inch-deep baking dish set into a larger dish.
2. In a medium pot over high heat, bring 1 quart of water to a boil with the 1/2 teaspoon of salt. Add the pasta and cook until al dente—1 minute less than the shortest cooking time given on the package. Drain, using a cheesecloth-lined colander if the pasta is smaller than the colander holes. Toss with the granulated sugar and set aside to cool.

3. In a medium, heavy-bottomed stainless steel saucepan, combine the milk, cream, powdered sugar, lemon and orange zests, and the remaining pinch of salt. Split the vanilla bean and scrape the seeds into the milk mixture, along with the pod. Bring to a scald over medium heat. Remove from the heat and allow the mixture to steep uncovered for 20 minutes.

4. Combine the egg, egg yolks, and mascarpone in a stainless steel bowl and whisk until the mixture is smooth.

5. Strain the milk mixture into a small pot, discard the solids, and return the liquid to the stove. Warm it over medium heat until the mixture just begins to bubble; do not allow it to boil. Begin whisking the egg mixture, and gently drizzle some of the hot milk mixture into it. Continue gradually adding and whisking until one third of the milk mixture is incorporated; then pour the warmed egg mixture back into the milk, whisking as you pour. Strain the milk mixture into a clean stainless steel bowl or a measuring cup large enough to accommodate all the custard (you will have about $2^1/_3$ cups).

6. Spread the cooked pasta on the bottom of the smaller baking dish and pour the warm custard over it. Stir to fully coat the pasta. Pour warm water into the outer baking dish to come $1^1/_2$ to 2 inches up the outside of the smaller dish (don't use boiling water—it will start to cook the eggs). Bake uncovered on the middle shelf until slightly firm and golden, 30 to 45 minutes. Remove from the oven and allow to cool in the water bath for 15 minutes. Divide the pudding among four dessert plates and serve warm with fresh fruit.

You will find almost everything you need at your local ethnic and gourmet markets, farmers' markets, and fine supermarkets. Here are some telephone and Internet sources, as well.

ARTISANAL PASTA

www.flyingnoodle.com

www.chefshop.com

Earthy Delights: www.earthy.com

CHEESES

Murray's Cheese Shop and Murray's by Mail catalogue: 888-692-4339;
  e-mail: murray's_cheese@msn.com

Mediterranean Foods (Greek feta cheese): 718-728-6166;
  www.mediterraneanfoods-inc.com

TRUFFLES, TRUFFLE PRODUCTS, AND WILD MUSHROOMS

Urbani USA: 718-392-5050; www.urbaniusa.com

Earthy Delights: www.earthy.com

Dean & DeLuca: 800-221-7714; www.deandeluca.com

Oakshire Mushroom Farm: 800-255-2077; www.mushroomlovers.com

Marché aux Délices: 888-547-5471; www.auxdelices.com

D'Artagnan: 800-327-8246; www.d'artagnan.com

RAMPS

Earthy Delights: www.earthy.com

ALEPPO PEPPER

Kalustyan's: 212-685-3451; www.kalustyans.com

Adriana's Caravan: 800-316-0820

Dean & DeLuca: 800-221-7714; www.deandeluca.com

RAS EL HANOUT

Adriana's Caravan: 800-316-0820

FOIE GRAS

Urbani USA: 718-392-5050; www.urbaniusa.com

Dean & DeLuca: 800-221-7714; www.deandeluca.com

D'Artagnan: 800-327-8246; www.d'artagnan.com

meat and potatoes

ACKNOWLEDGMENTS

Writing *Meat and Potatoes* has been a pleasure, in large part because of the talented and generous people who offered their support and worked along with me from start to finish. My sincere gratitude to Jane Dystel, Stacey Glick, Mary Bahr, Laura Ford, Eve Lindenblatt, Keith Dresser, and David Blasband.

Special thanks to the amazing chefs who contributed their vision to this book. For me, and for everyone who tastes the delights that follow, meat and potatoes will never be the same.

1.

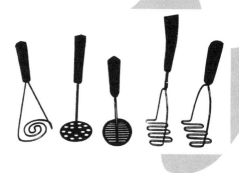

Introducing Meat and Potatoes

*A*DMIT IT, WHEN YOU'RE HUNGRY, YOU WANT MEAT AND potatoes! Put the two together and you need very little else to make a meal; their synergy in a dish always promises sustenance and comfort. But although comfort food was what I was after as I set out to collect recipes from America's finest chefs, I soon learned that the pairing of meat and potatoes goes way beyond the homey and nourishing—it provides a feast for the imagination.

The chefs who contributed to this book work their magic with beef, lamb, veal, and pork, and combine these meats with both white and sweet potatoes (including boniatos, which are a bit of each). The meats are grilled, roasted, braised, fried, or sautéed; the potatoes—whole, sliced, chunked, diced, or mashed—are braised, fried, sautéed, boiled, or simmered. The results are such creative leaps as Slow-Braised Veal and Vanilla Sweet Potato Shepherd's Pie (Gerry Hayden); Beef Short Rib Hash with Sunny Eggs and Balsamic Syrup (Deborah Stanton); Potato-Crusted Lamb Cakes (Daniel Angerer); Indian-Spiced Rack of Lamb with Potato Tikki and Mint Yogurt (Thomas John); and Roasted New Potatoes with Bacon, Chive Flowers, and Green Tomato Dressing (Ilene Rosen).

Much of the time, at home and in restaurants, meat and potatoes are cooked separately and presented together at the table. Grilled steak, for example, is just plain wonderful served with a creamy, herbal potato salad or beside a rich gratin that accents its simple perfection.

But when meat and potatoes are married in the pot, the finished dish is even more complex and nuanced, as with rib-eye steak that is oven-roasted over a bed of potatoes so that the savory and herbal flavors of the meat and its seasonings permeate the potatoes (Mitchel London); mashed potatoes that are formed into crusty cakes and stuffed with chili-spiced, braised short ribs (Andrew DiCataldo); diced potatoes combined with chorizo and layered over tortillas, to make crisp quesadillas (Sue Torres); and jalapeño-spiked mashed sweet potatoes that stuff a tender pork roulade (Glenn Harris).

Cook them separately or cook them together—both approaches show how meat and potatoes can work with one another, each highlighting the qualities of its partner. The final harmonious dish can be hot or cold, spicy or mild, sentimental or cutting edge. Just as macaroni and cheese is always greater than the sum of its parts, so is meat and potatoes.

A few words of advice: Although some of the dishes can be cooked relatively quickly, most of these recipes are not instant. Braises and roasts will require prep time and cooking time, and you should read each recipe carefully and plan ahead. But the good news is that nothing smells as wonderful as meat and potatoes that are gently simmering or roasting along with aromatic vegetables and herbs, wafting an atmosphere of well-being and plenty through your kitchen. Such cooking embodies the best qualities of slow food, whose preparation is a calming and gratifying activity—more pleasure than work and offering rewards you can taste.

Nevertheless, to make them more manageable, many recipes can be broken down into components that are made and refrigerated ahead and combined just before serving. A number of dishes can be cooked ahead and reheated later, and their flavor will deepen and mellow. And the bonus is that when you cook and later reheat, you get to enjoy the sensual experience (but not the work) twice.

As you become acquainted with these recipes, they will feed your own creative talents. Once you feel comfortable with the mechanics of braising, slow-roasting, and grilling, it becomes easy to choose a cut of meat and a variety of potatoes and pair them with the appropriate method. You can invent a recipe from scratch or deconstruct one of ours and reshuffle components to come up with a spontaneously delightful meal. Meat and potatoes are not only inspiring, they are forgiving.

About Meat

Buy the freshest and best-quality meat, from a butcher or supermarket you trust. If possible, buy ground meat from a butcher who grinds it to your order, rather than from a market where it has been preground and wrapped. Of course, check the date carefully on all packaged meat. As soon as possible after purchase, rewrap and refrigerate meat; use ground meat within two days and solid pieces within four days.

You will find that the more tender the cut of meat, the less time it needs to cook. Steaks and chops take only minutes from grill to table, while beef short ribs and oxtails—where flavorful morsels are hidden among the bones and fat—require longer braising. Leg and shoulder of lamb need a good amount of time in the oven to reach optimum flavor and texture. Although you can let each individual recipe be your guide, here are brief descriptions of the cooking methods used in this book:

Braising: Brown the meat in a little oil, then cook, partially submerged in a flavorful liquid, in a heavy, tightly covered pot or pan. Meat can be braised on the stovetop, in a Crock-Pot, or in the oven. Braising is the preferred method for tougher cuts of meat.

Grilling: Light an outdoor charcoal or gas grill and cook the meat quickly at a high temperature. Indoors, you can substitute an electric grill (make sure it provides enough heat to sear the meat), a stovetop grill pan, or a broiler.

Roasting: Cook the meat in a preheated oven, at a moderate to high temperature.

Sautéeing: Cook the meat in a skillet or sauté pan, in oil that has been heated until it shimmers, over medium or medium-high heat. Stir the meat as it cooks.

Stewing: Cover the meat with a flavorful liquid and cook at a simmer. This may be done on the stovetop, in a Crock-Pot, or in the oven.

The following meats are called for in our recipes:

BEEF

Cheeks
Meat near the face of the steer. Cheeks are a rich cut, with a gelatinous texture and a very intense flavor.

Chuck
Juicy and inexpensive cut from the shoulder and neck. Ground chuck goes into stew, meat loaf, and hamburger, and becomes the stuffing for chili peppers.

Oxtail
Tail of the steer; very bony meat. Chunky pieces (not from the end of the tail) are the meatiest, and become flavorful and tender when braised. Generally sold in 1- to 3-inch cross sections.

Rump
A cut from the bottom round; flavorful, a bit tougher than chuck, but very tender when braised.

Short Ribs
Cut from the prime rib and the next lower three ribs, these tasty, meaty ends of beef ribs require long cooking to become tender. They have layers of fat, meat, and bone. Fat must be removed both before and after cooking.

Same as chuck.

Steaks

Filet Mignon: Cut from the beef tenderloin. This is the tenderest steak, but it has a milder flavor than other steaks.

Rib Eye: Cut from the rib section. Juicy, flavorful, marbled with fat; not as tender as filet mignon.

Shell, or Strip Loin, Steak: A boneless cut from the beef short loin. Tender and mild-flavored.

Skirt Steak: Long, narrow steak, cut from the breast. A little fatty, but tender.

LAMB

Chops

Loin: From the hind saddle of the lamb. These are the tenderest lamb chops.

Rib: Cut from the rack. Tender and flavorful.

Shoulder: Cut from the lamb chuck. Juicy and marbled with fat, but not as tender as rib or loin chops. Arm chops, with a round bone, come from the lower part of the shoulder. Blade chops, with a narrow bone, are cut from the beginning of the shoulder.

Leg

Last half of the hind saddle of the lamb. A whole leg weighs from 6 to 11 pounds, but you can buy the shank end, which has more meat and less fat, or the sirloin end, which is tender but has more bone. A leg of lamb can be boned and then either butterflied or rolled and tied.

Rack

The attached lamb ribs, usually seven or eight ribs (each would be a chop if they were separated). The rack, which is the beginning of the foresaddle, is tender and delicious.

Shank

Includes part of the arm chop and bone. The foreshank is meatier than the hind shank.

Shoulder; Boneless Shoulder

A bit less tender than the leg, and more economical. A boneless shoulder can be rolled and roasted.

PORK

Bacon

Very fatty meat from the underside of a pig, sold sliced or in slabs. It is cured and smoked. Applewood-smoked bacon has excellent flavor and texture.

Chorizo

Cuban-style pork sausage made with paprika, wine, sugar, garlic, and fat.

Ham

Cured pork leg or shoulder. Black Forest ham is cut in one piece from the tenderest portion of the ham and smoked over corncobs or pinewood. It has excellent flavor and texture.

Kielbasa

Polish smoked sausage made from pork or a combination of beef and pork (it may also be made from beef).

Loin

The pork loin is divided into the blade end, which has the most fat; the sirloin end, which has the most bone; and the center, tenderloin portion, which is the leanest and most tender.

Tenderloin: The fillet cut from the center of the loin, usually 8 to 12 ounces; lean and tender.

Pancetta

Flavorful, moist Italian bacon that is cured, not smoked. It is usually sold in a sausage shape.

Prosciutto

Italian cured, air-dried ham that is firm, with a delicate flavor.

Breast; Boneless Breast

The breast includes the lower end of the ribs and weighs 9 to 10 pounds with bones. Chewy and flavorful.

Chops

Loin: These are the tenderest veal chops. Tournedos are boneless loin chops, very lean and tender. They are thin, so be careful not to overcook.

Rib: Cut from the rack. Very tender.

Rack, or Veal Rib Roast

The first part of the veal foresaddle, the rack looks like several attached rib chops. The first six bones have the tenderest meat.

About Potatoes

Textural wizards, potatoes can morph from dense to fluffy, chewy to crisp, depending on their preparation. A number of varieties are available at greenmarkets and supermarkets, and for more unusual types, contact the specialty suppliers listed in Sources. In our recipes, each chef states his or her preference, but if it isn't available, feel free to try another potato that is similar.

White (and gold) potatoes are classified as

STARCHY, with high starch and low water content

WAXY, with low starch and high water content

ALL PURPOSE, with medium starch and water content

NEW, with low starch and high water content (harvested when
young and thin-skinned, these potatoes
can be of any variety).

More starch generally makes potatoes good for baking, frying, and mashing; less means they are best roasted, boiled, or braised. That said, you may enjoy russet potatoes in some braises, as I do. They crumble a bit as they cook and thicken the sauce.

If you aren't sure which category your spuds fall into, put them in a bowl of salted water (2 tablespoons of salt to 11 ounces of water). High-starch potatoes will sink; waxy potatoes will float.

Shop for tubers that have firm, unwrinkled skin, without sprouts, cuts, or blemishes. Avoid those with green spots under the skin, which indicate that the potatoes have been stored in the light. (In a pinch, green spots, sprouts, and blemishes can be cut off, and the rest of the potato can be cooked.) Remove potatoes from their plastic bag and store them in a pantry that is cool, dark, and well ventilated. Although you should never refrigerate mature white or sweet potatoes, because their starch will convert to sugar, you can refrigerate new potatoes, which are lower in starch.

A general rule is three medium potatoes per pound; each pound makes about 2 cups mashed.

The following potatoes are called for in our recipes:

Peruvian Blue or Purple
Skin and flesh range from blue or lavender to dark purple. They have a dense texture, a subtle flavor, and a medium starch content. They originated in South America.

Boniato, or Cuban Sweet Potato
White-fleshed sweet potatoes that are less sweet than regular sweet potatoes, with a more subtle flavor, and a fluffy texture when cooked. Their skin color ranges from red to tan.

Fingerling
Shaped like a finger, 1 to 8 inches long. These are baby long white potatoes, with thin, light skin and a firm, creamy texture. They are all-purpose, with medium starch.

German Butterball
Yellow-fleshed round or oblong potatoes with a buttery taste, smooth deep yellow skin, and medium starch. This variety originated in Europe and was renamed in the United States.

New

Small, round, red- or brown-skinned potatoes that have been harvested before reaching maturity. They have low starch.

Red Bliss

Small, round, red-skinned new potatoes grown in California, Minnesota, and the Dakotas. They have a firm, smooth texture, white flesh, and less moisture than other red varieties, and they are low in starch. The spring and summer crops are sold immediately and have a sweeter, milder flavor than the fall crop, which is stored for later shipment.

Round Red

"Boiling potatoes." These have reddish-brown skin, waxy flesh, and medium starch.

Ruby Crescent Fingerling

Slightly larger fingerlings with pink-tan skin, yellow flesh, and low starch.

Russet, or Idaho

Rough brown skin with many eyes; white flesh; a light, fluffy texture when cooked; and high starch. This is the most widely used potato variety in the United States.

Sweet

Although there are many varieties, with orange, red, or white flesh, the darker-skinned orange-fleshed potatoes and the paler-skinned yellow-fleshed potatoes are the most common. The orange-fleshed, commonly called yams, are sweet and moist; the yellow-fleshed are less sweet and drier in texture. Both are long and tapered. (True yams are another tuber entirely, not related to sweet potatoes. They are large, starchy, and bland, with white, pink, or yellow flesh.)

Yukon Gold

Tan skin; oval shape; buttery, light yellow flesh; and a creamy texture. These are all-purpose potatoes, with medium starch.

Sources

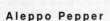

Most of the ingredients called for in the recipes are available at good supermarkets, specialty stores, butcher shops, ethnic markets, greenmarkets, and farmers' markets. Here are some telephone and Web sources, as well.

Aleppo Pepper

    ADRIANA'S CARAVAN: 800-316-0820;
        WWW.ADRIANASCARAVAN.COM
    DEAN & DELUCA: 800-221-7714; WWW.DEANDELUCA.COM

Beef Cheeks

    OTTOMANELLI & SONS: PHONE: 212-675-4217; FAX: 212-620-7286

Borlotti (Cranberry) Beans, Dried

    BUONITALIA: 212-633-9090

Chilies, Dried

    THE CMC COMPANY: 800-262-2780; WWW.THECMCCOMPANY.COM
    CULINARY PRODUCE: 908-789-4700; WWW.CULINARYPRODUCE.COM
    KALUSTYANS: 212-685-3451; WWW.KALUSTYANS.COM
    PENZEYS: 800-741-7787; WWW.PENZEYS.COM

Chili Powders and Ground Chili Peppers

    INTERNATIONAL SPICEHOUSE: 516-942-7248; WWW.SPICEHOUSEINT.COM
    KALUSTYANS: 212-685-3451; WWW.KALUSTYANS.COM
    PENZEYS: 800-741-7787; WWW.PENZEYS.COM

Demi-Glace

    WWW.GATEWAYGOURMET.COM
    MORE THAN GOURMET: 800-860-9385; WWW.MORETHANGOURMET.COM

Duck Fat

WWW.LUVADUCK.COM

Galangal

PENZEYS: 800-741-7787; WWW.PENZEYS.COM

Hickory Smoke Powder

INTERNATIONAL SPICEHOUSE: 516-942-7248; WWW.SPICEHOUSEINT.COM

LET'S SPICE IT UP!: 847-433-6309; WWW.LETSSPICEITUP.COM

Kaffir Lime Leaves

IMPORTFOOD.COM: 888-618-THAI; WWW.IMPORTFOOD.COM

Lemongrass

PENZEYS: 800-741-7787; WWW.PENZEYS.COM

Oregano

ADRIANA'S CARAVAN: 800-316-0820; WWW.ADRIANASCARAVAN.COM

Pomegranate Molasses

ADRIANA'S CARAVAN: 800-316-0820; WWW.ADRIANASCARAVAN.COM

KALUSTYANS: 212-685-3451; WWW.KALUSTYANS.COM

Potatoes

CULINARY PRODUCE: 908-789-4700; WWW.CULINARYPRODUCE.COM
(RUBY CRESCENT FINGERLINGS)

WWW.BIGELOWFARMS.COM (GERMAN BUTTERBALLS)

Truffle Butter

WWW.URBANI.COM

Truffle Oil, Black and White

      WWW.URBANI.COM

Truffles, Black

      WWW.URBANI.COM

Venison

      WWW.ATLANTICGAMEMEATS.COM

      WWW.AVENISON.COM

      D'ARTAGNAN: 800-327-8246; WWW.DARTAGNAN.COM

2.

Beef and Potatoes

ROBUST AND SATISFYING, BEEF SEEMS TO BE the favorite selection of meat-and-potato chefs. In fact, in sheer number of recipes, beef wins by a landslide, paired imaginatively with Yukon Gold, russet, boniato, red-skinned, purple, fingerling, Red Bliss, sweet, and new potatoes.

Steak is our starting point, the simplest and most tender cut chosen. It needs no more than to be simply grilled or roasted—but every cook has a unique perspective on what makes its best accompaniment. Keep your eye on the potatoes, because they are far more than an embellishment; they provide the variety and flair that define each dish.

Nora Pouillon marinates and grills strip steaks, and complements them with a rich gratin of potatoes, cream, and truffles; Philip McGrath's steak of choice is tender filet mignon, which he combines with the best of summer: beefsteak tomatoes and potato salad tossed with fresh tarragon; and Anita Lo pairs grilled shell steaks with crisp pancakes of grated potatoes stuffed with melted raclette cheese. Mitchel London roasts rib-eye steaks over and surrounded by potatoes, so that some spuds emerge crusty, while others become creamy and infused with meat juices. In a mélange of contrasts, Craig Cupani's steak becomes the center of a salad with portobello mushrooms, sweet caramelized onions, and *rösti* potatoes stuffed with bacon.

Less tender cuts require longer cooking times than steaks, but they can be made ahead and reheated, and they gain in flavor when served the next day. Short ribs are a favorite for braising: Felino

Samson combines them with creamy mashed boniatos; Laura Frankel incorporates them into the complex flavors of her Moroccan-Spiced Cassoulet; Dan Barber and Michael Anthony braise the ribs and serve them with delicate Ruby Crescent fingerlings. Deborah Stanton braises and minces these meaty ribs and turns them into a surprising Beef Short Rib Hash with Sunny Eggs and Balsamic Syrup; and Andrew DiCataldo treats them to a barbecue spice rub before cooking, in his Spicy Short Rib–Stuffed Potatoes.

Shepherd's pie, traditionally a casserole of savory ground or minced meat topped with buttery mashed potatoes, defines the meat-and-potato genre, but you won't recognize your old favorite in this section (see "Lamb, Venison, and Potatoes" for the classic pie). Here it is reborn three times: with tender braised short ribs and borlotti beans, in Hugh Acheson's dish; with gelatin-rich oxtail, in John Sundstrom's take on the original; and with beef shanks braised in fruity Zinfandel, in Henry Archer Meer's delicious version.

Cyril Renaud introduces us to meltingly tender beef cheeks, served with a super-rich purée of fingerling potatoes. Beef shanks offer rich, meaty flavor, and Arthur Schwartz first roasts them with root vegetables and then braises the oven-browned shanks and vegetables along with potatoes.

Juicy beef chuck, the definitive stew meat, is gently boiled with potatoes and other vegetables Provençal style, by Antoine Bouterin, a master of that cuisine. And Levana Kirschenbaum tells us how to adapt the classic boeuf bourguignon to cooking in a laborsaving Crock-Pot. In the hands of gifted chef Patricia Yeo, chuck becomes exotic Malaysian Beef Rendang with Sweet Potato–Coconut Purée.

Simple ground chuck shows its versatility, as well, moving from Ron Crismon's all-American Crispy Meat Loaf with Chanterelle-Buttermilk Gravy and Potato Gratin, and Matthew Kenney's savory Meat Loaf Stuffed with Mashed Potatoes and Cheddar, to a Tex-Mex favorite from Diana Barrios Treviño, Chiles Rellenos with Warm Mild Tomato Sauce. And if you crave Mediterranean flavors, Keith Dresser introduces us to meat and potatoes Italian style, in his fluffy Potato Gnocchi with Ragù Bolognese.

Grilled Rosemary-Marinated New York Strip Steak with Potato Gratin

Makes 4 servings

Nora Pouillon, of Nora, America's first certified organic restaurant, and Asia Nora, in Washington, D.C., infuses steaks with flavor by way of a bold marinade, and pairs them with a creamy, truffle-perfumed potato gratin. She suggests serving this rich combination with the simplest steamed vegetables, such as broccoli or green beans. Try to use organic ingredients.

FOR THE GRILLED ROSEMARY-MARINATED STEAKS:

2 tablespoons tamari or soy sauce
1 tablespoon minced onion
2 tablespoons minced garlic
2 tablespoons olive oil
1 teaspoon minced fresh rosemary

1 (3-inch) piece of fresh ginger, peeled
  and minced
1 tablespoon Dijon mustard
4 New York strip steaks (about
  8 ounces each)

1. In a medium nonreactive bowl, whisk together the tamari, onion, garlic, olive oil, rosemary, ginger, and mustard. Put the steaks in a glass or other nonreactive dish and pour the marinade over them. Allow them to marinate in the refrigerator for at least 2 hours or up to 8 hours.

2. When ready to cook the steaks, bring them to room temperature and preheat the grill or broiler.

3. Grill the steaks to the desired doneness (about 4 minutes on each side for medium-rare).

FOR THE POTATO GRATIN:

2 tablespoons unsalted butter, plus extra for
    the gratin dish
1 clove garlic, minced
2 pounds russet potatoes, peeled and sliced
    into 1/2-inch-thick rounds
1/2 teaspoon sea salt

1/4 teaspoon freshly ground black pepper
1/8 teaspoon freshly grated nutmeg
1 to 2 black truffles, thinly sliced or chopped
    (optional; see Sources)
1 cup heavy cream or half-and-half

1. Preheat the oven to 350°F.

2. Butter a shallow, preferably earthenware, dish and sprinkle with the garlic.

3. Layer the potato slices in the dish, sprinkling each layer with the salt, pepper, nutmeg, and black truffles, if using. Pour the cream over the potatoes; it should come three-quarters of the way up the contents of the dish. Dot with the 2 tablespoons butter, cut into small pieces, and bake for 1 to 1 1/2 hours, until the potatoes are soft and the top is browned and crisp.

TO SERVE, place a steak on each plate and accompany with a portion of the gratin.

Grilled Filet Mignon with Tarragon Potato Salad, Beefsteak Tomatoes, and Mustard Vinaigrette

Makes 4 servings

Chef McGrath, of the Iron Horse Grill, in Pleasantville, New York, was inspired to create this dish by the backyard barbecues of his youth. He combines the fondly remembered tastes on a single plate—where they most easily and successfully complement one another and present a beautiful picture. His superb potato salad is more than likely to erase your memories of all others.

FOR THE MUSTARD VINAIGRETTE:

5 tablespoons sherry vinegar
3 tablespoons Dijon mustard
1 cup extra-virgin olive oil

Kosher salt
Freshly ground black pepper

Combine the vinegar and the mustard in a small bowl. Slowly whisk in the olive oil. Season to taste with salt and pepper. This makes about 1 1/2 cups; it can be refrigerated for up to 3 days.

FOR THE TARRAGON POTATO SALAD:

2 pounds Yukon Gold potatoes, unpeeled
Kosher salt
4 scallions (white and 3 inches of green), minced

1 tablespoon minced fresh tarragon
Freshly ground black pepper
Mustard Vinaigrette

1. Put the potatoes in a saucepan, cover them with cold water, and bring to a boil over medium-high heat. Add salt and cook the potatoes until tender. Drain the potatoes, and when cool enough to handle, peel and cut into large dice.

2. In a large bowl, combine the diced potatoes, scallions, tarragon, and salt and pepper to taste. Toss with enough of the Mustard Vinaigrette to lightly coat the potatoes. Reserve the remaining vinaigrette. If you are going to serve the potato salad soon, cover and leave it at room temperature. Or refrigerate it for up to 1 day.

FOR THE GRILLED FILET MIGNON AND THE TOMATOES:

4 filet mignon steaks (about 8 ounces each)
Kosher salt
Freshly cracked black pepper (see Note)

Freshly cracked mustard seeds (see Note)
4 scallions, ends trimmed
4 beefsteak tomatoes, thickly sliced

1. Preheat the grill or broiler.

2. Season the steaks with salt, pepper, and mustard seeds.

3. Grill the steaks to the desired doneness (6 to 8 minutes on each side for medium-rare), grilling the scallions along with the steaks for 4 to 6 minutes (take care that they do not burn).

4. Arrange the tomatoes in a circle around the rim of each serving plate, season with salt and pepper, and drizzle with about 1 teaspoon of the reserved vinaigrette.

TO SERVE, place a generous scoop of potato salad in the center of each plate and top with a filet mignon. Garnish each steak with a grilled scallion.

NOTE: For cracked black pepper or mustard seeds, wrap peppercorns or seeds in a dish towel and smash them with a heavy pan.

Grilled Shell Steak with Raclette Potato Pancakes

Makes 4 servings

In this extraordinary version of steak and potato pancakes from Chef Lo, of Annisa Restaurant, in Manhattan, the cakes are stuffed with silky wilted leek and creamy melted cheese, and the juicy grilled shell steaks sit atop a rich mustard sauce. The components of this beautiful dish can be done ahead and assembled at the last minute, when the steaks have been grilled.

FOR THE RACLETTE POTATO PANCAKES:

2 large russet potatoes, peeled and
    julienned
Kosher salt
Freshly ground black pepper
Vegetable or canola oil
1 tablespoon unsalted butter

1 large leek (white part only), washed and cut
    into small dice
1 teaspoon combined chopped fresh chives,
    tarragon, thyme, and parsley
4 ounces ripe raw-milk French raclette cheese,
    cut into flat squares

1. Season the julienned potatoes with salt and pepper and put in a strainer set over a bowl. Press down on the potatoes to squeeze out as much liquid as possible.

2. Place four 5-inch, 3-inch-high, ring molds in a large frying pan over high heat. Pour in 1/4 inch of oil, heat, and flip the ring molds so that the oil coats the interior.

3. Divide the potato mixture among the molds and press down with a spatula, gathering up and discarding any strands of potato that go outside the molds. Cook until the bottom of each pancake is golden brown, then flip the filled molds and cook until the cakes are golden brown on the second side. Push the pancakes out of the molds and drain the cakes

on paper towels. Set aside until cool enough to handle. (To make the potato pancakes without molds, form the potato mixture into 4 thick, round, even cakes, and cook as above.)

4. Meanwhile, in a medium frying pan over medium heat, melt the butter and add the diced leek. Season to taste with salt and pepper. Cook until wilted but not browned, and place in a bowl to cool. When the leek has cooled, stir in the chopped chives, tarragon, thyme, and parsley.

5. When the potato pancakes are cool enough to handle, halve each one crosswise. Spread the leek mixture evenly over the 4 bottom halves and top with a square of raclette cheese. Reserve the top halves. You can make the cakes up to this point 3 hours ahead of time, cover loosely, and keep at room temperature.

6. When ready to serve, preheat the oven to 300°F. Place the halved potato pancakes on a baking sheet and put in the oven until the cheese has melted. Reassemble the cakes.

FOR THE SAUCE:

4 tablespoons plus 1 teaspoon unsalted butter
1 shallot, minced
1/2 cup veal stock, or substitute chicken stock
    or canned low-sodium chicken broth

1 tablespoon Dijon mustard
2 tablespoons coarse-grain mustard
Kosher salt
Freshly ground black pepper

In a medium saucepan over medium-high heat, melt 1 teaspoon of the butter and cook the shallot until softened but not colored. Add the stock and cook until reduced by three-quarters. Stir in the Dijon and coarse-grain mustards. Whisk in the remaining butter by tablespoons, making sure each is incorporated before adding the next. Season with salt and pepper and keep warm over very low heat. The sauce can be refrigerated for up to 1 day and reheated before serving.

FOR THE OPTIONAL GARNISH:

---

4 cups loosely packed baby arugula leaves
1/2 teaspoon red wine vinegar

1 1/2 teaspoons extra-virgin olive oil

Put the arugula in a large bowl. Combine the vinegar and olive oil and pour over the leaves, tossing to cover the arugula with the mixture.

FOR THE GRILLED STEAKS:

---

4 well-marbled shell steaks (about
8 ounces each)

Kosher salt
Freshly ground black pepper

Preheat the grill or broiler (alternatively, set a heavy skillet, preferably cast iron, over high heat until it is heated through). Season the steaks with salt and pepper, and grill to the desired doneness (6 to 8 minutes on each side for medium-rare). Allow the steaks to rest in a warm spot, tented with foil, for 5 minutes.

TO SERVE, divide the sauce among 4 plates. Slice each steak 1/2 inch thick across the grain and arrange over the sauce. Place a potato pancake on each plate and garnish with the arugula, if desired.

Seared Rib-Eye Steak with Crisp and Creamy Potatoes

BEEF

Makes 4 servings

You don't always need a grill to make a great steak, as this memorable dish from Mitchel London happily proves. And what is more, oven-roasting steak along with potatoes allows our two favorite foods to cook together in a way that brings out the finest qualities of both.

2 fresh thyme sprigs
Freshly cracked black pepper (see Note)
4 or 5 cloves garlic, unpeeled, crushed with
*   the broad end of a knife blade*
2 tablespoons extra-virgin olive oil

2 rib-eye steaks, bone in (about
*   1 3/4 pounds each)*
2 large russet potatoes, unpeeled, thinly sliced
Kosher salt
Chopped flat-leaf parsley

1. In a large bowl, combine the thyme, pepper, garlic, and 1 tablespoon of the olive oil. Add the steaks and cover with the marinade. Marinate for 2 hours at room temperature, or in the refrigerator if the room is very warm.

2. Preheat the oven to 475°F.

3. Place a large, heavy ovenproof pan, preferably cast iron, on the stove over high heat until it becomes very hot. Sear the steaks for 2 minutes on each side and remove from the pan.

4. Reduce the heat to medium, add the remaining 1 tablespoon olive oil to the pan, and heat until very hot. Toss the potatoes with salt and pepper, add to pan, and cook until brown on both sides and nearly cooked through. Place the steaks on top of some of the potatoes, and arrange the remaining potatoes around the steaks. Place the pan in the middle of the preheated oven and cook the steaks to the desired doneness (15 minutes for

medium-rare). The potatoes that have cooked under the steaks will be creamy, and those that surround the steaks will be crisp.

5. Remove the steaks to a cutting board, tent with foil, and let them sit for 5 minutes.

6. Slice the steaks as desired, and serve with the potatoes. Sprinkle with salt and garnish with chopped parsley.

NOTE: For cracked black pepper, wrap peppercorns in a dish towel and smash them with a heavy pan.

Sliced Steak and Mushroom Salad with Caramelized Onions and Bacon-Rösti Potatoes

Makes 6 servings

In this colorful dish, Chef Cupani, of Manhattan's Patroon Restaurant, makes juicy grilled steak the center of a hearty salad with tomatoes, basil, and grilled onions and mushrooms. Alongside (and very much a part of the picture) are crisp potato pancakes filled with bacon and onions.

This recipe is simpler than it may appear at first reading, because several steps can be done ahead. The steak should be marinated for 6 to 12 hours before cooking, and the bacon-and-onion filling for the potato pancake can be prepared 2 to 3 days before using. The potatoes can be baked up to 1 day before you shred them for the pancake.

Start the potato pancake on top of the stove, and just before you put it into the oven to finish cooking, put the steak, onions, and mushrooms on the grill. You can keep the pancake in the warm oven, if necessary, while you complete the salad.

FOR THE MARINATED STEAK:

2 tablespoons finely chopped shallots
1 tablespoon finely chopped garlic
1 tablespoon finely chopped fresh parsley
Freshly ground black pepper

1/2 cup red wine vinegar
1/2 cup packed brown sugar
1 cup olive oil
4 pounds skirt steak

In a large nonreactive bowl, combine the shallots, garlic, parsley, pepper, vinegar, brown sugar, and olive oil. Add the steak, cover, and refrigerate for at least 6 hours or up to 12 hours.

4 large russet potatoes, unpeeled
8 ounces bacon (preferably applewood
    smoked), cut into small dice
2 large white onions, sliced
Kosher salt

Freshly ground black pepper
Black truffle oil (optional; see Sources)
1 tablespoon chopped flat-leaf parsley
2 tablespoons olive oil

1. Preheat the oven to 400°F.

2. Bake the potatoes for 45 to 50 minutes, until cooked through but not quite soft. The baked potatoes can be refrigerated for up to 1 day.

3. Let the potatoes cool (if you haven't refrigerated them); peel and shred coarsely, using a box grater or a food processor.

4. In a large skillet over medium heat, sauté the bacon for 5 minutes. Discard the excess fat, add the onions, and continue cooking until the onions are dark golden brown, about 15 minutes. Season with salt, pepper, and truffle oil, if using, and stir in the chopped parsley. The bacon-and-onion mixture can be refrigerated for up to 3 days.

5. Preheat the oven to 200°F.

6. Place a 12-inch ovenproof skillet, preferably cast iron, over medium-high heat, add the olive oil, and heat until almost smoking. Add half the shredded potatoes, lightly shaking the pan. Spread the bacon-and-onion mixture evenly over the potatoes, and cover with the remaining grated potatoes. Using a rubber spatula, scrape down the sides of the skillet to keep the potato mixture uniform and round. Keep the pan on the stove just long enough to shape the potato pancake, then put the skillet in the oven for 15 minutes.

7. Carefully remove the skillet from the oven, and using a spatula, flip the potato pancake over (the potato should be golden brown). Return the skillet to the oven for an additional 15 minutes. Remove the potato pancake from the skillet. You can keep the pancake in the warm oven until ready to serve.

Kosher salt
3 red onions, sliced 1/4 to 1/2 inch thick
4 portobello mushrooms, caps only
3 plum tomatoes, sliced into 1/4- to
        1/2-inch-thick rounds

10 fresh basil leaves
Freshly ground black pepper
Olive oil

1. Preheat the grill or broiler.

2. Remove the steak from the marinade and shake off the excess liquid. Season the steak with salt, and grill to the desired doneness (3 to 4 minutes on each side for medium-rare). Grill the onions and mushrooms for 3 to 4 minutes on each side.

3. Remove the steak from the grill and let it sit, tented with foil, for 5 minutes; slice crosswise 1/4 inch thick. Slice the mushrooms crosswise 1/2 inch thick.

4. In a large bowl, separate the grilled onions into rings. Add the sliced mushrooms, plum tomatoes, fresh basil leaves, and finally, the sliced steak. Season with salt, pepper, and a little olive oil, and mix well.

TO SERVE, cut the warm potato pancake into wedges and divide among 6 plates. Evenly distribute the sliced steak and mushroom salad among the plates.

FELINO SAMSON

Bomboa's Braised Short Ribs with Mashed Boniatos and Gingered Baby Bok Choy

Makes 4 servings

If you haven't yet tried mashed boniatos, you are about to discover something wonderful. In Chef Samson's dish from Chicago's Bomboa Restaurant, the boniatos are unbelievable and the ribs are tender and tasty. Crisp bok choy is a simple companion to this Brazilian-accented combination.

While the meat is cooking, you can prepare the boniatos, and when it is just about done, you can quickly cook the bok choy. When shopping for boniatos in your supermarket, ask for white sweet potatoes—the tubers are often easier to find by that name.

FOR THE BRAISED SHORT RIBS:

4 beef short ribs (10 to 12 ounces each)
Kosher salt
Freshly ground black pepper
2 tablespoons canola oil
2 carrots, finely chopped
1 onion, finely chopped

2 to 3 stalks celery, finely chopped
1 (750-milliliter) bottle red wine
1/4 cup packed light brown sugar
6 cups veal stock, or substitute beef stock
 or canned low-sodium beef broth

1. Preheat the oven to 325°F.
2. Season the short ribs all over with salt and pepper.
3. In a large casserole or a roasting pan over medium-high heat, heat the canola oil and brown the meat (4 to 5 minutes on each side).

4. Combine the carrots, onion, and celery (this is a *mirepoix*) and add the vegetables to the meat. Reduce the heat to medium and cook until the vegetables are softened but not browned and some moisture has evaporated, about 5 minutes. Add the red wine and simmer for 5 minutes.

5. In a large saucepan, combine the brown sugar, 1 tablespoon of pepper, and the veal stock and bring to a boil. Pour the boiling stock over the meat and vegetables and cook in the oven, tightly covered, for about 2 hours, or until the meat is tender.

6. Strain, reserving the meat and the braising liquid separately. Discard the solids.

FOR THE MASHED BONIATOS:

4 boniatos (about 2 pounds), peeled
    and quartered
3 tablespoons unsalted butter

1/4 cup heavy cream
Kosher salt
Freshly ground black pepper

Put the boniatos in a large saucepan, cover with cold water, and bring to a boil over high heat. Boil gently until tender, 20 to 30 minutes. Drain and mash the boniatos, or put them through a food mill or ricer into a mixing bowl. Mix in the butter and cream, and season with salt and pepper

4 baby bok choy, split lengthwise

2 tablespoons extra-virgin olive oil

1 teaspoon grated or finely chopped
     fresh ginger

Kosher salt

Freshly ground black pepper

1. Bring a large pot of salted water to a boil and blanch the bok choy for 1 minute. Drain.

2. In a large sauté pan over medium heat, heat the olive oil, add the bok choy, and stir. Add the ginger, season with salt and pepper, and stir or toss to combine well; cook for about 2 minutes. The bok choy should be well coated and just lightly cooked.

TO SERVE, place a large mound of mashed boniatos in the center of each plate. Make a well and sink a short rib into the center of each mound of boniatos. Spoon the braising liquid on and around the meat and potatoes, and accompany with the bok choy.

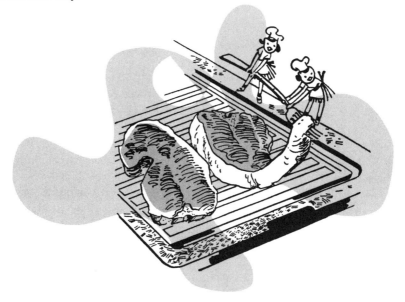

Braised Short Ribs with Pan-Roasted Ruby Crescent Fingerlings

Makes 8 servings

In this winning combination from Manhattan's Blue Hill Restaurant, Chefs Barber and Anthony braise short ribs until the meat is meltingly tender, and combine it with golden pan-roasted fingerling potatoes, the best the greenmarket or your nearest farm stand has to offer.

FOR THE BRAISED SHORT RIBS:

10 pounds beef short ribs
Kosher salt
Freshly ground black pepper
2 tablespoons vegetable oil, plus more
     as needed
2 large onions, coarsely chopped
2 carrots, sliced 1 inch thick
2 stalks celery, sliced 1 inch thick
1 head garlic, unpeeled, halved crosswise

1/4 cup packed dark brown sugar
2 tablespoons Worcestershire sauce
2 fresh bay leaves, or substitute dried
2 cups red wine
1 cup Madeira, or substitute another cup
     of red wine
About 8 cups chicken stock or canned
     low-sodium chicken broth, or
     substitute water

1. Preheat the oven to 225°F.

2. Season the short ribs all over with salt and pepper.

3. In a large sauté pan over high heat, heat the vegetable oil and sear the short ribs until golden brown. You will have to do this in batches. Remove the ribs from the pan and set aside.

4. Pour off all but 2 tablespoons of the fat remaining in the pan. Reduce the heat to low and add the onions, carrots, celery, and garlic to the sauté pan. Gently sauté until the onions are golden, about 5 minutes.

5. Put the reserved ribs and the sautéed vegetables in a deep roasting pan or a Dutch oven. Add the brown sugar, Worcestershire sauce, bay leaves, red wine, and Madeira, and season to taste with salt and pepper. Add enough stock to cover the ribs. Tightly cover the pan with foil and/or a lid. Cook in the oven for 3 to 3 1/2 hours, until the meat separates from the bones.

6. Remove the ribs from the pan and pull the meat from the bones; reserve the meat.

7. In the roasting pan over medium high heat, bring the braising liquid to a gentle boil and reduce it until thick and saucelike. Strain the liquid and return the meat and the liquid to the pan until ready to serve.

FOR THE PAN-ROASTED RUBY CRESCENT FINGERLINGS:

16 Ruby Crescent fingerling potatoes, unpeeled
(see Sources; or substitute another
variety of fingerling, or Red Bliss)
Kosher salt

2 tablespoons olive oil
1 clove garlic, crushed with the broad end of a
knife blade and peeled
Freshly ground black pepper

1. Put the potatoes in a large pot and cover with cold water by 1 inch. Add 1 tablespoon of salt and bring to a gentle boil. Cook the potatoes until tender, 40 to 45 minutes. Drain the potatoes, and peel them while they are still warm. Leave the potatoes whole if they are small; halve or quarter them if they are larger.

2. In a large skillet over medium-high heat, heat the oil with the garlic, and sauté the potatoes until golden, about 4 minutes on each side. Season with salt and pepper.

TO SERVE, divide the meat with its juices among 8 plates and accompany with the potatoes.

BEEF

Moroccan-Spiced Cassoulet

Makes 6 to 8 servings

This is a glorious potpourri of Middle Eastern and traditional Western flavors, from Laura Frankel's Manhattan restaurant, Shallots, and its Chicago sibling. You can prepare this cassoulet ahead, relax, and then reheat it when you are ready to serve a truly special meal.

Olive oil

10 pounds short ribs, each rib cut into thirds and trimmed of excess fat (the butcher can do this)

Kosher salt

Freshly ground black pepper

2 large Spanish onions, cut into small dice

3 leeks (white and tender green parts), washed and thinly sliced

4 cloves garlic, crushed with the broad end of a knife blade, peeled, and finely chopped

2 sweet potatoes, peeled and cut into small dice

2 Yukon Gold potatoes, peeled and cut into small dice

1 butternut squash, peeled, seeded, and cut into small dice

1 acorn squash, peeled, seeded, and cut into small dice

3 cups beef or chicken stock, or substitute canned low-sodium beef or chicken broth, plus more as needed

1/2 cup pearl barley

1/4 cup tomato paste

1 tablespoon ground cinnamon

1 tablespoon ground coriander

1/2 teaspoon red pepper flakes

1/2 teaspoon ground cumin

1/4 cup chopped pitted Medjool dates

1/4 cup chopped dried apricots

1/4 cup chopped dried figs (preferably Calimyrna)

1/4 cup chopped fresh parsley

1. Coat the bottom of a large Dutch oven or heavy casserole with olive oil and set the pot over medium-high heat.

2. Season the short ribs all over with salt and pepper and brown them in batches in the oil (adding more oil if needed). Remove the browned ribs to a large roasting pan, and pour off the fat from the pot. Wipe out the pot with paper towels.

3. Preheat the oven to 325°F.

4. Coat the bottom of the Dutch oven with fresh olive oil, place over medium heat, and cook the onions, leeks, and garlic, stirring occasionally, until golden, about 10 minutes. Add the onion mixture to the roasting pan, and repeat the cooking with the sweet potatoes, Yukon Gold potatoes, butternut squash, and acorn squash. Cook all the vegetables in small batches, so as not to overcrowd the Dutch oven, adding olive oil as needed, and seasoning each batch with salt and pepper. Add each cooked batch to the roasting pan.

5. Meanwhile, put the stock and barley in a medium pot and simmer over medium-high heat until the barley is cooked through, about 30 minutes.

6. Add the tomato paste to the Dutch oven and cook quickly until it darkens, 2 to 3 minutes. Stir in the cinnamon, coriander, red pepper flakes, and cumin and cook for 1 to 2 minutes. Add the stock and cooked barley. Add the dates, apricots, and figs.

7. Add the tomato mixture to the roasting pan, and mix well with the meat and vegetables. Add more stock, if needed, to come three-quarters of the way up the contents of the pan. Cover the pan tightly, place it in the oven, and cook for 2 hours.

8. Pour the meat and vegetables into a strainer set over a large bowl and return the strained juices to the roasting pan. Return the cooked vegetables to the pan. Pull the meat from the rib bones, removing the excess fat, and add the meat to the vegetables and juices. Cover the roasting pan and return it to the oven to cook for about 30 minutes more.

9. To serve, divide the meat and vegetables among 6 to 8 plates and spoon the juices over them. Sprinkle with the chopped parsley.

Short Rib Shepherd's Pies with Borlotti Beans and Chive Potato Crust

Makes 4 servings

Try these individual shepherd's pies from the Five-and-Ten Restaurant, in Athens, Georgia, the creation of Chef Hugh Acheson. In his imaginative take on what has surely become our favorite cut for braising, savory short ribs are mixed with sturdy pink-flecked beans and then covered with a golden crust of creamy mashed potatoes. The defining herbal flavors here are chives, rosemary, and thyme.

FOR THE SHORT RIBS AND BORLOTTI BEANS:

1 cup dried borlotti (cranberry) beans, rinsed
   and picked over (see Sources; or
   substitute 2 cups drained canned
   Roman beans such as Goya brand)
3 pounds beef short ribs, trimmed of excess fat
Kosher salt
Freshly ground black pepper
2 tablespoons vegetable oil
1 onion, diced

1 carrot, diced
1/2 cup diced celery
2 cups red wine
2 cups chicken or beef stock, or substitute
   canned low-sodium chicken or
   beef broth
1 bay leaf
1 tablespoon chopped fresh thyme
1 tablespoon chopped fresh rosemary

1. Quick-soak the beans, if desired (see Note).
2. Preheat the oven to 325°F.
3. Season the short ribs all over with salt and pepper.
4. In a large ovenproof pot over medium-high heat, heat the vegetable oil until very hot and sear the ribs on all sides. Remove them to a plate.

5. Pour off all but 1 tablespoon of the oil from the pot and add the onion, carrot, and celery. Sauté the vegetables over medium heat for 5 minutes; they will turn lightly golden and release some of their sugars.

6. Add the wine, increase the heat to medium-high, and cook, scraping the browned bits from the bottom of the pan. Add the stock and bring to a gentle boil. Reduce the heat to medium and bring the mixture to a simmer.

7. Return the ribs to the pot, add the bay leaf, thyme, and rosemary, and cover the pot tightly. Braise in the oven for 2 1/2 hours.

8. While the ribs are cooking, put the beans in a pot, cover with cold water by 2 inches, and bring to a boil. Skim off any foam that rises, reduce the heat to medium, and simmer the beans, covered, until cooked, about 35 minutes if they have been quick-soaked, 45 to 90 minutes if they haven't. When the beans have softened, add 2 teaspoons salt. Drain and set aside.

FOR THE CHIVE POTATO CRUST:

2 pounds Yukon Gold potatoes, peeled
Kosher salt
3 tablespoons unsalted butter, at room
  temperature

1 cup heavy cream
Freshly ground black pepper
1/2 cup chopped fresh chives

Put the potatoes in a saucepan, cover them with cold water, and bring to a boil over medium-high heat. Add 1 tablespoon salt and cook the potatoes until tender. Drain and pass the potatoes through a food mill or ricer into a mixing bowl. While they are still hot, add the butter and cream, combine well, and season with salt and pepper. Fold in the chives.

1. Remove the ribs from the pot and strain the braising liquid. Return the pot, with the braising liquid, to the stove and reduce by half over medium heat. Turn off the heat and add the cooked borlotti beans to the reduced braising liquid. Pull the meat from the rib bones, removing the excess fat, and add the meat to the braising liquid.

2. Increase the oven heat to 400°F.

3. Divide the meat, beans, and braising liquid evenly among 4 ovenproof bowls or small casseroles. Top each with a layer of mashed potatoes and smooth the potatoes over with a knife. Place the 4 bowls on a baking sheet and bake in the oven for 15 minutes.

NOTE: To quick-soak the borlotti beans, put the beans in a small pot and pour boiling water over them to cover by 2 inches. Soak until the beans have doubled in size, about 1 hour. Drain and discard the soaking liquid. Set the beans aside until ready to cook.

ANDREW DICATALDO

Spicy Short Rib–Stuffed Potatoes

Makes 10 appetizer or 5 main-dish servings

Short ribs are treated to a spicy and sweet barbecue rub before they are braised in stock and dark beer; then the tender meat becomes the filling for crusty potato cakes that combine crisp, creamy, chewy, sweet, and spicy in each mouthful. Chef DiCataldo, of Patria, in Manhattan, suggests serving these satisfying cakes with a simple green salad sprinkled with some blue cheese.

You can make the ribs in advance and refrigerate or freeze them in their cooking liquid. If you do this, don't reduce the liquid completely, and finish the reduction when you reheat the meat.

FOR THE BARBECUE SPICE RUB:

1/4 cup granulated sugar
1/4 cup packed light brown sugar
1/4 cup kosher salt
2 tablespoons garlic powder
2 tablespoons onion powder
1/4 cup paprika
2 tablespoons ground ancho chili pepper
  (see Sources)

1 tablespoon ground cumin
2 tablespoons ground chipotle pepper
  (see Sources)
2 tablespoons mulatto (dark American)
  chili powder (see Sources)
1 tablespoon hickory smoke powder
  (see Sources)

Combine all the ingredients and store at room temperature in an airtight container. You will have more than you need for this recipe, but the spice rub will keep for up to 6 months. Makes about 1 1/2 cups.

2 pounds beef short ribs, trimmed of excess fat

1/4 cup Barbecue Spice Rub

1/4 cup canola oil

1 (12-ounce) bottle dark beer, such as Guinness

4 cups chicken stock or canned low-sodium
     chicken broth

1 onion, cut into large chunks

3 cloves garlic, peeled

2 stalks celery, cut into large pieces

3 carrots, cut into large pieces

2 bay leaves

3 tablespoons chopped fresh thyme leaves

Kosher salt

Freshly ground black pepper

1. Rub the short ribs generously with the Barbecue Spice Rub and refrigerate, covered (or in a Ziploc bag), for at least 4 hours or up to 12 hours.

2. Preheat the oven to 350°F.

3. Heat the canola oil in a large, heavy, ovenproof pot over medium-high heat and brown the ribs, turning to cook on all sides (because of the spice rub, they will turn deep brown). Add the beer, stock, onion, garlic cloves, celery, carrots, bay leaves, and thyme, and bring to a boil. Season with 1 1/2 teaspoons salt and 1/2 teaspoon pepper. Loosely top with foil and place in the oven until the meat is very tender and falling off the bone, about 2 1/2 hours.

4. Remove the short ribs from the pot with tongs and put them on a plate or into a high-sided pan. Strain the braising liquid and discard the solids. Return the liquid to the pot and simmer over medium-high heat until the liquid is reduced by half, 25 to 30 minutes. Season with salt and pepper. Shred the meat, discarding the bones and excess fat, and add the meat to the reduced braising liquid. Allow the mixture to cool slightly.

3 pounds purple potatoes or white baking
     potatoes, unpeeled

Kosher salt

Freshly ground black pepper

Place the potatoes in a large pot and cover with cold water by 1 inch. Add 1 tablespoon salt and bring to a gentle boil. Cook the potatoes until tender, 40 to 45 minutes. Drain the potatoes, let them cool slightly, and peel them. Put the potatoes through a food mill or ricer, or mash them, and season to taste with salt and pepper. Divide the mashed potatoes into 10 equal portions.

FOR THE STUFFED POTATO CAKES:

1/2 cup all-purpose flour
4 large eggs, beaten
Kosher salt

3 cups plain bread crumbs
Canola oil

1. Dip your hands into cold water to prevent the potatoes from sticking. Flatten 1 portion of mashed potatoes between the palms of your hands into a circle 3 1/2 to 4 inches in diameter. Make a slight well in the center and fill it with 2 heaping teaspoons of the braised short ribs, reserving the sauce. Fold the potato circle over the meat. Press the edges together to seal, and with both hands, shape the potato cake into a ball and flatten slightly. Repeat until all the stuffed potato cakes have been formed.

2. Set out 3 medium bowls. Put the flour into one, beat the eggs lightly with 2 teaspoons salt in another, and put the bread crumbs into the third. Dredge the cakes in the flour, gently shaking off the excess. Dip them into the beaten eggs, and roll them in the bread crumbs until they are well coated.

3. Pour canola oil about 1/2 inch deep into a large saucepan or a large, high-sided skillet. Over medium-high heat, heat the oil to 375°F. Carefully put the potato cakes into the hot oil and fry them until golden, about 1 minute on each side. You may have to do this in batches.

4. Remove the cakes from the oil with a slotted spoon, and drain on paper towels. Serve with the reserved sauce.

BEEF

Beef Short Rib Hash with Sunny Eggs and Balsamic Syrup

Makes 6 servings

Chef Deborah Stanton, of Deborah, in Greenwich Village, has been praised for spinning classics into gold, and this recipe demonstrates her wizardry. It takes simple beef hash to new levels—and it will become your favorite brunch or Sunday supper dish. The balsamic syrup, short ribs, and potatoes can be made ahead and refrigerated, making the final preparation simple and quick.

FOR THE BALSAMIC SYRUP:

2 cups balsamic vinegar

In a small saucepan over very low heat, cook the vinegar until reduced to a syrup. Remove, let cool, and reserve in an airtight container. May be refrigerated for up to 1 week.

FOR THE SHORT RIBS:

2 tablespoons canola oil
Kosher salt
Freshly ground black pepper
3 pounds beef short ribs, cut into 3-inch pieces and trimmed of excess fat (the butcher can do this)
All-purpose flour
2 large Spanish onions, quartered
2 bulbs fennel, halved
5 cloves garlic, peeled

1/2 (750-milliliter) bottle Cabernet, or substitute a quality red wine such as Zinfandel or Shiraz
6 cups chicken stock or canned low-sodium chicken broth
1 (24-ounce) can plum tomatoes, with their juice
3 bay leaves
1 teaspoon red pepper flakes

1. In a large pot, heat the canola oil over medium heat. Lightly salt and pepper the short ribs and roll them in flour, shaking off the excess. Put the ribs in the pot and brown on all sides; remove from the pot.

2. Pour off any excess fat and add the onions, fennel, and garlic cloves to the pot. Cook, stirring frequently to deglaze the beef flavors from the bottom, and to give a bit of color to the vegetables, about 5 minutes.

3. Add the wine and boil gently for 5 minutes, until the alcohol has cooked off. Add the chicken stock and tomatoes and combine well. Return the ribs to the pot and evenly distribute them.

4. Add the bay leaves and red pepper flakes. Taste and season with salt and pepper. Bring the mixture to a boil, cover, and reduce the heat to low. Keep the heat low so that the liquid doesn't reduce too quickly. Simmer until the ribs are fork-tender and falling off the bone, about 1 hour and 20 minutes. (Begin by cooking the ribs for 1 hour, then check every 10 minutes for doneness.)

5. Let the pot stand off the heat for an additional 20 minutes; remove the ribs to a platter and let cool. Hand-shred the meat, remove the fat, and reserve the cooking liquid. The meat and juices can be refrigerated for up to 3 days.

FOR THE POTATOES:

2 pounds Yukon Gold potatoes, unpeeled, cut into 1/8-inch dice

Kosher salt

Put the potatoes in a large saucepan and cover with cold water. Add 1 tablespoon salt and bring to a boil over high heat. The potatoes should be done at this point; if they are not, reduce the heat to medium and cook at a gentle boil until fork-tender. Drain, place on a plate or tray, and let cool in the refrigerator. The potatoes can be refrigerated for up to 1 day.

1 tablespoon canola oil, plus more, as needed

1 teaspoon finely chopped garlic, plus more,
    as needed

1 bunch of kale, washed and cut into
    1/2-inch-thin ribbons

1 to 2 tablespoons unsalted butter

6 large eggs

Kosher salt

Freshly ground black pepper

2 scallions (white and 3 inches of green),
    thinly sliced

1. Heat 1 tablespoon canola oil in a large sauté pan over medium-high heat. Add 1 teaspoon chopped garlic and lightly brown. Add 1 cup of cut kale and sauté until softened. Add 1 cup of the cooked potatoes and 1 cup of the shredded beef, and mix well. Add 1/8 cup of the reserved beef-cooking liquid, cook until the mixture is slightly thickened, and remove to a bowl or plate. Repeat until all the kale, potatoes, and beef have been cooked. Return all the ingredients to the pan and reheat briefly.

2. Meanwhile, in a large, preferably nonstick, skillet over medium heat, melt the butter. Break the eggs into the skillet, sprinkle with salt and pepper, cover, and cook until set, 4 to 6 minutes.

TO SERVE, transfer the hash to a large serving platter. Top with the sunny-side-up eggs, and drizzle with balsamic syrup. Sprinkle with the sliced scallions.

Roasted Beef Shanks with Vegetables and Potatoes

Makes 4 to 6 servings

Food commentator and cookbook author Arthur Schwartz was inspired to create this oven-cooked dish when he caramelized some meaty beef shanks, along with vegetables, to make brown stock. He praises this meat for its deep flavor and the richly textured sauce it produces, both ideally suited to the chunky potatoes (peeled or not—it's your call) that complete the dish. Serve this with plenty of crusty bread to soak up the delicious sauce.

4 to 6 (1-inch-thick) slices of beef shank
    (about 3 1/2 pounds total)
Kosher salt
Freshly ground black pepper
8 carrots
8 small onions
2 or 3 parsnips, peeled, tips cut off,
    and heavier tops halved
2 tablespoons olive oil
16 cloves garlic, peeled

1 (14 1/2-ounce) can regular or low-sodium
    beef broth
1 (1-pound) can plum tomatoes, with their
    juice
2 pounds Yukon Gold or Red Bliss potatoes,
    peeled or unpeeled, cut into 2-inch
    chunks
4 fresh parsley sprigs
1/2 teaspoon fresh thyme leaves
1 large bay leaf

1. Preheat the oven to 450°F.

2. In a roasting pan (approximately 15 by 11 inches), arrange the slices of beef shank, preferably without overlapping them. Sprinkle the meat with salt and pepper. Arrange the carrots, onions, and parsnips over and between the pieces of meat. Drizzle on the olive oil. Sprinkle the vegetables with salt and pepper.

3. Place the roasting pan in the oven for 15 minutes. Turn the meat over and rearrange the vegetables. Cook for another 15 minutes, or until the meat is brown. Remove the roasting pan and reduce the oven temperature to 350°F.

4. Add all the remaining ingredients to the pan, breaking up the tomatoes slightly with the side of a wooden spoon. Cover with heavy-duty foil and return to the oven for 1 1/2 to 2 hours, until the meat and vegetables are very tender. The dish may be served with the juices as they are, or the juices may be reduced (see step 5).

5. If you prefer a thicker sauce, remove the meat and all the vegetables except the garlic to a platter; cover with foil to keep warm. Strain the juices into a saucepan, pushing through any tomato bits and the pulp from the garlic. Skim off the surface fat. Place over high heat and reduce the juices slightly, stirring frequently. Pour the thickened juices over the meat and vegetables.

TO SERVE, divide the meat and vegetables, with the sauce, among 4 to 6 deep plates or shallow bowls.

Shepherd's Pie of Beef Shank Braised in Zinfandel

Makes 8 servings

Chef Meer, of Manhattan's City Hall Restaurant, chooses a meaty beef shank when he pre-pares his shepherd's pie, braising it in Zinfandel and topping it with cheese-spiked mashed potatoes. For perfect potatoes, he urges us never to allow the potatoes to boil, but to sim-mer them slowly until done, and to be sure the potatoes and the milk are hot when we mix them together.

This cut provides the bonus of rich beef marrow—try it spread on a garlicky toasted baguette.

FOR THE ZINFANDEL-BRAISED BEEF SHANK:

1 beef shank (about 6 pounds)
Kosher salt
Freshly ground black pepper
5 to 6 tablespoons canola oil
6 carrots, cut into medium dice
2 onions, cut into medium dice

1 bunch of celery, cut into medium dice
1 head garlic, unpeeled, halved crosswise
2 bay leaves
1 (750-milliliter) bottle Zinfandel
4 cups water

1. Preheat the oven to 375°F.

2. Season the beef shank well with salt and pepper. In a large casserole over medium-high heat, heat the oil until very hot and sear the beef until browned, 3 to 4 min-utes on each side. Cover the casserole tightly with foil and put it in the oven for 45 minutes.

3. Reduce the oven temperature to 300°F.

4. Remove the shank to a plate and skim off any excess fat from the cooking juices. Add the carrots, onions, celery, garlic, and bay leaves to the juices in the casserole and cook over medium-high heat for 12 to 15 minutes. Add the Zinfandel and cook until the liquid is reduced by half, about 30 minutes. Add the water and beef shank, cover tightly with foil and the lid, and return to the oven. Cook for 2 hours.

5. Remove the beef shank and vegetables and allow the meat to cool to room temperature. Remove the meat from the bone, discarding the excess fat and reserving the bone (see Note). Cut the meat into bite-sized cubes.

6. Remove and discard the bay leaves and garlic from the cooking juices. Return the meat to the casserole with the vegetables and add about 2 cups of the cooking juices, just enough to cover the meat. (There will be more liquid than you need. You can reduce the juices over medium-high heat until thickened, or you can reserve the extra liquid for other uses.) The meat can be refrigerated for up to 2 days; reheat when ready to finish the recipe.

FOR THE MASHED-POTATO TOPPING:

3 pounds Yukon Gold potatoes, peeled
   and cut into large chunks
Kosher salt
1 to 1 1/2 cups milk
4 1/2 tablespoons unsalted butter, at room
   temperature

8 ounces Parmigiano-Reggiano cheese,
   freshly grated
Freshly ground black pepper

1. Put the potatoes in a large pot and cover with cold water. Add 1 tablespoon salt and bring to a simmer over medium-high heat. Simmer until tender, 25 to 30 minutes.

2. While the potatoes are cooking, heat the milk in a small pot over medium heat.

3. Drain the potatoes, put them in a large bowl, and mash with a potato masher until smooth. With a wooden spoon, mix in the butter, then mix in the warm milk. Add the Parmigiano-Reggiano cheese and combine well. Season with salt and pepper.

TO MAKE THE SHEPHERD'S PIE:

1. Preheat the oven to 350°F.
2. Spoon the mashed potatoes over the meat-and-vegetable mixture in the casserole. Place in the oven for about 30 minutes, or until the potatoes are browned and the meat mixture is bubbling. Serve from the casserole.

NOTE: You can enjoy the marrow from the shank bone along with the shepherd's pie. Stand the reserved shank bone on end and split it down the middle with a cleaver. Spoon out the marrow. Halve a baguette lengthwise and toast it. Rub 1 clove of garlic over the surface of the bread and spread with the roasted marrow. Season with salt and pepper to taste.

If you have refrigerated the cooked bone, before splitting, reheat it in a 300°F oven for 10 minutes.

JOHN SUNDSTROM

Shepherd's Pie of Merlot-Braised Oxtail

Makes 4 to 6 servings

Oxtail requires long, slow braising to unlock its deep flavor and tenderness. But be generous with your time, and the result will be unusually rich and satisfying. Infused with earthy wild mushrooms, topped with creamy truffled mashed potatoes, and perfumed with black truffle, Chef Sundstrom's dish from Seattle's Earth and Ocean is a knockout.

FOR THE MERLOT-BRAISED OXTAILS:

2 carrots, diced

1 onion, diced

2 stalks celery, diced

1 head garlic, cloves crushed with the broad end of a knife blade and peeled

2 bay leaves

1 tablespoon black peppercorns

2 cups Merlot

3 to 4 pounds oxtails, cut into chunks and trimmed of excess fat

3 tablespoons olive oil

4 cups chicken, veal, or beef stock, or canned low-sodium chicken or beef broth

3 tablespoons kosher salt

1. In a large nonreactive bowl, combine the carrots, onion, celery, garlic cloves, bay leaves, peppercorns, and Merlot. Add the oxtails and toss to coat well with the marinade. Cover and refrigerate for 5 hours or up to 24 hours.

2. Remove the oxtails with a slotted spoon or tongs, and separately reserve the meat; the carrots, onion, and celery; and the wine. Pat the meat dry with paper towels.

3. In a large roasting pan over medium-high heat, heat the olive oil until very hot, and brown the oxtails well on all sides. Remove the meat from the pan. Add the reserved

carrots, onion, and celery and cook for 15 minutes. Add the reserved wine and boil gently until the alcohol has cooked off, about 5 minutes.

4. Return the oxtails to the pan and add the stock. Sprinkle well with the salt. Increase the heat to high, and bring to a boil. Reduce the heat to low, cover, and simmer on the stovetop until the meat is very tender and beginning to fall off the bone, 3 to 3 1/2 hours. (Or place the covered pan in a preheated 300°F oven for 3 to 3 1/2 hours.)

5. Remove the meat and set it aside to cool. Pour the contents of the roasting pan into a strainer set over a large pot and discard the vegetables. Skim any fat from the braising liquid, then gently simmer over medium-low heat until slightly thickened and concentrated. Reserve. Remove the oxtail meat from the bones and reserve.

FOR THE RAGOUT:

1 tablespoon unsalted butter
1 cup combined red and white pearl onions,
     or substitute all white pearl onions
     (or use frozen pearl onions)
1 teaspoon minced garlic
2 cups combined assorted wild (and/or domestic) mushrooms (such as porcini, morels, chanterelles, cremini, and shiitakes), cut or torn into bite-sized pieces

1/2 cup Merlot
Kosher or sea salt
Freshly ground black pepper

1. In a large sauté pan over medium heat, melt the butter, and sauté the pearl onions until tender. Add the garlic and mushrooms, and sauté until the garlic is just golden.

2. Add the Merlot and simmer until reduced by half. Add the oxtail meat and 1 cup of the braising liquid. Simmer until the vegetables are well coated and the sauce is reduced

by half; adjust the seasoning. The ragout can be refrigerated for up to 3 days; reheat before continuing with the recipe.

FOR THE TRUFFLED-MASHED-POTATO TOPPING:

3 Yukon Gold potatoes, peeled and cut into
    large dice
Kosher or sea salt
1 cup heavy cream
8 tablespoons unsalted butter, cut into
    small pieces

1 ounce black truffle, thinly sliced or shaved
    (see Sources)
Freshly ground white pepper

1. Cover the potatoes with cold water in a large saucepan, add 1 tablespoon salt, and simmer over medium heat until tender. Drain, then pass through a fine-mesh sieve, food mill, or ricer into a large bowl.

2. Mix in the cream, butter, and truffle. Season with salt and white pepper.

TO MAKE THE SHEPHERD'S PIES:

1/2 cup freshly grated Parmesan cheese

1. Preheat the oven to 400°F or preheat the broiler.

2. Divide the oxtail ragout among 4 to 6 individual casserole dishes set on a sheet pan and press the mixture down. Top each with truffled mashed potatoes, press down again, and smooth the tops. Sprinkle with the grated Parmesan cheese. Bake or broil until

the tops are light golden and the pies are heated through. (The mixture can also be baked in a 9 by 9-inch casserole.)

3. Meanwhile, in a small saucepan over medium heat, simmer the reserved braising liquid until slightly reduced.

4. Place the individual casseroles on serving plates and drizzle with the warmed braising liquid.

Braised Beef Cheeks with Fingerling Potato Purée

Makes 4 servings

The unusually delicious and silky cut of beef blends perfectly with a buttery purée of fingerlings, in this recipe from Chef Renaud of Manhattan's Fleur de Sel. The combination is rich and memorable. Should there be any leftovers, they will be even better the next day.

Beef cheeks are not always easy to find at your neighborhood butcher, but widen your search—they are worth it.

FOR THE BRAISED BEEF CHEEKS:

1 (750-milliliter) bottle Malbec, or substitute
Merlot or Cabernet
2 pounds beef cheeks, cut into 16 pieces,
trimmed of excess fat but some fat left
for flavor (see Sources; or substitute beef
round or veal shank)
Kosher salt
Freshly ground black pepper

1/2 cup canola oil
6 shallots, thinly sliced
1 head garlic, cloves peeled and roughly
chopped
8 cups veal stock, or substitute canned
low-sodium beef broth combined with
4 ounces tomato paste

1. In a medium saucepan over medium-high heat, bring the wine to a boil. Cook at a low boil until the wine is reduced by half.

2. Preheat the oven to 450°F.

3. Season the beef cheeks on all sides with salt and pepper.

4. In a large ovenproof saucepan, heat the canola oil over medium-high heat until it smokes slightly. Add the beef cheeks, fat side down, and cook, turning to brown them on all sides. Remove the meat from the pan.

5. Reduce the heat to medium and add the shallots and garlic to the pan. Season with salt and pepper, and cook until the shallots are softened and translucent but not colored, about 10 minutes. Return the meat to the pan, add the reduced wine and the veal stock, and bring to a boil, skimming off any scum that forms.

6. Cover with foil or a lid and place in the oven for about 2 hours, or until the beef is fork-tender. Pour the contents of the pan into a colander set over a large bowl and separate the meat and the sauce. Brush off any garlic or shallots that remain on the meat.

7. Pour the sauce through a fine-mesh strainer into a saucepan, and place over medium-high heat. Simmer until the sauce is reduced by about two-thirds or it is thick enough to coat the back of a spoon. Season with salt and pepper, and combine with the meat. Keep warm until ready to serve.

FOR THE FINGERLING POTATO PURÉE:

2 1/2 pounds fingerling potatoes, peeled
    (or substitute Red Bliss)
Kosher salt
1 1/4 pounds (5 sticks) unsalted butter, cut into
    small pieces

1 1/2 cups whole milk
3/4 cup heavy cream
Freshly ground black pepper

1. Put the potatoes in a large pot and cover with cold water. Add 1 tablespoon salt and bring to a simmer over medium-high heat. Simmer until the potatoes are fork-tender, about 35 minutes. Drain the potatoes and pass them through a food mill or ricer into a mixing bowl. Mix in the butter.

2. Warm the milk and cream in a small saucepan over medium heat. Add half to the potato mixture, stirring until it is absorbed. Continue adding and stirring until the purée is smooth; you may not need all the liquid. Season with salt and pepper.

TO SERVE, divide the meat and sauce among 4 plates, and spoon the potato purée alongside.

Provençal Bouilli (Boiled Beef and Vegetables)

Makes 6 servings

Chef Antoine Bouterin, of Manhattan's Bouterin Restaurant, remembers how his mother prepared this fragrant stew on cool days in Saint-Rémy-de-Provence when he was a child. She would let it cook gently all afternoon, so the flavors of the meat and farm-fresh vegetables melted into one another. It was—and is—a perfect family meal.

FOR THE BOUQUET GARNI:

3 flat-leaf parsley sprigs
2 fresh basil sprigs

2 fresh thyme sprigs
2 bay leaves

Wrap the parsley, basil, thyme, and bay leaves in a small square of cheesecloth. Tie with string, if necessary, to hold the package together.

3 pounds beef chuck, or substitute rump

2 large onions, 1 stuck with 4 cloves and
    1 halved

1 tablespoon kosher salt

1 tablespoon black peppercorns

3 large carrots

3 large leeks (white and tender green parts),
    washed

2 cloves garlic, unpeeled, crushed with the
    broad end of a knife blade

2 small turnips, peeled and quartered

3 stalks celery

1 large tomato, halved

2 small parsnips, peeled and thickly sliced

10 small potatoes (such as Red Bliss),
    unpeeled

1 small cabbage, quartered

6 allspice berries

1. Put the meat in a large pot and cover with water by 4 inches. Add the bouquet garni, onions, salt, and peppercorns and bring to a boil over high heat. Add the carrots, leeks, garlic, turnips, celery, and tomato. Reduce the heat to medium and boil gently, uncovered, for about 3 hours. Skim occasionally.

2. Add the parsnips, potatoes, cabbage, and allspice berries, and simmer until the potatoes and parsnips are tender, about 30 minutes. Strain the broth, reserving the meat and vegetables. Discard the bouquet garni, peppercorns, and cloves.

TO SERVE, slice the meat about 1/4 inch thick and return it to the broth, with the vegetables. Serve as a main-course soup, in large bowls; or serve the broth as a first course and the meat and vegetables as a main course.

Boeuf Bourguignon

BEEF

Makes 4 to 6 servings

Manhattan's Levana Restaurant is the source for this sophisticated yet simple stew. Preparation is a snap, but the deep flavors of the meat, vegetables, and herbs make the result extraordinary. This dish reheats very well, and improves after a day or two, making it perfect for a do-ahead dinner party. As a kosher cook, Levana uses meat that has been pre-salted, so her original recipe doesn't call for any additional salt. We have added some to the recipe for cooks who use unsalted meat.

3 tablespoons extra-virgin olive oil
3 pounds beef shoulder, cut into 2-inch cubes
6 cloves garlic, peeled
2 cups dry red wine
2 large tomatoes, cut into small dice
Kosher salt

1 tablespoon freshly ground black pepper
6 bay leaves
4 fresh thyme sprigs, leaves only
2 pounds very thin carrots (about 20)
20 very small potatoes, unpeeled
12 small onions

1. To cook in a Crock-Pot, layer the oil, beef, garlic cloves, wine, and tomatoes in a 6-quart Crock-Pot, seasoning each layer lightly with salt and pepper. Top with the bay leaves, thyme, carrots, potatoes, and onions. Set the Crock-Pot on low and cook for 10 to 12 hours.

2. To cook on the stovetop, place the oil, beef, and 8 cups of water in a wide, heavy pot over high heat and bring to a boil. Reduce the heat to medium and cook, covered, for 2 hours. Add the garlic, wine, tomatoes, salt, pepper, and bay leaves and cook for an addi-

tional 30 minutes. Add the thyme, carrots, potatoes, and onions, season to taste, and cook for another 30 minutes. The meat should be fork-tender.

3. Using a slotted spoon, transfer the meat and vegetables to a serving platter. If the liquid left in the pot is too thin, reduce it over high heat until it is thickened to the consistency of maple syrup. Pour the reduced liquid over the meat and vegetables, and serve hot.

Malaysian Beef Rendang with Sweet Potato–Coconut Purée

Makes 4 to 6 servings

Chef Yeo presents meat and potatoes in a brilliant and unexpected form in this Malaysian dish that she remembers as a childhood favorite. Rendang combines the complex notes of coconut and chilies and is served with a sweet potato purée that repeats and intensifies the coconut flavor.

FOR THE BEEF RENDANG:

1 pound shredded unsweetened dried coconut

10 assorted dried chilies (such as Thai bird, guajillo, and ancho), soaked for at least 2 hours or overnight, drained, seeded, and stemmed (see Sources)

4 cups coarsely chopped shallots

2 1/2 pounds beef stew meat (such as chuck), cut into 1-inch pieces

2 kaffir lime leaves (see Sources)

2 stalks lemongrass, tough ends trimmed off, tender stalks cut into 3-inch pieces and crushed (see Sources)

2 (2-inch) pieces of galangal (see Sources; or substitute fresh ginger)

5 cups unsweetened coconut milk

Kosher salt

Freshly ground black pepper

1. Preheat the oven to 325°F.

2. Spread the coconut out on a large sheet pan and toast, stirring every 8 to 10 minutes, for about 25 minutes, or until golden and fragrant.

3. In a food processor, combine 2 tablespoons of the toasted coconut with the soaked chilies and the shallots. Process to a paste and transfer to a large, heavy pot.

4. Add the beef and toss to coat well. Place the pot over medium-high heat, add the remaining ingredients, and bring to a boil. Reduce the heat to a simmer and cook, stirring occasionally, until the meat is tender, about 30 minutes.

5. Increase the heat to medium-high and cook the rendang, stirring constantly, until the coconut oil starts to separate from the sauce and the sauce is thick and fairly dry (this may take up to 30 minutes). The coconut will be browned and toasty, and the dish will be dry and not too saucy. Taste and adjust the salt and pepper.

FOR THE SWEET POTATO–COCONUT PURÉE:

1 (14-ounce) can unsweetened coconut milk
6 large sweet potatoes, peeled and cut into
   large chunks

Kosher salt
Freshly grated nutmeg
Freshly ground black pepper

1. In a saucepan over medium-high heat, simmer the coconut milk until reduced by one-quarter.

2. Meanwhile, boil the sweet potatoes in a large pot of lightly salted water until very tender. Drain well and transfer to a food processor or mixer. Add the reduced coconut milk and a few gratings of nutmeg and pulse together just until smooth. Season to taste with additional nutmeg, salt, and pepper, and serve hot.

SERVE the beef rendang with the sweet potato–coconut purée.

Meat Loaf Stuffed with Mashed Potatoes and Cheddar

Makes 4 to 6 servings

Everyone loves savory meat loaf served with fluffy mashed potatoes, and Chef Kenney combines the two favorites in a single dish—accented with Cheddar cheese. As the potatoes cook, they are flavored with the meat's juices and the melting cheese, and each generous slice of meat loaf offers layers of color and texture.

FOR THE MASHED POTATOES:

1 pound russet potatoes, unpeeled
Kosher salt
1 tablespoon unsalted butter, at room
     temperature

1/4 cup light cream or milk
Freshly ground black pepper

1. Put the potatoes in a medium pot and cover with cold water. Add 1 tablespoon salt and bring to a simmer over medium-high heat. Cook until the potatoes are tender, 25 to 30 minutes.

2. Drain, peel, and quarter the potatoes. In a mixing bowl, mash them coarsely with a potato masher or fork, blending in the butter. Mix in the cream, as needed. Season with salt and pepper. Small pieces of potato are fine; this should not be a purée.

Olive oil
1 pound ground beef chuck
3/4 cup plain bread crumbs
1 small onion, finely chopped
3 cloves garlic, minced
1/3 cup ketchup

1 large egg, lightly beaten
1 teaspoon Tabasco sauce
1 teaspoon kosher salt
1/2 teaspoon freshly ground black pepper
2 to 3 ounces Cheddar cheese, thinly sliced

1. Preheat the oven to 400°F. Lightly oil a large loaf pan or a high-sided sheet pan.

2. In a large mixing bowl, combine the ground beef, bread crumbs, onion, garlic, ketchup, egg, Tabasco, salt, and pepper.

3. On a sheet of foil, pat out the meat into a square of approximately 10 by 10 inches. Arrange the cheese slices over the meat, leaving a narrow border all around. Spoon the mashed potatoes in an even layer over the cheese. Using the foil as a guide, fold one side of the meat up over the other, and press down all around to seal. Gently form the meat into a loaf shape.

4. Place the meat loaf in the prepared pan, seam side down, and brush the top lightly with olive oil. Bake for about 45 minutes, or until cooked through. Cut into thick slices to serve.

Crispy Meat Loaf with Chanterelle-Buttermilk Gravy and Potato Gratin

Makes 8 servings

Bubby's Pie Company, in Tribeca, is famous for this crisp-topped home-style meat loaf, served alongside the easiest gratin I've ever encountered—and one of the best. But it is Chef Crismon's mushroom gravy that puts the dish over the top. It is fragrant with golden chanterelles, garlic, and herbs, and smoothed with a combination of buttermilk and rich cream.

FOR THE CRISPY MEAT LOAF:

1 tablespoon unsalted butter
1 yellow onion, thinly sliced
1 clove garlic, chopped
1 teaspoon chopped fresh tarragon
1/4 cup freshly grated Parmesan cheese
1 teaspoon chopped fresh thyme

1 1/4 cups cornflake crumbs
3/4 cup ketchup
2 large eggs
2 pounds ground beef chuck
1 teaspoon salt
1/2 teaspoon freshly ground black pepper

1. Preheat the oven to 375°F. (If you are not making the potato gratin at the same time, preheat the oven to 400°F.)

2. In a medium skillet, melt the butter over medium heat. Add the onion and reduce the heat to medium-low. Cook, stirring, until the onion softens and then gradually turns a golden caramel color, about 25 minutes.

3. In a large bowl, combine the caramelized onion with the garlic, tarragon, Parmesan cheese, thyme, 1 cup of the cornflake crumbs, 1/2 cup of the ketchup, the eggs, ground beef, salt, and pepper. Mix thoroughly.

4. On a sheet of parchment paper or foil, shape the meat into a loaf; or form it in a large loaf pan. Brush with the remaining 1/4 cup ketchup, then sprinkle with the remaining 1/4 cup cornflake crumbs. Bake in a loaf pan or in a high-sided sheet pan for 40 to 45 minutes, until browned.

FOR THE POTATO GRATIN:

Unsalted butter

2 pounds russet potatoes, peeled, sliced 1/8 inch thick, and put into a bowl of cold water

1 yellow onion, halved lengthwise and thinly sliced

1 cup heavy cream

Pinch of ground nutmeg

Pinch of ground cloves

1/4 teaspoon ground cinnamon

6 ounces Cheddar cheese, freshly grated

6 ounces Parmesan cheese, freshly grated

Kosher salt

Freshly ground black pepper

1. Preheat the oven to 375°F. Lightly butter a 12 by 8-inch baking pan.

2. Drain the potatoes and dry them with paper towels. Put them in a mixing bowl and add the onion, cream, nutmeg, cloves, cinnamon, 4 ounces of the grated Cheddar cheese, 4 ounces of the grated Parmesan cheese, and salt and pepper to taste. Combine well and pour into the prepared baking pan. Top with the remaining 2 ounces Cheddar and 2 ounces Parmesan, and bake for 45 to 50 minutes, until the potatoes are soft and the top is golden brown.

3 tablespoons unsalted butter

1 tablespoon finely diced red onion

1/2 clove garlic, finely chopped

8 ounces chanterelle mushrooms, thickly sliced

2 tablespoons all-purpose flour

2 cups chicken stock or canned low-sodium
    chicken broth

1 tablespoon chopped fresh thyme

1/2 cup heavy cream

1/2 cup buttermilk

Kosher salt

Freshly ground black pepper

2 tablespoons chopped fresh parsley

1. In a large saucepan over medium-high heat, melt the butter. Add the onion and garlic and sauté until sizzling. Add the mushrooms and cook, stirring, until softened. Add the flour and mix until smooth. Cook, stirring frequently, for 4 minutes.

2. Add the chicken stock and stir constantly for 1 to 2 minutes. Add the thyme, reduce the heat to low, and simmer for 20 minutes. Add the cream and buttermilk, season with salt and pepper, and simmer, stirring occasionally, for 8 to 10 minutes. Stir in the parsley.

TO SERVE, cut the meat loaf into thick slices and divide among 8 plates. Spoon the gratin alongside the meat loaf, and pass the gravy separately.

-And Don't forget the Gravy

Chiles Rellenos with Warm Mild Tomato Sauce

Makes 8 servings

Chef Barrios Treviño presides over San Antonio's famous Los Barrios Restaurant, the place to go for authentic Tex-Mex cuisine. In her take on this classic dish, poblanos are stuffed with a spicy mixture of meat and potatoes, dipped in flour and egg, and fried until golden. Serve them under a mantle of fresh tomato sauce that mellows their heat.

FOR THE WARM MILD TOMATO SAUCE:

4 tomatoes, quartered
1/4 cup vegetable oil
1 onion, thinly sliced
1/2 green bell pepper, thinly sliced

1/4 teaspoon garlic powder
1/8 teaspoon ground cumin
1/2 teaspoon kosher salt
1/4 teaspoon freshly ground black pepper

1. Put the tomatoes in a blender and blend until puréed.

2. In a medium skillet, heat the oil over medium heat and cook the onion and bell pepper until soft, 3 to 5 minutes. Add the puréed tomatoes, garlic powder, cumin, salt, and pepper and bring to a simmer. Reduce the heat to low and simmer gently for about 45 minutes.

1/4 cup olive oil

2 pounds ground beef chuck

1/2 teaspoon kosher salt

1/2 teaspoon freshly ground black pepper

1/2 teaspoon garlic powder

1/2 teaspoon ground cumin

1 russet potato, peeled and diced

1 carrot, diced

8 roasted and peeled poblano chilies
     (see Note)

5 large eggs, separated and yolks beaten

All-purpose flour

Vegetable oil

1. In a large skillet, heat the olive oil over medium heat and add the ground beef. Season with the salt, pepper, garlic powder, and cumin, and cook, stirring to break up any lumps, until the meat is browned, 6 to 8 minutes. Add the potato and carrot and cook, stirring occasionally, until they are fork-tender, 8 to 10 minutes. Remove from the heat.

2. Make a slit down the side of each peeled poblano chili and remove the seeds. Stuff the chiles with the meat mixture.

3. In a large bowl, beat the egg whites until they form stiff peaks. Beat in the egg yolks.

4. Spread the flour on a sheet of waxed paper.

5. Pour 1 inch of vegetable oil into a large, deep skillet and heat until very hot. One at a time, roll the stuffed peppers in the flour to coat, then dip into the egg mixture and add to the pan. Cook one at a time until lightly browned on one side, 30 to 60 seconds. Turn and brown on the second side. Remove with a slotted spoon and drain briefly on paper towels.

TO SERVE, place the stuffed chiles on a platter and top with the tomato sauce.

NOTE: To roast poblano chilies, preheat the oven to 350°F. Lightly brush the chilies with vegetable oil and place on a cookie sheet. Roast, turning the chilies every 10 minutes, for about 30 minutes, or until the skin begins to split and peel. Put the chilies in a plastic bag, seal the bag, and let the chilies sit until they are cool enough to handle. Then peel off the skin.

Potato Gnocchi with Ragù Bolognese

Makes 4 main-course or 6 first-course servings

Inspired by a recent trip through Italy, Keith Dresser, of *Cook's Illustrated* magazine, created this robust Mediterranean-style meat-and-potato combination. The meaty, long-simmered sauce marries perfectly with the flavor and texture of light, chewy potato gnocchi. Keith advises that while homemade gnocchi are the best by far, you can substitute a good-quality prepared product, if necessary.

FOR THE RAGÙ BOLOGNESE:

2 tablespoons tomato paste
3/4 cup chicken stock or low-sodium canned
    chicken broth
2 tablespoons extra-virgin olive oil
2 ounces pancetta, finely chopped
1 1/2 pounds coarsely ground beef chuck

1 large carrot, finely chopped
2 small stalks celery, finely chopped
1/2 onion, finely chopped
1/2 cup dry white wine
1 1/2 cups whole milk

1. Combine the tomato paste and chicken stock, and set aside.

2. Put the olive oil and pancetta in a Dutch oven over medium heat and cook until the pancetta has rendered most of its fat, about 7 minutes.

3. Raise the heat to medium-high, add the beef, and cook, stirring frequently, until the beef is well browned, 8 to 10 minutes. Stir in the carrot, celery, and onion, and sauté until the onion is translucent, about 3 minutes.

4. Stir in the wine and diluted tomato paste. Reduce the heat to low and simmer for 10 minutes. Stir in 1/2 cup of the milk and simmer for 25 minutes. Repeat the process of adding 1/2 cup of the milk and simmering for 25 minutes two more times, until all the milk is used and the sauce is the consistency of a thick soup.

FOR THE POTATO GNOCCHI:

1 1/2 pounds russet potatoes, unpeeled   1 1/2 teaspoons kosher salt
1 cup all-purpose flour, plus more as needed

1. Preheat the oven to 400°F.

2. Bake the potatoes for about 1 hour, or until a thin-bladed paring knife slides in without resistance.

3. While the potatoes are still hot, peel them with a paring knife. Pass the potatoes through a food mill or ricer into a large bowl. Let the potatoes cool slightly, about 10 minutes.

4. Sprinkle the flour and salt over the potatoes. Mix with a wooden spoon until a soft, smooth dough has formed. If the mixture is sticky, add more flour as needed, 1 tablespoon at a time.

5. Divide the dough into 4 equal pieces. Roll each piece of dough into a 1-inch-thick rope (if the dough breaks apart while rolling, put it back into the bowl and add more flour).

6. Sprinkle a tray or sheet pan lightly with flour. Cut each rope into 1-inch pieces. Holding a fork in one hand and a 1-inch dough piece in the other, gently press and roll the dough against the fork tines, and flick the gnocchi off the tines onto the lightly floured tray. Each piece of gnocchi should have a slight indentation on one side, from your finger, and grooves on the other, from the fork. The gnocchi can be refrigerated for up to 2 hours or frozen for up to 1 month.

Kosher salt

1/2 cup freshly grated Parmesan cheese, or to
      taste

Bring 6 quarts of water to a boil in a large pot. Add 1 tablespoon of kosher salt. Add half of the gnocchi and cook until they float to the surface, 1 1/2 to 2 minutes. Remove the gnocchi from the water with a slotted spoon and place in a warmed serving dish or in individual bowls. Repeat with the remaining gnocchi. Top with the *ragù*, sprinkle with the Parmesan cheese, and serve immediately.

3.

Veal, Mixed Meats, and Potatoes

*T*HIS SHORT LIST CAPTURES THE VERSATILITY OF VEAL AND ITS COMPATABILITY WITH different preparations—and several types of potatoes. Sweet, russet, Yukon Gold, and German Butterball potatoes complement this subtle, delicate meat in a variety of dishes.

Laurent Gras pairs lean, sautéed tournedos of veal with potatoes cooked two ways: caramelized and creamy. He tops this complex mix of textures with fruity, sweet sautéed apple slices, in a virtuoso dish. Country-Style Veal Chops with Potatoes and Mushrooms, from my kitchen, is a version of a traditional farm supper, easy to cook, tender, and wonderfully fragrant.

Allen Susser roasts a rack of juicy veal and accompanies it with pancakes that combine grated potatoes (familiar) with roasted red bell peppers (unexpected). Adding another surprise, he crusts the veal roast with crisp celery seeds.

Walter Potenza gently cooks veal shoulder in a tangy, herbaceous tomato sauce with eggplant and zucchini and bakes it with feathery potato gnocchi, under a mantle of melting Pecorino Romano cheese. Gerry Hayden works magic with Slow-Braised Veal and Vanilla Sweet Potato Shepherd's Pie, combining sweet and savory flavors with tender braised veal breast.

I love the light yet chewy texture of ground veal, and in my Veal Croquettes with Dilled New Potatoes, it is highlighted by a bit of cream. Fresh dill, tossed with buttery potatoes, is the perfect herbal accent.

If one tender, delicious cut of meat is good, three must be better! Two unusual dishes are enriched by a mixture of several meats: Philippe Bertineau's Baeckeofe, a meat-and-potato casserole from Alsace, combines chunks of beef, lamb, and pork with potatoes, for traditional slow baking; and Carla Pellegrino's La Svizzera with Prosciutto Mashed Potatoes, a sophisticated yet home-style Italian burger, puts ground beef, veal, and pork to excellent use.

VEAL

Veal Tournedos with Caramelized and Creamy Potatoes and Sautéed Apple Slices

Makes 4 servings

Adapted from Chef Gras's elegant creation, served at San Francisco's Fifth Floor Restaurant, this version of veal tournedos is somewhat simpler than the original but is based on his classic yet imaginative concept. Delicate veal tournedos are joined with potatoes done two ways—creamy and caramelized—and sweetened by golden sautéed apple slices. The combination equals pure poetry!

FOR THE CREAMY POTATOES:

3/4 cup chicken stock or canned low-sodium
    chicken broth
2 pounds German Butterball potatoes,
    unpeeled (see Sources; or substitute
    Yukon Gold)

Kosher salt
8 tablespoons (1 stick) unsalted butter
1 flat-leaf parsley sprig, roughly chopped

1. In a small saucepan over high heat, bring the stock to a boil. Remove from the heat and reserve.

2. Put the potatoes in a pot large enough to accommodate them and cover with lightly salted cold water. Bring to a simmer and cook over medium-high heat until fork-tender, about 30 minutes, depending on the size of the potatoes.

3. Drain and peel the potatoes and pass them through a food mill or ricer into a large pan set over low heat. Add the reserved chicken stock and 4 tablespoons of the butter, and

mix well. Stir in the remaining 4 tablespoons butter and season with salt. Just before serving, stir in the chopped parsley.

FOR THE CARAMELIZED POTATOES:

4 russet or Yukon Gold potatoes, peeled and
   sliced lengthwise about 1/2 inch thick
   (there should be about 8 pieces)
2 tablespoons clarified unsalted butter
   (see Notes)

1/2 cup veal stock, or substitute beef stock
   or canned low-sodium beef broth
Fleur de sel or other sea salt, or substitute
   kosher salt
Freshly ground black pepper

In a large skillet over medium-high heat, sauté the potato slices in the clarified butter until golden, 4 to 5 minutes on each side. Add the stock (be careful that it doesn't splatter) and cook until the stock is reduced and the potatoes are caramelized, another 4 to 5 minutes. Sprinkle with fleur de sel and pepper.

FOR THE SAUTÉED APPLE SLICES:

1 Golden Delicious apple, peeled, halved, and
   sliced 1/4 inch thick (there should be
   about 16 slices)
1 tablespoon clarified unsalted butter
   (see Notes)
1 tablespoon demi-glace (see Sources) or veal
   stock, or substitute beef stock or canned
   low-sodium beef broth

Fleur de sel or other sea salt, or substitute
   kosher salt
Freshly cracked black pepper (see Notes)

In a medium skillet over medium heat, sauté the apple slices in the clarified butter until golden and softened, about 10 minutes. Brush with demi-glace (or toss with the stock) and sprinkle with fleur de sel and pepper.

FOR THE VEAL TOURNEDOS:

4 boneless veal loin chops (about 4 ounces each)
Fleur de sel or other sea salt, or substitute kosher salt

Freshly ground black pepper
2 tablespoons canola oil
Demi-glace (see Sources), veal stock, beef stock, or canned low-sodium beef broth

1. Preheat the oven to 300°F.
2. Season the veal chops with fleur de sel and pepper on one side only. In a large skillet over medium-high heat, heat the canola oil until very hot and sear the veal on both sides until golden, 2 to 3 minutes on each side. Place the veal on a baking sheet, brush with the demi-glace, and bake for about 10 minutes, or until cooked through. (Be careful not to overcook and dry out the meat.)

TO SERVE, place one tournedo of veal on the bottom half of each plate and place the caramelized potatoes on the top half. Spoon the creamy potatoes across the center, and arrange the apple slices over all.

NOTES: To clarify butter, melt it over low heat and simmer briefly. Pour off and use the clear yellow portion, and discard the milky solids. You will lose about one-quarter of the butter this way, so start with some extra. Or microwave the butter for 1 to 2 minutes, skim off the foam, and use the clear yellow portion. Discard the milky solids.

For cracked black pepper, wrap peppercorns in a dish towel and smash them with a heavy pan.

Country-Style Veal Chops with Potatoes and Mushrooms

Makes 4 servings

The simplest, best ingredients, combined with the easiest of methods, make this a family favorite. And your kitchen smells heavenly while the veal, potatoes, and mushrooms cook.

4 russet or Yukon Gold potatoes (1 1/2 to 2 pounds), unpeeled
1/4 cup olive oil, plus extra for the baking dish
2 large onions, thinly sliced
4 cloves garlic, crushed with the broad end of a knife blade, peeled, and minced

10 ounces domestic white mushrooms, thickly sliced
Kosher salt
Freshly ground black pepper
1/2 cup chopped flat-leaf parsley
4 rib or loin veal chops, 1/2 to 3/4 inch thick, trimmed of excess fat

1. Microwave the potatoes until they are barely cooked through. When they are cool enough to handle, peel and slice 1/2 inch thick.

2. Preheat the oven to 350°F. Lightly oil a baking dish large enough to accommodate the veal chops in one layer.

3. In a large skillet over medium heat, heat 2 tablespoons of the olive oil and cook the onions and garlic until the onions are softened but not colored. Add the mushrooms and cook until softened. Season with salt and pepper and pour into a mixing bowl. Add the parsley and mix well.

4. Season the veal chops with salt and pepper. Add the remaining 2 tablespoons oil to the pan and heat over medium-high heat. Sear the veal chops until browned on both sides, 5 to 6 minutes total. Turn off the heat and leave the chops in the pan.

5. Layer half the potatoes in the baking dish, and season with salt and pepper. Top with all 4 veal chops, reserving the pan juices. Spoon the onion mixture over the chops. Top with the remaining potatoes, and season with salt and pepper. Pour the reserved pan juices over the potatoes.

6. Cover the dish tightly with foil or a lid and bake for about 45 minutes, or until the chops are very tender. Serve from the baking dish.

Celery Seed–Crusted Veal Roast with Red Pepper–Potato Pancakes

Makes 6 servings

Both the tender rack of veal and the crisp potato pancakes—perfect partners—are given a surprising new twist by Allen Susser, of Chef Allen's, in Miami Beach. The roast is crusted with crisp celery seeds, and the pancakes are brightened with juicy chunks of red bell pepper. When you carve this roast, Chef Allen reminds you to reserve the meaty bones, for an especially tasty treat.

FOR THE CELERY SEED–CRUSTED VEAL:

2 tablespoons minced fresh thyme
1 tablespoon minced fresh rosemary
1 tablespoon crushed garlic
1 tablespoon black peppercorns
1 tablespoon kosher salt
2 tablespoons olive oil

1 (5-pound) rack of veal, shoulder blade and
  flap of meat over the rack removed,
  bones trimmed, and the rack tied
  so that it will sit better in the pan
  (the butcher can do this)
3 tablespoons celery seeds

1. Preheat the oven to 375°F.

2. In a small bowl, combine the thyme, rosemary, garlic, black peppercorns, salt, and olive oil. Rub the mixture into the veal.

3. Put the veal on a rack in a roasting pan, with the bones down, and place it in the center of the oven. Roast for 30 minutes, then turn the meat over, reduce the heat to 350°F, and roast for another 20 minutes. Remove the veal from the oven and roll it in the celery seeds. Return it to the oven until well browned, about 15 minutes more.

4. Remove the veal from the oven and let it rest for 10 minutes, tented with foil, in a warm spot over the oven, before slicing.

FOR THE RED PEPPER–POTATO PANCAKES:

1 large red bell pepper

1 tablespoon olive oil

3 red-skinned potatoes, peeled

1/2 Spanish onion

1 large egg

2 tablespoons matzo meal

Kosher salt

Freshly ground black pepper

1/2 cup peanut oil

1. Rub the red bell pepper with the olive oil and roast it in the oven with the veal until well cooked. Place it in a bowl, cover with a dish towel, and set aside for 15 minutes. Peel, skin, and seed the pepper, then cut the flesh into half-inch dice.

2. Grate the potatoes and onion on a hand grater into a large mixing bowl. Mix in the red pepper, egg, and matzo meal, and season with salt and pepper.

3. In a sauté pan over medium-high heat, heat the peanut oil until shimmering. Drop in the batter by tablespoons, making silver dollar–sized pancakes. Brown the pancakes for about 1 minute on each side, and cook until crisp and cooked through, 3 to 4 minutes more on each side. Reduce the heat to medium if the pancakes are becoming too brown. Drain on paper towels.

4. Place the pancakes on a sheet pan and keep them warm in the oven (reduce the oven temperature to 250°F while the veal is resting).

TO SERVE, slice the meat 1 inch thick and place on individual plates. Place 2 pancakes alongside each serving.

Veal Stew Baked with Gnocchi

Makes 4 to 6 servings

Chef Potenza, the Providence restaurateur, cooking teacher, and food historian, recommends that you bake this *tegamata di vitello e gnocchi* in a terra-cotta casserole, for true Italian flavor. The stew is first cooked on the stovetop, and while it is simmering, you can prepare the potato gnocchi. Then combine the meat and potatoes under a sprinkling of grated Romano, and bake. The tender meat and chewy gnocchi drift in a light aromatic sauce, topped by melting cheese.

FOR THE MARINATED VEAL:

1/3 cup extra-virgin olive oil
1 1/2 cups red wine
3 fresh sage leaves
1 fresh rosemary sprig
1 fresh thyme sprig

*3 cloves garlic, crushed with the broad end of a
    knife blade and peeled*
*3 pounds veal shoulder, chuck, or neck,
    cut into 1-inch cubes*

In a large nonreactive bowl, combine the olive oil, wine, sage, rosemary, thyme, and garlic. Add the veal and mix well with the marinade. Cover and refrigerate for 4 to 8 hours, or overnight.

----

1 large onion, minced
1 stalk celery, thinly sliced
1 small carrot, thinly sliced
6 cups chicken stock or canned low-sodium
    chicken broth
2 tablespoons tomato paste

1/2 to 1/3 pound eggplant, peeled and cut into
    1-inch cubes (about 3 1/4 cups)
1 zucchini, cut into 1/2-inch slices
Kosher salt
Freshly ground black pepper

In a medium stockpot over medium heat, combine the veal, marinade, onion, celery, carrot, stock, and tomato paste and simmer gently, stirring occasionally, for 15 minutes. Reduce the heat to medium-low, add the eggplant and zucchini, and season with salt and pepper. Continue cooking until the meat is tender, about 1 1/2 hours. Reserve. Can be refrigerated for up to 3 days.

FOR THE GNOCCHI:

----

1 1/2 pounds russet potatoes, unpeeled
Kosher salt

1 3/4 cups unbleached all-purpose flour
Pinch of freshly grated nutmeg

1. Put the potatoes in a medium pot and cover with cold water. Add 1 tablespoon salt and bring to a simmer over medium-high heat. Simmer until tender, 40 to 50 minutes, depending upon the size of the potatoes.

2. Spread the flour on a work surface. While the potatoes are still hot, peel them and pass them through a food mill or ricer onto the flour. Sprinkle the potatoes with nutmeg and salt. Let them cool to room temperature.

3. Combine the potatoes with the flour, using your fingers and a dough scraper, and gather the dough into a ball. Cut the dough into 8 pieces. Roll each piece into a thin log

(about the width of your finger), and cut into 1/2-inch pieces with a sharp knife. Roll each of the gnocchi over a fork or a grater to obtain grooves. (The gnocchi can be refrigerated for up to 2 days. Toss with a little flour or cornmeal so the pieces don't stick to one another. Bring to room temperature before cooking.)

4. Bring a large pot of water to a boil and add the gnocchi. Let them cook for 3 to 4 minutes; they will rise to the surface when done. Remove with a slotted spoon and add to the veal stew. (The gnocchi can be refrigerated for up to 2 hours or frozen for up to 1 month.)

TO COMPLETE THE STEW:

1 cup freshly grated Pecorino Romano or
    Parmigiano-Reggiano cheese

1. Preheat the oven to 350°F.

2. Spoon the stew into a medium ovenproof casserole, preferably terra-cotta, and top with the grated Pecorino Romano. Bake for about 15 minutes, or until the cheese is melted and the stew is heated through. Serve from the casserole.

GERRY HAYDEN

Slow-Braised Veal and Vanilla Sweet Potato Shepherd's Pie

Makes 4 servings as a side dish

Expect the unexpected from Chef Hayden, of Manhattan's Amuse Restaurant. In this tantalizing combination of opposites, the sweetness of the potatoes and the earthiness of the mushrooms play counterpoint to savory veal. This fusion of sweet potatoes, leeks, and mushrooms makes a rich accompaniment to your favorite grilled veal chops.

FOR THE BRAISED VEAL:

8 ounces boneless veal breast
Kosher salt
Freshly ground black pepper
2 tablespoons canola oil

8 ounces demi-glace (see Sources; or substitute veal or chicken stock or canned low-sodium chicken broth)

1. Preheat the oven to 325°F.

2. Season the veal breast with salt and pepper. In an ovenproof sauté pan large enough to accommodate the meat, heat the canola oil over medium-high heat until very hot, and sear the veal breast on both sides. Drain the excess oil, add the demi-glace, and bring to a boil.

3. Cover the pan with foil and place it in the oven. Braise for 1 hour, or until the meat starts to separate when pulled at with a fork.

4. Pour the contents of the pan into a colander set over a large bowl and separate the meat and the juices. Cut the meat into 1/4-inch dice and reserve both the meat and the juices.

1 1/2 pounds sweet potatoes, peeled
1/2 vanilla bean
6 tablespoons unsalted butter, at
    room temperature
1 tablespoon maple syrup
Kosher salt

Freshly ground black pepper
2 large leeks (white and 1/2 inch of green),
    washed and cut into 1/2-inch dice
8 shiitake mushroom caps, cut into
    1/2-inch dice
1 tablespoon chopped fresh chives

1. Cut up enough sweet potatoes to make 1 cup of 1/2-inch dice, and reserve the rest for the purée. Put the sweet potato dice in a medium pot of cold salted water and bring to a boil. Cook for 1 minute and drain. Let the potatoes cool; they should have a slight bite. Reserve.

2. Put the remaining sweet potatoes in another pot of cold salted water and bring to a boil. Cook until very tender (20 to 30 minutes), and drain. Keep the potatoes in the covered pot, off the heat, for 2 minutes, to steam. Transfer the steamed potatoes to a food processor. Scrape in the vanilla bean seeds, and add 2 tablespoons of the butter, the maple syrup, and salt and pepper to taste. Process to a very smooth purée. Let cool and reserve.

3. In a sauté pan over medium heat, melt 2 tablespoons of the butter. Add the diced leek and cook for 2 minutes. Add the diced shiitake and cook for 2 minutes more, or until the vegetables are soft. Season to taste with salt and pepper. Let cool and reserve.

4. In a mixing bowl, combine the reserved diced veal, the sweet potato dice, the leek-and-shiitake mixture, the chives, and the remaining 2 tablespoons butter. Add the reserved veal juices, season to taste with and salt and pepper, and mix well.

1. Preheat the oven to 375°F.

2. Spread the veal mixture evenly over the bottom of a medium casserole dish, then spread the sweet potato purée evenly over the top of the veal. Cover with foil and bake for 20 minutes, or until the mixture is heated through (when the tip of a knife inserted and removed is hot to the touch). Remove the foil and bake for 10 minutes more, or until the top is slightly golden. Serve from the baking dish.

JOAN SCHWARTZ

Veal Croquettes with Dilled New Potatoes

Makes 4 servings

Golden, delicate cakes of ground veal need a gentle accompaniment, and they find their ideal match in new potatoes perfumed with sprigs of fresh dill. The light flavors of the veal and the potatoes delicately complement one another, and your favorite bright green vegetable will complete the plate.

FOR THE VEAL CROQUETTES:

12 ounces ground veal
3/4 cup plain bread crumbs
1/2 teaspoon kosher salt
1/4 teaspoon freshly ground black pepper

1/4 teaspoon ground nutmeg
1/2 cup half-and-half
2 tablespoons canola oil

1. In a mixing bowl, combine the veal, 1/2 cup of the bread crumbs, the salt, pepper, and nutmeg. Mix in the half-and-half with a wooden spoon until completely absorbed.

2. Divide the veal mixture into 4 portions and form each into an even patty, about 1/2 inch thick. Put the patties on a plate and sprinkle on both sides with the remaining 1/4 cup bread crumbs, pressing the crumbs into the meat.

3. In a medium skillet, preferably nonstick, heat the canola oil over medium-high heat. Cook the veal croquettes until golden, about 3 minutes on each side; reduce the heat to medium-low and cover the pan. Continue cooking until the croquettes are cooked through, 5 to 7 minutes more.

2 pounds new potatoes, unpeeled

Kosher salt

3 tablespoons unsalted butter, at room temperature, cut into small chunks

1/2 cup minced fresh dill, plus fresh dill sprigs

Freshly ground black pepper

1. Put the potatoes in a medium pot and cover with cold water. Add 1 tablespoon salt and bring to a simmer over medium-high heat. Simmer until the potatoes are tender, 25 to 30 minutes.

2. Drain the potatoes in a colander and immediately return them to the pot. With a wooden spoon, mix in the butter and minced dill. Smash the potatoes slightly with the spoon, and season with salt and pepper.

SERVE   the potatoes alongside the croquettes, and garnish with fresh dill sprigs.

PHILIPPE BERTINEAU

Baeckoefe (Alsatian Meat-and-Potato Casserole)

Makes 6 servings

Chef Bertineau, of Manhattan's Payard Pâtisserie and Bistro, tells us that in the Alsatian countryside, farmers traditionally brought casseroles of mixed meats and potatoes to the village baker to cook while they were working in the fields. Although the casseroles baked most of the day until the farmers' return, in your home oven, the dish can be done in considerably less time.

Lard is traditional for greasing the terrine, but you can also use butter or duck fat.

FOR THE MARINATED BEEF, LAMB, AND PORK:

1 (750-milliliter) bottle Alsatian Pinot Blanc
   wine, or substitute Riesling
2 onions, cut into small dice
2 whole cloves
1 fresh thyme sprig
8 cloves garlic, crushed with the broad end of a
   knife blade and peeled
Kosher salt

Freshly ground black pepper
1 pound beef top round, cut into 1 1/2-inch
   chunks
1 pound boneless lamb leg or shoulder,
   cut into 1 1/2-inch chunks
1 pound pork shoulder or butt, cut into
   1 1/2-inch chunks

In a large nonreactive bowl, combine the wine, onions, cloves, thyme, garlic, and salt and pepper to taste. Add the beef, lamb, and pork, and stir to cover well with the marinade. Cover and refrigerate for at least 8 hours or overnight.

1 to 2 tablespoons unsalted butter, plus extra for greasing the terrine (or substitute lard or duck fat, see Sources)
2¹/2 pounds Yukon Gold potatoes, unpeeled
1 large onion, thinly sliced

Kosher salt
Freshly ground black pepper
1¹/3 cups beef stock or canned low-sodium beef broth

1. Drain the meat in a colander set over a bowl. Reserve the marinade and the meat, and discard the other solids.

2. Preheat the oven to 325°F. Lightly butter a 13 by 9-inch casserole or a round 3- to 4-quart casserole.

3. Peel and slice the potatoes 1/4 inch thick and immediately begin to layer them in the casserole. Do not put the potatoes in water; it is important that they retain their starch.

4. Starting and ending with the potatoes, make layers of potatoes, onion, and meat, seasoning each layer with salt and pepper. The final layer of potatoes can be formed into a decorative pattern by making a rectangle or circle of potatoes just within the outer rim of the casserole and then forming increasingly smaller inner rectangles or circles until you reach the middle. Decorate the top with any leftover slices.

5. Combine 1¹/3 cups of the reserved marinade with the stock, and pour the liquid into and around the layers, coming just to the top of the potatoes but not covering them. Dot the top with the butter.

6. Cover tightly with a lid and place in the oven for 2 hours. Remove the lid and bake for 1 hour more, to reduce the juices and caramelize the top. If the meat and potatoes are not yet tender, continue baking until the desired doneness is reached.

SERVE from the casserole with a green salad and the same Pinot Blanc or Riesling used in the marinade.

La Svizzera (Italian-Style Hamburgers) with Prosciutto Mashed Potatoes

Makes 4 servings

Chef Pellegrino, of Manhattan's Baldoria Restaurant, tells us that in northern Italy, hamburgers are called *Svizzera* because the Swiss were the first Europeans to fall in love with the American creation. Whatever the name, this is a fabulous Italian dish!

A few tips: This recipe will make 4 generous burgers; you can make 6 smaller portions, if you prefer. It's a good idea to start the potatoes first and prepare the burgers while they are cooking. And for a great meatball recipe, simply add an egg to the meat mixture—but if you do, be sure to cook the meatballs at a lower temperature.

FOR THE PROSCIUTTO MASHED POTATOES:

2 pounds russet potatoes, peeled and
    quartered
Kosher salt
1 cup whole milk
1/4 cup corn oil
1 large onion, thinly sliced

1/2 pound (2 sticks) plus 2 tablespoons
    unsalted butter, the 1/2 pound diced
Freshly ground white pepper
Pinch of ground nutmeg
8 ounces prosciutto, cut into 1/2-inch dice

1. Put the potatoes in a large pot and cover with cold water. Add 1 tablespoon salt and bring to a low boil over medium-high heat. Cook until tender when pierced with the tip of a knife, about 25 minutes.

2. While the potatoes are cooking, bring the milk to a boil in a small pot over medium heat.

3. Place a medium sauté pan over medium heat for 3 minutes. Add the corn oil and heat until smoking. Reduce the heat to medium-low, add the sliced onion, and cook, stirring occasionally, until translucent, about 15 minutes. Add the 2 tablespoons butter and cook, stirring often, until the onion turns a caramel color, another 12 to 15 minutes.

4. Drain the potatoes and pass through a food mill or ricer back into their cooking pot, off the heat. Add half of the diced butter and mix well until the butter is fully incorporated. Gradually mix in the remaining diced butter. Add 3/4 cup of the hot milk, mix well, and add the remaining 1/4 cup, as needed. Season with white pepper, the nutmeg, and additional salt, if needed.

5. Place the pot over low heat and stir in the caramelized onion and the prosciutto. Cook, stirring often, for 3 minutes.

FOR THE HAMBURGERS:

1 pound ground beef chuck

8 ounces ground veal

8 ounces ground pork

1/2 teaspoon minced garlic

2 tablespoons freshly grated Parmesan cheese

2 tablespoons finely chopped shallots
    or white onion

1/4 cup corn oil

Kosher salt

Freshly ground black pepper

4 good-quality hamburger buns, halved

4 slices Swiss, Cheddar, or American cheese
    (optional)

Mayonnaise (optional)

4 slices beefsteak tomato

4 Boston lettuce leaves, washed and patted dry

1. Preheat the oven to 400°F.

2. In a large nonreactive bowl, using your hands, combine the beef, veal, and pork. Add the garlic, Parmesan cheese, shallots, and 2 tablespoons of the corn oil, and mix well. Season with salt and pepper.

3. Divide the meat mixture into 4 patties, about 1 inch thick, and flatten the surfaces.

4. Heat a large ovenproof sauté pan over medium heat for 3 minutes; add the remaining 2 tablespoons corn oil and heat for 2 to 3 minutes more. Add the hamburgers and sear until brown, 4 to 5 minutes on each side.

5. Put the pan in the oven and cook to the desired doneness (3 to 4 minutes for medium-rare, 12 minutes for medium-well). Put the buns in the oven for about 3 minutes, to toast.

6. If you want to make cheeseburgers, top each patty with a slice of the cheese for the last 2 minutes of cooking.

7. Spread 4 of the bun halves with the mayonnaise, if using, and place a burger, a slice of tomato, and a lettuce leaf on each. Top with the other half of the bun.

SERVE   the *Svizzera* alongside a mound of the prosciutto mashed potatoes.

4.

Lamb, Venison, and Potatoes

*P*OTATOES HAVE ALWAYS BEEN NATURAL PARTNERS FOR the assertive flavor of lamb, and these recipes include Red Bliss, creamer, russet, Yukon Gold, red new, purple, and fingerling. Sometimes the potatoes provide a quiet balance to the meat, and sometimes they do the unexpected and yell even louder.

In John Sundstrom's Herb-Grilled Lamb Chops with Chanterelle and Potato Hash, golden, red, and purple potatoes more than hold their own beside herb-accented grilled loin chops. In Jean-Louis Gerin's Lamb Chops Champvallon, both the chops—this time from the shoulder—and the potatoes are treated gently, simply layered with onions and baked until succulent. In Thomas John's Indian-Spiced Rack of Lamb with Potato Tikki and Mint Yogurt, the lamb is cut into separate chops after the rack has been roasted; it is served with cumin-and-coriander-spiced potato cakes and a cooling minted yogurt sauce.

Lamb shanks require a longer cooking time than chops or a rack of lamb, but for Daniel Angerer's Potato-Crusted Lamb Cakes, the meat can be slowly braised and then crusted with thinly sliced potatoes ahead of time, and reheated quickly when you are ready to serve.

Roast leg of lamb with potatoes is a perfect party dish, and you can give it either a French or a Greek accent. Sandro Gamba flavors his roast with curry and lemon and accompanies it with his grandmother Jeannette's beyond-heavenly truffled mashed potatoes. Cooking in a different style, Jim Botsacos flavors leg of lamb with lusty garlic, Greek oregano, and olive oil, and roasts it along with onions and potatoes. He completes the picture with a spicy, colorful okra, onion, and tomato stew.

Mark Franz's Slow-Roasted Lamb Shoulder with Potatoes, Garlic, and Rosemary is a boneless rolled roast that is herbaceous and delicious, and its potatoes absorb aromatic juices as the dish slowly cooks.

I had been searching for an old-fashioned Irish stew, but Frank Coe offered a much more exciting dish ("I haven't made Irish stew for years," he informed me). His lamb and potatoes are flavored with a variety of herbs and spices, along with dried figs and apricots and pomegranate molasses. I turned to my kitchen for a shepherd's pie that is a lot like the favorite you remember from your own childhood, with savory ground lamb under a topping of golden-crusted mashed potatoes. And for a touch of Middle Eastern style, try Lamb-Stuffed Potato Kubbeh, crusty mashed-potato cakes filled with a mixture of sautéed ground lamb and sweet raisins.

In an elegant dish from their Maine restaurant, Mark Gaier and Clark Frasier pair lean, marinated venison with rich sweet potatoes. Arrows' Leg of Venison with Roasted Yams is not an everyday meat-and-potatoes combination, but it is a perfect one.

Herb-Grilled Lamb Chops with Chanterelle and Potato Hash

LAMB

Makes 6 servings

Forget hash browns! This is the most beautiful potato hash ever, resplendent with gold, purple, and white potatoes and golden mushrooms, from Chef Sundstrom of Seattle's Earth and Ocean. Juicy grilled lamb chops that have been bathed in an herbal marinade complete the striking dish.

FOR THE MARINATED LAMB CHOPS:

$^{1}/_{4}$ cup extra-virgin olive oil

6 fresh summer savory sprigs, leaves stripped
    and chopped

6 fresh rosemary sprigs, leaves stripped and
    chopped

6 fresh thyme sprigs, leaves stripped and
    chopped

4 cloves garlic, minced

Kosher or coarse salt

Freshly ground black pepper

12 double-cut lamb loin chops, Frenched

In a large bowl, combine the olive oil, savory, rosemary, thyme, garlic, salt, and pepper. Add the lamb chops and toss to coat them well with the marinade. Cover and refrigerate for at least 4 hours or up to 24 hours.

4 tablespoons unsalted butter

1 pound Yukon Gold potatoes, unpeeled,
    cut into 3/8-inch dice

Kosher salt

Freshly ground black pepper

1 pound red new potatoes, unpeeled,
    cut into 3/8-inch dice

1 pound purple potatoes, unpeeled,
    cut into 3/8-inch dice

1 pound golden chanterelle mushrooms,
    quartered

2 yellow onions, cut into 1/4-inch dice

4 cloves garlic, minced

1 bunch of scallions (white and 3 inches of
    green), thinly sliced

1. Heat a large nonstick pan over medium heat. Melt 1 tablespoon of the butter and cook the Yukon Gold potatoes, allowing them to brown slightly on all sides and to become crisp yet tender. Toss often and season lightly with salt and pepper. Remove to a plate.

2. Repeat with 1 tablespoon of butter and the red new potatoes.

3. Repeat with 1 tablespoon of butter and the purple potatoes.

4. Add the remaining 1 tablespoon butter and cook the chanterelles and onions until the mushrooms are tender and the onions are softened, about 8 minutes. Add the garlic and cook until softened, about 2 minutes. Leave the mushroom mixture in the pan. Return all the potatoes to the pan and combine well. Add the scallions and cook for 1 minute. Season again with salt and pepper, and reserve.

Canola oil
Kosher salt
Freshly ground black pepper

1. Preheat a charcoal or gas grill and brush the rack with an oiled paper towel. (Or preheat a heavy stovetop grill pan or the broiler.)

2. Remove the lamb chops from the marinade and let them come to room temperature. Season them with salt and pepper, and grill to the desired doneness (8 to 10 minutes for medium-rare). Let the chops rest in a warm place for 5 to 6 minutes before serving.

TO SERVE:

Chopped flat-leaf parsley

Divide the chanterelle and potato hash evenly among 6 serving plates and top with the lamb chops. Garnish with chopped parsley.

Lamb Chops Champvallon

Makes 4 servings

A simple, earthy pairing of tender lamb chops and sliced potatoes, this classic French dish, from the chef and owner of Restaurant Jean-Louis, in Greenwich, Connecticut, is said to have first been introduced in the court of Louis XIV. Champvallon is for true potato lovers—there will be generous leftovers to enjoy.

4 shoulder lamb chops, about ¹/₂ inch thick
Kosher salt
Freshly ground black pepper
2 tablespoons unsalted butter
6 cups unsalted chicken stock or canned
*   low-sodium chicken broth*
1 bay leaf

1 fresh thyme sprig
4 to 5 russet potatoes, peeled and sliced
*   ¹/₄ inch thick (6 cups)*
3 to 4 onions, sliced ¹/₄ inch thick (2 cups)
2 tablespoons minced scallions (white and
*   2 inches of green)*

1. Preheat the oven to 350°F.
2. Season the lamb chops with salt and pepper.
3. In a large skillet over medium-high heat, melt the butter and sauté the chops until lightly browned, about 2 minutes on each side. Add the chicken stock, bay leaf, and thyme, and bring to a boil. Remove from the heat.
4. Place half of the potato slices in a thin layer on the bottom of a gratin dish, sprinkle lightly with salt and pepper, and cover with half of the onion slices. Arrange the lamb

chops over the onions. Top with the remaining onion slices, and finish with a layer of the remaining potato slices. Season with salt and pepper.

5. Pour the chicken stock mixture over the dish and cover tightly with foil. Bake for 40 minutes, then remove the foil and continue baking for 15 to 30 minutes more, until the potatoes and meat are tender and the potatoes are golden. Remove the bay leaf and thyme sprig, sprinkle with the scallions, and serve immediately on warmed plates.

Indian-Spiced Rack of Lamb with Potato Tikki and Mint Yogurt

Makes 2 servings

Herbs and freshly toasted spices—cilantro leaves, fresh mint, cumin and coriander seeds—are Chef John's gift to meat and potatoes. In his Mantra Restaurant, in Boston, tender rack of lamb is paired with crisp, spicy Indian potato cakes, and the combination is served with a cooling minted yogurt sauce.

FOR THE MINT YOGURT:

1/2 cup fresh mint leaves
1/2 cup fresh cilantro leaves
1 clove garlic, peeled
2 tablespoons coarsely chopped white onion

1 tablespoon freshly squeezed lime juice
1/4 cup plain yogurt, regular or fat-free
1/4 teaspoon kosher salt

Purée all the ingredients in a blender until smooth. The sauce can be refrigerated for up to 3 days; bring it to room temperature before serving.

1¹/2 teaspoons freshly cracked black pepper
    (see Note)
1 tablespoon cumin seeds
¹/2 teaspoon kosher salt, or to taste
2 tablespoons red wine vinegar

1 tablespoon extra-virgin olive oil
1 tablespoon plain yogurt, regular or fat-free
1 rack of lamb, chine bone removed and
    trimmed of excess fat (the butcher can
    do this)

1. Combine the black pepper, cumin seeds, salt, vinegar, olive oil, and yogurt in a large bowl. Add the lamb, cover, and marinate for 30 minutes or up to 1 hour.

2. Preheat the broiler.

3. Remove the lamb from the marinade, shaking off any excess liquid. Place the lamb under the broiler, meat side up, and cook to the desired doneness (15 minutes for medium-rare). Remove the lamb from the broiler and let it rest for 5 minutes, tented with foil. Slice into chops, using a sharp knife.

1 large russet potato, unpeeled
¹/2 teaspoon cumin seeds
¹/2 teaspoon coriander seeds
1 clove garlic, minced

2 tablespoons minced white onion
Juice of ¹/2 lemon
Kosher salt
1 tablespoon grapeseed oil

1. Preheat the oven to 350°F and bake the potato for about 45 minutes, or until tender (or microwave the potato until tender).

2. In a small dry pan, toast the cumin and coriander seeds over medium-high heat until fragrant, about 4 minutes, shaking the pan often. Grind the seeds to a powder in a spice grinder, coffee grinder, or mortar and pestle.

3. When the potato is cool enough to handle, peel and grate it finely. Place the grated potato in a mixing bowl and add the garlic, onion, ground cumin and coriander, lemon juice, and salt. Mix lightly and form the mixture into 2 square cakes, 1/2 to 1 inch thick

4. In a medium pan, heat the grapeseed oil over medium-high heat and cook the cakes until brown and crisp on both sides and warmed through, 6 to 8 minutes.

TO SERVE, place 1 sautéed potato cake in the center of each plate. Arrange the lamb chops around the potato cake, and ladle mint yogurt around the lamb.

NOTE: For cracked black pepper, wrap peppercorns in a dish towel and smash them with a heavy pan.

Potato-Crusted Lamb Cakes

LAMB

Makes 4 servings

Chef Angerer, of Fresh restaurant in Tribeca, braises lamb shanks with fragrant spices and herbs, and uses the classic technique of wrapping in caul fat, in his preparation of individual crisp-crusted cakes. You can cook the lamb ahead of time and form the cakes up to 4 days before you are ready to do the final cooking. This elegant entrée will then take less than half an hour to put on the table.

FOR THE BRAISED LAMB SHANKS:

3 large lamb shanks (3 to 4 pounds total)
Kosher salt
Freshly ground black pepper
2 tablespoons canola oil
2 carrots, cut into 1-inch dice
2 onions, cut into 1-inch dice
1 celery root, cut into 1-inch dice

3 cups red wine, preferably Merlot
2 cups chicken stock or canned low-sodium
    chicken broth
2 tablespoons coriander seeds
2 tablespoons pink peppercorns
2 bay leaves
2 fresh rosemary sprigs

1. Preheat the oven to 350°F.

2. Sprinkle the lamb shanks generously with salt and pepper.

3. In a large ovenproof pot over medium-high heat, heat the canola oil and brown the meat evenly on all sides. Transfer the meat to a plate and pour off all but 1 tablespoon of the fat.

4. Add the carrots, onions, and celery root to the pot and cook until browned, about 10 minutes. Add the red wine and chicken stock. Wrap the coriander seeds, peppercorns,

bay leaves, and rosemary in a square of cheesecloth and add the sachet to the pot. Bring the liquid to a boil, add the lamb shanks, and cover.

5. Transfer the pot to the oven. Braise the lamb shanks until the meat falls off the bone, 2 to 2½ hours.

6. Drain the meat and vegetables in a colander over a large bowl, reserving the braising liquid. Discard the herbs and bones.

FOR THE POTATO-CRUSTED LAMB CAKES:

2 large russet potatoes, peeled

2 ounces caul fat (lining of a pork stomach, may be ordered from your butcher), soaked in water, patted dry, and cut into 4 equal pieces

2 tablespoons canola oil

1. Put the lamb-and-vegetable mixture into four 4-inch, 1-inch high, ring molds (see Note). Press the mixture down with a spoon. Refrigerate for about 30 minutes, or until firm.

2. Meanwhile, slice the potatoes paper thin (using a mandoline, if possible).

3. When the lamb cakes are cool, layer the potatoes onto the top of each, dividing the potatoes equally. Remove the cakes from the molds and wrap each tightly with the caul fat, as thinly as possible. The cakes may be refrigerated, well covered, for up to 4 days. In fact, they will taste even better after 1 day's refrigeration and will be more compact and easier to sear. They may be frozen, well wrapped, for up to 3 months.

4. If the oven has been turned off, preheat it again to 400°F.

5. In a large ovenproof sauté pan, heat the canola oil over medium-high heat until shimmering, and sear the lamb cakes, potato crust down, until well browned, about 5 minutes. Turn over and transfer to the oven for 10 minutes, or until heated through. If they have been refrigerated or defrosted, the cakes may take longer to reheat.

6. Serve the cakes hot from the oven.

NOTE: If you don't have ring molds, pack the meat into 1/2-pint plastic containers (the kind you get food in at the deli), or shape rings out of aluminum foil.

SANDRO GAMBA

Roasted Leg of Lamb with Grandmother Jeannette's Truffled Mashed Potatoes

Makes 6 to 8 servings

Chef Gamba, of Chicago's NoMI, pairs his grandmother's famous potato dish (from her renowned restaurant, Les Cinq Ponts, in Neufchâteau, France) with tender leg of lamb marinated in curry and lemon. The result is an elegant version of childhood memories.

FOR THE ROASTED LEG OF LAMB:

1 cup sweet curry powder
4 cups lemon olive oil (available in specialty
    grocery stores) or extra-virgin olive oil
1 (5- to 7-pound) leg of lamb, butterflied
Kosher salt
Freshly ground black pepper
2 tablespoons canola oil
2 carrots, cut into thick disks

2 stalks celery, cut into 1-inch pieces
2 onions, cut into 1-inch dice
1 head garlic, halved crosswise
1/4 cup black peppercorns
2 bay leaves
2 cups apple juice
2 cups chicken stock or canned low-sodium
    chicken broth

1. In a deep nonreactive bowl that is large enough to accommodate the lamb, combine the curry powder and the lemon olive oil.

2. Spread the lamb on a work surface and brush on the marinade. Roll the lamb into a cylinder (keep the fattier side outside) and tie it with butcher's string. Put the lamb into the marinade bowl, coat with the remaining marinade, cover, and refrigerate for 24 hours.

3. Preheat the oven to 350°F.

4. Remove the lamb from the bowl and shake off any excess marinade. Season the lamb with salt and pepper. In a large sauté pan over medium-high heat, heat the canola oil and sear the lamb until golden brown on all sides; remove it from the pan.

5. Add the carrots, celery, onions, and garlic to the pan and sauté them in the remaining oil, over medium-high heat, until lightly browned. Season the vegetables with salt and pepper.

6. Lay the vegetables, peppercorns, and bay leaves in the bottom of a roasting pan (about 12 by 9 by 4 inches) and place the lamb on top of them. Add the apple juice and chicken stock. Roast the lamb until the internal temperature reaches 140°F for medium-rare, 1 1/4 to 1 1/2 hours. Strain the cooking liquid and reserve. If you want a thicker sauce, reduce the liquid over high heat to the desired thickness.

FOR THE TRUFFLED MASHED POTATOES:

2 pounds Yukon Gold potatoes, peeled
Kosher salt
1 cup whole milk

2 tablespoons heavy cream
4 ounces truffle butter (see Sources)
Freshly ground black pepper

1. Put the potatoes in a medium pot and cover with lightly salted cold water. Bring to a simmer over medium-high heat and cook until fork-tender, 35 to 40 minutes. Do not allow the water to boil; lower the heat, if necessary, to keep it at a simmer. Drain the potatoes and pass them through a food mill or ricer into a mixing bowl.

2. Meanwhile, in a small pan over low heat, gently heat the milk and the heavy cream to a simmer.

3. Add the milk, cream, and truffle butter to the potatoes. Mix, using a wooden spoon, until the potatoes are smooth and creamy. Be careful not to overmix the potatoes, or they will become pasty. Season with salt and pepper

TO SERVE, allow the lamb to rest for 15 minutes, tented with foil. Remove the string and slice thickly. Accompany with the truffled mashed potatoes

Roasted Greek Leg of Lamb with Rustic Potatoes and Okra, Onion, and Tomato Stew

Makes 8 servings

This is the Greek way to roast lamb and potatoes—Chef Jim Botsacos, of Manhattan's Molyvos, reinterprets a classic, beautiful dish. The colorful okra and tomato stew heightens the mellow flavors and velvety texture of the meat and potatoes.

Make the okra stew while the lamb is roasting. You will need to stir in 1 cup of the lamb cooking juices, and you can take this amount out of the roasting pan shortly before the lamb is done—the juices won't be needed until the last 15 minutes of cooking the okra.

FOR THE ROASTED LEG OF LAMB:

1 (6- to 7-pound) leg of lamb (weight with
    bone in), boned, rolled, and tied
1 clove garlic, quartered
1/4 cup plus 1 tablespoon extra-virgin olive oil
Kosher salt
Freshly ground black pepper
1 tablespoon dried Greek oregano, plus
    1 teaspoon crumbled (or substitute
    Turkish or Mediterranean, see Sources)

4 yellow onions, thinly sliced
16 small, thin-skinned potatoes (such as
    Red Bliss or creamer), unpeeled,
    quartered
Juice of 1 lemon
1/2 cup white wine
2 cups chicken stock or canned low-sodium
    chicken broth, plus more as needed

1. Make 4 random slits in the lamb and insert the garlic quarters. Rub the lamb with 1 tablespoon olive oil, and sprinkle with salt, pepper, and the 1 teaspoon crumbled oregano. Place in a nonreactive dish, cover, and refrigerate for at least 3 hours or up to 8 hours.

2. Preheat the oven to 450°F.

3. Put the lamb in a roasting pan or a casserole large enough to accommodate it (as well as the onions and potatoes that you will add later), and roast, uncovered, for 25 minutes.

4. Meanwhile, in a large nonreactive bowl, combine the onions, the potatoes, 1 tablespoon dried oregano, 1/4 cup olive oil, and the lemon juice. Season with salt and pepper, and toss lightly to combine.

5. Remove the roasting pan from the oven and reduce the oven temperature to 400°F. Pour the wine into the pan and add the onion and potato mixture, taking care to distribute it evenly around the lamb. Add the chicken stock.

6. Return the lamb to the oven and roast, uncovered, basting frequently, for another 2 hours, or until an instant-read meat thermometer reaches 140°F (this will be medium-rare). Add additional stock or water to the pan during roasting if needed. There should be at least 2 cups of lamb juices; remove 1 cup of juice about 30 minutes before the lamb is done, and use it for the okra, onion, and tomato stew, below.

7. Remove the lamb from the oven and let it rest, tented with foil, for 10 minutes before slicing.

1/4 cup plus 2 tablespoons olive oil
1 pound okra, washed and trimmed
Kosher salt
Freshly ground black pepper
4 onions, julienned
3 cloves garlic, thinly sliced
1/2 teaspoon dried Greek oregano
    (or substitute Turkish or
    Mediterranean, see Sources)

1/4 teaspoon Aleppo pepper (see Sources)
2 cups canned crushed whole tomatoes, with
    their juice (from a 28-ounce can; there
    will be some left over)
1 cup reserved lamb juices, strained
2 tablespoons sliced pitted kalamata olives
2 tablespoons chopped fresh parsley
2 tablespoons extra-virgin olive oil

1. In a large saucepan, heat 1 tablespoon of the olive oil over medium-high heat, add half the okra, and sauté until lightly seared, 2 to 3 minutes. Season with salt and black pepper. Transfer to a bowl and reserve. Reheat the pan, add another tablespoon of the olive oil, and repeat with the remaining okra.

2. In a large, heavy pot, heat the 1/4 cup olive oil over medium-high heat and add the onions. Season with a pinch of salt, stir, and cook until soft and translucent, 10 to 15 minutes. Stir in the garlic, reduce the heat to medium, and cook, stirring occasionally, until the onions are lightly caramelized, about 8 minutes more. Add the oregano and Aleppo pepper, stir, and cook for 1 minute.

3. Reduce the heat to low, stir in the tomatoes, and cook for 5 to 6 minutes. Add the reserved okra and stir to combine the ingredients. Add the lamb juices and simmer (still over low heat) for 15 to 20 minutes. When the okra is slightly tender, fold in the olives, parsley, and extra-virgin olive oil. Season with salt and black pepper.

TO SERVE, place the lamb on a large platter and remove the string. Slice the lamb to the desired thickness, and arrange the potatoes and onions around it. Serve with the okra, onion, and tomato stew.

Slow-Roasted Lamb Shoulder with Potatoes, Garlic, and Rosemary

Makes 6 to 8 servings

Chef Franz, of San Francisco's Farallon Restaurant, makes this garlicky, herbaceous lamb in his kitchen at home. Slow roasting ensures that the lamb is tender and delicious and that the potatoes are infused with aromatic, flavorful juices.

20 cloves garlic, peeled
Kosher salt
1 (6-pound) boneless lamb shoulder,
    rolled and tied

1/2 cup chopped fresh rosemary
1/2 cup olive oil
Freshly ground black pepper
6 large russet potatoes, peeled

1. Preheat the oven to 300°F.

2. Using a mortar and pestle, crush 6 of the garlic cloves and mash into a paste with some of the kosher salt. Rub the paste into the lamb. Sprinkle the lamb all over with 1/4 cup of the rosemary and then rub with some of the olive oil. Season with more salt and the black pepper.

3. Quarter the potatoes and toss them in a bowl with the rest of the olive oil.

4. Put the lamb in a large roasting pan and tuck the potatoes and the remaining 14 garlic cloves all around (but not under) the lamb. Sprinkle with the remaining 1/4 cup rosemary. Seal the pan tightly with a double layer of foil and put it in the oven. Roast the lamb for 2 hours and then remove the foil. Increase the heat to 350°F and continue to roast the lamb for another 30 minutes.

5. Remove the lamb from the oven and allow it to rest loosely covered with the foil for 20 minutes.

6. Place the lamb on a platter and remove the string. Carve the lamb into thick slices and arrange the potatoes and garlic alongside. Pour the accumulated juices over the meat and potatoes.

Chef Frank's Flavorful Lamb Stew

LAMB

Makes 4 servings

This isn't your mom's Irish stew! Chef Coe, of Long Island's Wild Goose Restaurant, calls his herbaceous, fruit-accented blending of lamb and potatoes sweet, sassy, and seductive. It looks and smells irresistible, and provides a satisfying balance of flavors.

Pinch of cumin seeds

1/4 cup extra-virgin olive oil

1 1/2 pounds boneless lamb shoulder, cut into 2-inch cubes

Sea salt or kosher salt

Freshly ground black pepper

2 shallots, finely diced

1 stalk celery, strings removed, finely diced

1 carrot, finely diced

1 leek (white and tender green parts), washed and finely diced

1/2 parsnip or celery root, peeled and finely diced

4 cloves garlic, finely diced

1 tablespoon grated orange zest (an organic orange is best)

3 tablespoons pomegranate molasses (see Sources)

4 dried figs, coarsely chopped

2 dried apricots, coarsely chopped

2 pitted prunes, coarsely chopped

12 fingerling potatoes, peeled

1 tablespoon chopped fresh thyme

1 tablespoon chopped fresh tarragon

1 tablespoon chopped fresh rosemary

1/4 teaspoon saffron threads

2 cups demi-glace (see Sources); or substitute veal or chicken stock. (Do not use canned chicken broth.)

1/2 cup tomato concassée (see Note)

1 tablespoon chopped fresh marjoram

1 tablespoon chopped fresh mint

1. In a small dry pan over medium heat, toast the cumin seeds for about 3 minutes, shaking the pan so the seeds do not burn. Reserve.

2. Preheat the oven to 300°F.

3. In a large ovenproof skillet or Dutch oven, heat 2 tablespoons of the olive oil over medium-high heat. Sprinkle the lamb cubes with salt and pepper, and sear until golden brown on all sides, about 5 minutes. Reduce the heat to low.

4. In another large skillet, heat the remaining 2 tablespoons olive oil over medium heat. Add the shallots, celery, carrot, leek, and parsnip, and cook until the vegetables are softened but not colored, 6 to 8 minutes. Add the garlic and cook until softened, 1 or 2 minutes more.

5. Add the vegetables to the lamb. Add the orange zest, reserved cumin seeds, and pomegranate molasses, and combine well. Add the figs, apricots, prunes, potatoes, thyme, tarragon, rosemary, and saffron. Add the demi-glace and tomato concassée, stir to combine, and season with salt and pepper.

6. Raise the heat to medium, bring the stew to a simmer, and place in the oven. Cook until the meat and potatoes are tender, about $1^1/2$ hours.

7. Spoon into a serving bowl and sprinkle with the chopped marjoram and mint.

NOTE: To make $1/2$ cup tomato concassée, bring a small pot of lightly salted water to a boil and immerse 1 ripe tomato, about $1/3$ pound, cored, with a small X cut on the bottom, for 10 to 15 seconds. Remove from the water and peel—the skin should slip off easily. Halve the tomato and squeeze gently to remove the seeds and juice. Cut the flesh into $1/4$-inch dice.

JOAN SCHWARTZ

Old-Fashioned Shepherd's Pie

Makes 4 to 6 servings

In compiling the recipes for this book, I've learned a lot about shepherd's pies! This version is the mother of them all—simple, rustic, delicious, and a real lifesaver for the busy cook.

FOR THE MASHED-POTATO TOPPING:

1¹/₂ pounds Yukon Gold or russet potatoes,
    unpeeled
Kosher salt
¹/₂ cup milk

2 tablespoons unsalted butter, at room
    temperature
¹/₄ teaspoon freshly ground black pepper

1. Put the potatoes in a medium pot and cover with cold water. Add 1 tablespoon salt and bring to a simmer over medium-high heat. Simmer until tender, 25 to 30 minutes. Drain the potatoes, and peel as soon as they are cool enough to handle.

2. Meanwhile, in a small pot over medium heat, or in the microwave, warm the milk.

3. Pass the potatoes through a food mill or ricer into a mixing bowl, or mash with a potato masher. Add the butter and milk, mix well with a wooden spoon, and season with ¹/₂ teaspoon salt and the pepper, or to taste.

2 tablespoons olive oil

1 onion, finely chopped

1 carrot, finely chopped

1 stalk celery, finely chopped

1 pound ground lamb

2 tablespoons chopped fresh rosemary

1 teaspoon kosher salt, or to taste

1/2 teaspoon freshly ground black pepper,
     or to taste

2 tablespoons plain bread crumbs or
     matzo meal

1 large egg, lightly beaten

1 cup frozen tiny peas (they do not have to
     be thawed)

1 tablespoon unsalted butter, cut into
     small chunks

1. Preheat the oven to 400°F.

2. In a medium skillet over medium heat, heat the olive oil and cook the onion, carrot, and celery until softened, about 10 minutes. Add the lamb and press down with a fork to break up any lumps. Cook, stirring, until the meat is browned, about 15 minutes. Add the rosemary, salt, and pepper, and remove the mixture to a mixing bowl.

3. Add the bread crumbs to the meat mixture and mix well. Add the egg and combine well.

4. Pour the mixture into an ungreased 8- or 9-inch square ovenproof pan. Spoon the peas evenly over the meat. Spoon the mashed potatoes over the top, leaving a rough surface, and dot with the butter. Place in the oven for 30 to 35 minutes, until heated through and slightly browned on top. Serve from the pan.

Lamb-Stuffed Potato Kubbeh

Makes 6 servings

These crusty, savory cakes of mashed potatoes stuffed with lamb and sweet raisins are a delicious staple in Middle Eastern Jewish households. This version is adapted from the tempting *kubbeh* served at the New York home of Rachel Meer, and from the recipe created by her mother, Touba Anwarzadeh.

While the flavors are delicate, the potato cakes are hearty, and need only a simple salad as an accompaniment. Or serve single cakes as appetizers.

FOR THE LAMB STUFFING:

1/2 cup dark raisins
2 tablespoons olive oil
1 small onion, finely chopped
8 ounces ground lamb

Kosher salt
Freshly ground black pepper
2 tablespoons minced fresh parsley

1. Put the raisins in a cup and cover with warm water. Set aside until plump, about 5 minutes, and then drain.

2. In a large skillet over medium-high heat, heat the olive oil and cook the onion until golden and softened, about 5 minutes. Add the lamb, season with salt and pepper, and sauté until the meat is browned, 5 to 10 minutes, breaking it up as it cooks. Add the raisins and parsley, and set aside to cool.

2 pounds russet potatoes, unpeeled

Kosher salt

1/4 teaspoon freshly ground black pepper

1/4 cup all-purpose flour

Vegetable oil

1. Put the potatoes in a medium pot and cover with cold water. Add 1 tablespoon salt and bring to a simmer over medium-high heat. Simmer until tender, 25 to 30 minutes. Drain the potatoes, and peel as soon as they are cool enough to handle.

2. Pass the potatoes through a food mill or ricer into a mixing bowl, or mash with a potato masher. Season with 1/2 teaspoon salt and the pepper, add the flour, and mix well. Divide into 12 balls.

3. To form the *kubbeh,* flatten 1 ball of mashed potatoes into a disk between your hands. Put about 1 tablespoon of the lamb mixture in the center, and fold the potato over to enclose the meat. Press the edges together to seal, and with both hands, shape the potato cake into a ball. Flatten into a pancake. Repeat until all the stuffed potato cakes have been formed.

4. Wipe out the large skillet used to cook the lamb and place it over medium-high heat. Pour in the vegetable oil to a depth of 1/2 inch and heat the oil over medium-high heat to 375°F, or until a bit of potato sizzles when immersed. Place the potato cakes in the hot oil, and fry them until deep brown, 1 to 3 minutes on each side, taking care that they do not burn.

5. Remove the *kubbeh* from the oil with a slotted spoon and drain them on paper towels. Serve hot. The *kubbeh* can be refrigerated for up to 1 day or frozen. Reheat them in a little vegetable oil over medium heat.

Arrows' Leg of Venison with Roasted Yams

Makes 6 servings

This is a simple dish, as served at Arrows, the Ogunquit, Maine, rural restaurant owned by Chefs Gaier and Frasier, but the combination of marinated, roasted venison and herb-roasted sweet potatoes is inspired. Venison is a very lean meat, so be sure not to overcook it.

FOR THE ROASTED LEG OF VENISON:

2 cups red wine

2 tablespoons red wine vinegar

1 carrot, finely diced

2 stalks celery, finely diced

1 Spanish onion, finely diced

3 cloves garlic, finely sliced

2 tablespoons coarsely chopped fresh rosemary

1 tablespoon black peppercorns

1 cup plus 2 tablespoons olive oil

1 (2¹/₂- to 3-pound) leg of venison, in a single piece (available by special order from many butchers, or see Sources)

Kosher salt

Freshly ground black pepper

1. Combine the red wine, red wine vinegar, carrot, celery, onion, garlic, rosemary, peppercorns, and 1 cup olive oil in a nonreactive casserole. Place the venison in the casserole, cover, and refrigerate for 2 hours or up to 8 hours.

2. When ready to cook, preheat the oven to 375°F. Remove the venison from the marinade and sprinkle with salt and pepper.

3. In a large sauté pan over high heat, heat 2 tablespoons olive oil until very hot but not smoking, and add the venison. Reduce the heat to medium and sauté the venison until browned on one side, then flip the meat and sauté until browned on the other

side (2 to 3 minutes on each side). Turn the meat over again, put the pan in the oven, and roast until the internal temperature of the meat is 135°F for medium-rare, about 17 minutes per pound.

FOR THE ROASTED YAMS:

3 yams (about 2 pounds), peeled and cut into
    1/2-inch cubes
2 tablespoons finely chopped fresh rosemary
1/2 cup finely chopped flat-leaf parsley

3 to 4 tablespoons unsalted butter, cut into
    small chunks
Kosher salt
Freshly ground black pepper

1. Place the yams in a nonreactive ovenproof casserole, sprinkle with the herbs, and toss with the butter. Season with salt and pepper.

2. Roast the yams in the oven (with the venison) for about 30 minutes, or until soft.

TO SERVE, slice the venison across the grain about 1/4 inch thick and divide among 6 plates along with the yams.

5.

Pork and Potatoes

ERSATILE PORK CAN BE FOUND FRESH OR CURED, AND, IN FACT, IT MOST INSPIRES OUR chefs in its incarnations as bacon, ham, and sausage. Because they are so lean, the pork chops and loins in these recipes cook quickly (although you must allow some time for marination), and the cured cuts can be prepared in a flash. In all forms, this light, succulent meat pairs perfectly with Yukon Golds, russets, sweet potatoes, and red potatoes, both mature and new.

Deborah Stanton gives pork chops a citric marinade before grilling, in her Brine-Marinated Pork Chops with Scallion-Smashed Potatoes and Grilled Granny Smith Apple Slices. Bobby Flay treats tender pork and potatoes to a riot of flavors, in his New Mexican Rubbed Pork Tenderloin with Bourbon-Ancho Sauce and Roasted Garlic–Sweet Onion Potato Gratin. And for his Sweet Potato–Stuffed Roulade of Pork, Glenn Harris rolls and stuffs a lean pork loin with mashed sweet potatoes spiked with a surprising cilantro pesto.

Ham is a team player in Debra Ponzek's recipe, adding flavor and a touch of texture. Her simple and delicious Split Pea, Ham, and Potato Soup welcomes the cooler weather.

Sausage travels to Mexico, where smoky chorizo meets potatoes and tortillas, in the imaginative Chorizo, Potato, and Goat Cheese Quesadillas from Sue Torres. Maarten Pinxteren makes kielbasa a Dutch treat with bacon, mashed potatoes, and crisp greens, in his traditional Dutch Stamppot.

Crisp bacon and buttery-soft potatoes are surely a match made in heaven, and our chefs have found ingenious ways to present it. Alexandra Guarnaschelli's Bacon Lovers' Mashed Potatoes are the purest form

of this combination and will make bacon lovers of all who taste it. William Snell's golden Tartiflette de Cocotte, topped with melting Reblochon cheese, is his tempting version of a bistro favorite. And bacon and potatoes make the perfect spring salad, as Ilene Rosen found when she scouted the Union Square Greenmarket for the freshest ingredients for her Roasted New Potatoes with Bacon, Chive Flowers, and Green Tomato Dressing.

Brine-Marinated Pork Chops with Scallion-Smashed Potatoes and Grilled Granny Smith Apple Slices

PORK

Makes 4 servings

These pork chops and potatoes will look so beautiful on your table, you will imagine that you are dining at Deborah, a favorite Greenwich Village restaurant. The chops are brined, then roasted until they are golden brown and succulent. They are accompanied by silky mashed potatoes laced with scallions and accented with sweet golden apples that can be either grilled or sautéed—a delightful combination of flavors and textures.

Even given the marinating time, preparation is efficient; the dish can be served in about an hour and a half, start to finish.

FOR THE BRINE-MARINATED PORK CHOPS:

2 cups freshly squeezed orange juice, or
    substitute good-quality purchased
Juice of 1 lemon
Juice of 2 limes
$^1/_2$ cup kosher salt

$^1/_4$ cup sugar
2 tablespoons chopped garlic
4 center-cut boneless pork chops (about
    9 ounces each)

1. In a stainless steel or other nonreactive bowl, combine the orange, lemon, and lime juice. Whisk in the salt, sugar, and garlic.

2. Pour the brine mixture into a large plastic bag, preferably Ziploc. Add the pork chops, and squeeze the air out of the bag. Seal the bag and refrigerate for 30 minutes.

2 1/2 pounds Yukon Gold potatoes, unpeeled,
    cut into large dice
Kosher salt
2 cups heavy cream
4 tablespoons unsalted butter, cut into
    1/2-inch pieces

Freshly ground black pepper
2 scallions (white and 3 inches of green), finely
    chopped

1. Put the potatoes in a large pot and cover with cold water. Add 1 tablespoon salt and bring to a simmer over medium-high heat. Simmer until fork-tender, about 25 minutes.

2. While the potatoes are cooking, pour the cream into a small saucepan and bring to a scald over medium heat.

3. Drain the potatoes in a colander and put in a mixing bowl. Smash, using a potato masher or fork, blending in the butter, cream, and salt and pepper to taste. This should be a rough mixture, not a purée. Fold in the chopped scallions.

About 3 1/2 cups canola oil
1 leek (white and tender green parts), cleaned
    and sliced lengthwise into fine julienne
Kosher salt

Set a sauté pan, or a heavy stovetop grill pan that you can later use for the pork chops, over medium-high heat. Heat 1/2 inch of canola oil to 350°F and fry the leek until golden brown, 8 to 10 minutes. Drain on paper towels. Sprinkle with salt, and reserve.

1. Preheat a charcoal or gas grill to moderately hot and carefully brush the rack with an oiled paper towel. Or preheat the oven to 350°F, preheat a heavy stovetop grill pan, and brush the pan with an oiled paper towel.

2. Remove the pork chops from the marinade and rinse with cold water. Pat dry. If using a grill, sear the chops on both sides, and cook to an internal temperature of 140°F. Or sear over high heat in the heated pan for 3 minutes on each side, and place in the oven until cooked to an internal temperature of 140°F (this will take about 15 minutes per inch of thickness).

3. Allow the chops to rest for 5 minutes, then slice 1/2 inch thick.

FOR THE GRILLED APPLES:

2 Granny Smith apples, sliced 1/2 inch thick (if sautéing, cut the apples into small dice)

Canola oil (if sautéing, substitute 1 tablespoon unsalted butter)

Kosher salt

Freshly ground black pepper

1. Lightly coat the apple slices with canola oil, if grilling, and season with salt and pepper. If sautéing, season the diced apples with salt and pepper.

2. Place the apple slices on the grill with the chops until golden and softened, 8 to 10 minutes. Or in a medium skillet over medium heat, melt the butter and sauté the diced apples until golden and softened, 8 to 10 minutes.

TO SERVE, divide the smashed potatoes among 4 plates, spooning them down the center. Top with the sliced pork. Fan the grilled apple slices, or arrange the sautéed diced apples, alongside the pork, and top with the fried leek, if desired.

PORK

New Mexican Rubbed Pork Tenderloin with Bourbon-Ancho Sauce and Roasted Garlic–Sweet Onion Potato Gratin

Makes 4 servings

At first reading, you might think that the bourbon-ancho sauce could be optional, since there are so many contrasting, bold notes in the New Mexican spice rub. But be sure to include this sauce! Its mellow richness works magic in bringing together all the elements of this complex dish from Bobby Flay, of Manhattan's Mesa Grill and Bolo, and television's Food Network. It is nothing short of amazing.

Bobby accompanies the deep reddish-brown crusted pork roast with a gratin of potatoes, sweet onions, and melted cotija cheese.

Both the spice rub and the sauce can be made ahead; and the gratin can be constructed a few hours ahead and refrigerated, tightly covered, until cooking time.

FOR THE NEW MEXICAN SPICE RUB:

3 tablespoons ground ancho chili pepper
   (see Sources)
2 tablespoons packed light brown sugar
1 tablespoon ground pasilla chili pepper
   (see Sources)

1 tablespoon kosher salt
2 teaspoons ground chile de arbol
   (see Sources)
2 teaspoons ground cinnamon
2 teaspoons ground allspice

Combine all the ingredients in a small bowl and reserve. This is more than you will need for the pork; store the remainder tightly covered for up to 3 months. Makes just over 1/2 cup.

FOR THE ROASTED GARLIC–SWEET ONION POTATO GRATIN

2 cups heavy cream

1 head garlic, roasted, cloves peeled and
    puréed (see Note)

2 tablespoons olive oil

1 tablespoon unsalted butter

2 large sweet onions (such as Vidalia or Walla
    Walla), halved and thinly sliced

Kosher salt

Freshly ground black pepper

4 large russet or Yukon Gold potatoes, peeled
    and cut crosswise into 1/8-inch-thick
    slices

1/4 cup grated cotija cheese

1. Preheat the oven to 375°F.

2. In a medium nonreactive saucepan over medium heat, bring the cream to a simmer and whisk in the puréed roasted garlic.

3. In a large skillet over medium heat, heat the olive oil and butter and add the onions. Season with salt and pepper and cook until soft, about 20 minutes.

4. In a 9-inch square casserole, make a layer of one-eighth of the potato slices and season with salt and pepper. Top with one-eighth of the onions and drizzle with 1/4 cup of the cream. Repeat to make 8 layers.

5. Cover with foil and bake for 30 minutes. Remove the foil, sprinkle the cheese evenly over the top layer, and bake until the potatoes are tender and golden brown on top, about 20 minutes.

FOR THE BOURBON-ANCHO SAUCE:

2 tablespoons olive oil

1 red onion, finely chopped

2 cups plus 2 tablespoons bourbon whiskey

3 ancho chiles, soaked, stemmed, seeded, and
   puréed

6 cups chicken stock or canned low-sodium
   chicken broth

1 cup frozen apple juice concentrate, thawed

8 black peppercorns

1/4 cup packed light brown sugar

Kosher salt

1. In a medium saucepan over medium-high heat, heat the olive oil and cook the onion until softened, about 10 minutes. Add 2 cups bourbon and cook until it is completely reduced and almost dry, about 10 minutes. Add the ancho chile purée, chicken stock, apple juice concentrate, peppercorns, and light brown sugar, and cook until the mixture is reduced by half, about 20 minutes.

2. Strain through a fine-mesh sieve and return the mixture to the pan. Cook over medium heat to a sauce consistency (it should coat the back of a spoon). Add 2 table-spoons bourbon and cook for 2 minutes more. Season with salt. Reserve the sauce over very low heat. May be refrigerated for up to 2 days, or frozen. Makes 1 cup.

FOR THE PORK TENDERLOIN:

1 (2-pound) pork tenderloin

Kosher salt

New Mexican Spice Rub

2 tablespoons olive oil

1. Preheat the oven to 375°F.

2. Season the pork with salt on both sides. Dredge the pork in the spice rub and tap off any excess.

3. In a medium ovenproof sauté pan or skillet over high heat, heat the olive oil until smoking, and sear the pork until golden brown on both sides. Place the pan in the oven and cook the pork to medium doneness, 8 to 10 minutes. Tent with foil and allow to rest for 5 minutes.

TO SERVE, slice the tenderloin and divide among 4 plates; spoon some sauce over the slices. Spoon some gratin alongside the pork. Pass the remaining sauce separately.

NOTE: To roast a head of garlic, rub it with olive oil and wrap it loosely in foil. Roast at 300°F for 45 minutes, or until soft.

Sweet Potato–Stuffed Roulade of Pork

Makes 6 to 8 servings

This moist and fragrant combination of juicy pork, aromatic pesto, and mellow sweet potatoes comes from Manhattan's Jane Restaurant, where Glenn Harris creates tantalizing new American bistro food. He suggests your favorite roasted brussels sprouts as a crisp green accompaniment.

FOR THE SWEET POTATOES:

Kosher salt
2 large sweet potatoes, peeled and julienned

Bring a medium pot of salted water to a boil over medium-high heat. Add the sweet potatoes and boil gently until tender, about 3 minutes. Drain the potatoes and place on paper towels to dry and cool.

FOR THE MARINADE:

2 tablespoons dried oregano
1 tablespoon paprika
1 tablespoon ground cumin
1 tablespoon freshly ground black pepper
1 tablespoon ground fennel seeds (see Note)

1 cup sugar
1 tablespoon kosher salt
1 tablespoon olive oil
1/2 cup water

In a small dry skillet over medium heat, combine the oregano, paprika, cumin, pepper, and ground fennel, and toast, stirring, for 3 minutes. Pour into a bowl and stir in the sugar and salt. Add the olive oil and water and mix well. Reserve.

FOR THE PESTO:

2 jalapeño peppers, stemmed and seeded
    (wash your hands well after touching
    the peppers)
4 ounces pine nuts
1 bunch of fresh cilantro, washed, heavy stems
    removed, and coarsely chopped

3 cloves garlic, coarsely chopped
Kosher salt
Freshly ground black pepper

Put the jalapeños, pine nuts, cilantro, and garlic in a food processor and blend to a paste. Season with salt and pepper. Reserve.

FOR THE PORK ROULADE:

1 (2- to 3-pound) boneless center-cut pork loin,
    butterflied (the butcher can do this)

1. In a mixing bowl, combine the sweet potatoes and the pesto. Place the butterflied pork loin on a work surface and spread the sweet potato mixture evenly over it, leaving a 1/2-inch border all around. Roll as tightly as possible, as for a jelly roll, without squeezing out any of the filling, and tie with butcher's string.

2. Place the roll in a nonreactive pan and cover with the marinade. Cover and refrigerate for at least 1 hour or up to 8 hours.

3. When ready to cook, preheat the oven to 350°F.

4. Roast the roulade, uncovered, still in the marinade, until the internal temperature reaches 140°F, about 1 hour. Remove from the oven and let rest, tented with foil, for 20 minutes.

FOR THE SAUCE:

1¹/₂ cups balsamic vinegar   *3 cups apple cider*

In a medium pot over medium-high heat, combine the balsamic vinegar and the apple cider and bring to a gentle boil. Cook until reduced by two-thirds, about 1 hour.

TO SERVE, place the roulade on a platter and remove the string. Slice to the desired thickness. Spoon a little sauce over each serving.

NOTE: Fennel seeds are usually sold whole; grind them at home in a spice grinder, coffee grinder that you reserve for spices and seeds, or mortar and pestle.

Split Pea, Ham, and Potato Soup

Makes 4 to 6 servings

This simple, perfect soup from Chef Debra Ponzek of Aux Délices, in Greenwich, Connecticut, is the ideal way to welcome the first chilly days of autumn. Split peas and potato are flavored with fresh vegetables and herbs, as well as smoky bacon and Black Forest ham, in a smooth, fragrant brew.

*2 strips bacon, stacked and thinly sliced
    crosswise*
1 stalk celery, thinly sliced
1 carrot, thinly sliced
1 small onion, thinly sliced
6 ounces split peas
2 teaspoons chopped fresh thyme

*4 cups chicken or vegetable stock, or canned
    low-sodium chicken or vegetable broth*
3 ounces Black Forest ham, cut into small dice
1 russet potato, peeled and cut into small dice
Kosher salt
Freshly ground black pepper

1. Heat a medium saucepan over medium heat for 2 to 3 minutes. Add the bacon and cook for 3 to 4 minutes. Add the celery, carrot, and onion, and sauté for 10 to 12 minutes, until the vegetables are softened. Add the split peas, thyme, and stock.

2. Increase the heat to high and bring the soup to a boil. Reduce the heat to medium and simmer for 30 to 35 minutes. Add the ham and potato, and simmer until the potato is soft, another 12 to 15 minutes. Season with salt and pepper to taste, and serve hot.

PORK

Chorizo, Potato, and Goat Cheese Quesadillas

Makes 4 to 6 quesadillas, each 1 serving

If you don't usually think of tortillas and potatoes together, these crisp, fragrant tortilla "sandwiches" from chef Sue Torres, of Manhattan's Sueño, will change your point of view. Spicy chorizo and hot poblanos make great companions for creamy potatoes, melting cheese, and fragrant herbs.

FOR THE PEPPERS:

2 red bell peppers, skin well dried with paper towels

2 poblano peppers, skin well dried with paper towels

Place the peppers over a high, open flame and turn until roasted and blackened on all sides. Cover with plastic wrap or put into a Ziploc bag and allow to cool for 15 to 20 minutes. Under a thin stream of cold running water, peel off the burned skin. Remove the stem. Split the pepper open and rinse out the seeds. Pat dry and cut into julienne. Reserve.

1 pound russet potatoes, unpeeled
Kosher salt
2 tablespoons olive oil
1 tablespoon unsalted butter

1 onion, thinly sliced
Freshly ground black pepper
1 pound chorizo, casing removed and cut into
    2 1/2-inch pieces

1. Put the potatoes in a medium pot and cover with lightly salted water. Bring to a simmer over medium-high heat and cook for about 10 minutes. Reduce the heat to medium and cook until fork-tender, 30 to 35 minutes, depending on size. When cool enough to handle, peel and cut into small dice. Reserve.

2. In a medium skillet, heat 1 tablespoon of the olive oil and the butter over low heat until the butter has melted, and cook the onion until softened but not colored, about 20 minutes. Season with salt and pepper. Increase the heat to medium-low and continue cooking until the onion is golden. Remove to a bowl and reserve.

3. Return the skillet to medium-high heat and add the remaining 1 tablespoon olive oil. Cook the chorizo until browned, about 5 minutes. Cut into 1/4-inch circles and quarter the circles. Reserve.

TO MAKE THE TORTILLAS:

1/4 cup shredded fresh cilantro
2 cups shredded Monterey Jack cheese
2 cups crumbled goat cheese, or substitute
    another 2 cups Monterey Jack
Kosher salt
Freshly ground black pepper

8 to 12 (12-inch) flour tortillas, or substitute
    corn tortillas
Vegetable oil
Crème fraîche or sour cream (optional)
Sliced radishes (optional)

1. Preheat the oven to 400°F.

2. In a large mixing bowl, combine the reserved red bell peppers, poblanos, potatoes, onion, and chorizo. Add the cilantro, Monterey Jack cheese, and goat cheese. Season with salt and pepper.

3. Lay 1 tortilla flat on a work surface and spread with about 1 cup of filling, making a 1/2-inch-thick layer. Top with another tortilla, to make a quesadilla. Repeat with the remaining tortillas and filling.

4. Arrange the filled quesadillas on ungreased baking sheets, 2 to a sheet, and bake until crisp, 12 minutes.

TO SERVE, cut each quesadilla into 4 wedges. Garnish with crème fraîche and sliced radishes, if desired.

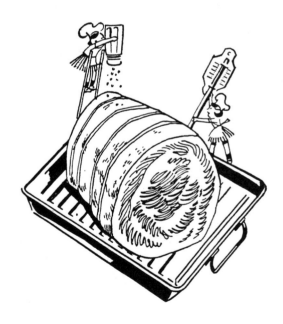

Dutch Stamppot

Makes 6 servings

This satisfying winter dish (the name means "hodgepodge") is traditional in Holland, and comes to us from the kitchen of NL, Manhattan's Dutch restaurant. Hot, buttery mashed potatoes are combined with crisp bacon and fresh escarole, and topped with a layer of smoked sausage slices. Chef Pinxteren gilds the lily, and you can do the same, with a touch of truffle oil.

3 pounds russet potatoes, peeled
Kosher salt
1 pound kielbasa, preferably half beef
   and half pork
1 pound bacon
1/2 cup milk
4 tablespoons cold unsalted butter,
   cut into 1/2-inch cubes

1 teaspoon white truffle oil (optional;
   see Sources)
1 pound escarole, washed and leaves cut into
   1-inch strips (or substitute watercress or
   arugula; see Note)
Freshly ground black pepper
1 tablespoon chopped fresh chives

1. Cut the potatoes lengthwise into 4 pieces, and place them in a bowl of cold water, so they won't discolor. Put them in a large pot and cover with salted cold water. Cook over high heat until the water begins to boil, then reduce the heat to medium and simmer for 20 minutes, or until the potatoes are done, and they begin to fall apart when pressed with a fork.

2. Meanwhile, in a small saucepan, cover the sausage with hot water and cook over medium heat until warm. To prevent the sausage from cracking, do not let the water boil. Drain, and reserve the sausage in the pot.

3. In a large skillet over high heat, fry the bacon until crisp. Drain on paper towels and crumble into 1/2-inch pieces.

4. In a small saucepan over low heat, or in a microwavable cup, warm the milk. Set aside.

5. Drain the potatoes in a sieve, shaking them dry, and put them into a large bowl. Mash with a potato masher, or pass through a food mill or ricer, until they are light and fluffy. With a wooden spoon, stir in the cold cubes of butter, one at a time. When the butter is fully incorporated, add the milk and stir well. Add the truffle oil, if using.

6. Add the escarole and bacon to the potatoes and mix thoroughly with a wooden spoon. Add salt and pepper to taste, and spoon the mixture into a serving bowl.

7. Slice the sausage and arrange the slices decoratively over the potatoes. Sprinkle with the chives and serve.

NOTE: If desired, you can briefly sauté the escarole in 2 tablespoons olive oil with 1 clove garlic, finely chopped. If you are using watercress or arugula, do not sauté.

PORK

Bacon Lovers' Mashed Potatoes

Makes 10 servings

Chef Guarnaschelli, of the Manhattan restaurant Butter, tells us that the renowned chef Joachim Bernard Spilchal created this dish, a perfect accompaniment to any grilled or roasted meat or poultry. For true bacon and potato fans, it can be a meal in itself.

*2 pounds Red Bliss potatoes, unpeeled,
  quartered*
*2 pounds Yukon Gold potatoes, peeled
  and quartered*
Kosher salt
*16 strips bacon, stacked and thinly
  sliced crosswise (see Note)*

¹/₄ cup cold water
2 white onions, finely chopped
1¹/₂ cups milk, plus more as needed
1 cup heavy cream
4 tablespoons unsalted butter
Freshly ground white pepper
2 tablespoons chopped fresh parsley (optional)

1. In a large pot, combine the Red Bliss and Yukon Gold potatoes. Fill the pot with water and bring to a boil over high heat; salt the water. Allow the potatoes to boil steadily until they are tender in the center when pierced with the tip of a knife.

2. Meanwhile, in a medium skillet, combine the sliced bacon and water (the water will draw some salt from the bacon). Cook over low heat until the water evaporates and the bacon is light brown and crisp. Add the onions, stirring with a wooden spoon to blend. Cook for 12 to 15 minutes, until the onions are tender. Drain any excess fat and set aside.

3. When the potatoes are tender, drain them in a colander, discarding the cooking water. Allow the potatoes to cool, and their excess liquid to drain off, for 5 minutes, but no longer. If the potatoes cool too much, the resulting dish can be gummy and elastic.

4. In a medium pot over medium heat, heat the milk, cream, and butter. In a large bowl, combine the potatoes with the milk mixture, mixing with a large whisk or a wooden spoon until the mixture is a chunky but homogeneous mass. Add the bacon and onions. Season to taste with salt and white pepper. Sprinkle with the parsley, if desired, and serve hot.

NOTE: If desired, set aside some of the cooked bacon and crumble it over the top of the potatoes just before serving.

Tartiflette de Cocotte (Potato Gratin with Cheese and Bacon)

Makes 4 to 6 servings

This "estimable early fall dinner" (*The New York Times*) comes from Chef William Snell of Brooklyn's Cocotte and LouLou restaurants. Departing from tradition, he adds garden-fresh zucchini and yellow squash to this popular French gratin. Serve the *tartiflette* with your favorite salad of delicate greens.

3 Yukon Gold potatoes, unpeeled,
    cut lengthwise into eighths
1 tablespoon chopped fresh tarragon
2 tablespoons chopped flat-leaf parsley
2 tablespoons canola oil
Kosher salt
Freshly ground black pepper
8 ounces very good quality bacon (preferably
    applewood smoked) strips, stacked and
    cut into 1/4-inch-wide pieces
1 cup small- to medium-diced seeded zucchini
1 cup small- to medium-diced seeded yellow
    squash

2 large Spanish onions, cut into small to
    medium dice
5 ounces shiitake mushrooms, stemmed and
    quartered (or substitute cremini or
    button mushrooms)
8 cloves garlic, very thinly sliced
1 (8 1/2 ounce) wheel of Reblochon cheese,
    halved lengthwise to form 2 disks
    (you may have to buy an 8 1/2-ounce
    portion of a larger wheel; if you can't
    find Reblochon, substitute Gruyère or
    Muenster)

1. Preheat the oven to 350°F.
2. In a mixing bowl, combine the potatoes, tarragon, 1 tablespoon of the parsley, and the canola oil, and season with a pinch of salt and pepper. Toss until most of the herbs

adhere to the potatoes. Put the potatoes into a shallow baking pan and roast for 30 to 35 minutes, until golden brown. Allow to cool slightly at room temperature.

3. Increase the oven temperature to 400°F.

4. In a large sauté pan over medium heat, cook the bacon until crisp but not well done, 6 to 10 minutes. Drain the bacon on paper towels, discarding all but 2 tablespoons of the bacon fat in the pan.

5. Add the zucchini, yellow squash, onions, and mushrooms to the reserved bacon fat. Cook over medium heat, stirring occasionally, for about 5 minutes. Add the garlic, season with salt and pepper, and cook, stirring constantly, for an additional 3 minutes (you may have to do this in batches; or use 2 pans, with slightly less fat in each pan). Remove the pan from the heat and stir in the reserved bacon.

6. Pour the vegetable mixture into a medium ovenproof casserole. Place the cheese disks on top, cut side down. Place in the oven for 12 to 15 minutes, until the cheese has completely melted and the rind is left on top of the vegetables. Let the *tartiflette* cool at room temperature for 3 minutes, sprinkle with the remaining 1 tablespoon parsley, and serve.

Roasted New Potatoes with Bacon, Chive Flowers, and Green Tomato Dressing

Makes 6 servings

Chef Rosen, of the City Bakery in Manhattan, created this light, herbaceous salad of roasted new potatoes with bacon. The nearby Union Square Greenmarket provided green tomatoes for the citric, fresh-tasting dressing, as well as beautiful chive flowers and greens. But even if you're not in the neighborhood, you can find most of these ingredients at your local market—and fresh chives can stand in for the flowers.

FOR THE GREEN TOMATO DRESSING:

3 small green tomatoes
1/4 cup plain rice vinegar (available at Asian markets and some supermarkets)
1 tablespoon seasoned rice vinegar (available at Asian markets and some supermarkets)

1 1/2 teaspoons Dijon mustard
3/8 cup canola oil
Kosher salt
Freshly ground black pepper

1. Bring a medium pot of water to a boil over high heat. Add the whole green tomatoes and cook for 10 minutes. Drain and allow to cool in a bowl of cold water. When they are cool enough to handle, peel, core, and quarter the tomatoes.

2. Put the tomatoes in a food processor, add the plain rice vinegar and the seasoned rice vinegar, and purée. With the machine running, add the mustard and drizzle in the canola oil. Season with salt and pepper. Can be refrigerated for up to 2 days.

1¹/2 pounds red new potatoes, unpeeled,
    halved or quartered, depending
    upon size
Canola oil
Kosher salt
Freshly ground black pepper
Green Tomato Dressing

5 to 8 strips bacon, stacked and cut into
    3/8-inch pieces, cooked and drained
12 purple chive flowers or 4 chives, cut into
    1-inch pieces
1 large handful of sturdy greens (such as
    arugula, escarole, bok choy, or spinach),
    washed

1. Preheat the oven to 350°F.

2. Toss the potatoes with canola oil to coat, and season with salt and pepper. Place the potatoes on a sheet tray in a single layer and roast for about 30 minutes, or until the cut sides are golden brown. Allow the potatoes to cool briefly.

3. In a large serving bowl, toss the potatoes with ¹/2 cup of the Green Tomato Dressing. Add the bacon and chive flowers, reserving some flowers for garnish. Adjust the seasoning. In another bowl, toss the greens lightly with the remaining dressing, or to taste.

TO SERVE, divide the potato mixture among 6 plates and garnish with the greens and reserved chive flowers.

Chefs' Biographies

JODY ADAMS, chef and partner of Rialto in Cambridge, and Red Clay in Chestnut Hill, Massachusetts, is known for her exciting combinations of New England ingredients with Mediterranean culinary traditions. Her passion for food began at her family's dinner table and was fueled by her time living and traveling in Europe. As a talented and veteran chef in Boston, Jody has received many honors throughout the years. In 1997 she won the James Beard Award for Best Chef: Northeast, and in Gourmet magazine's October 2000 restaurant issue, Rialto was ranked "#1 Restaurant in Boston." She and her husband, Ken Rivard, are writing a cookbook.

HUGH ACHESON, chef-owner of Five-and-Ten Restaurant, in Athens, Georgia, graduated high school in Ottawa, where his father is an economics professor, and studied political philosophy in college. He began his restaurant career as a dishwasher and cooked at various restaurants in Canada, all the while educating himself about food, wine, etiquette, food history, and food science. He was inspired by Chef Rob MacDonald of Ottawa's Cafe Henri Burger and followed him to Maplelawn Restaurant as sous-chef. Hugh moved to Athens, where he cooked at the Last Resort, while his wife, Mary, completed graduate studies at the University of Georgia. When she graduated, they moved to San Francisco, where Hugh worked with renowned chefs Mike Fennelly, at Mecca, and Gary Danko.

Returning to Athens, he opened Five-and-Ten and was named one of the Ten Best New Chefs of 2001 by Food & Wine magazine, which praised him for his success in "merging soul food with Old World cuisine."

DANIEL ANGERER, executive chef and owner of Fresh restaurant in Tribeca, was born in Austria and trained in Europe and the United States. He has worked with some of the world's most respected chefs and restaurateurs, including Joel Robouchon in Paris. He started his career in the Hotel Arlberg Hospiz, high in the mountains of Austria, and then moved on to Austria's Steirereck Restaurant. He moved to Germany, working under Heinz Winkler at the Relais & Chateaux. In America, Chef Angerer worked at Manhattan's San Domenico, Restaurant Jean Georges, and Bouley Bakery; and Palm Beach's Aquario.

In New York, Chef Angerer was associated with the French bistro Alouette, the bistro Barrio, and Steak Frites Restaurant.

MICHAEL ANTHONY, executive chef of Blue Hill Restaurant, in Manhattan, graduated at the top of his class from École Supérieure de Cuisine Française, in Paris. His love for cooking was fueled during his years in Japan, where he came to appreciate the clean and fresh Japanese aesthetic. In France, he trained at Chez Pauline, L'Auberge de Tal Moor, and Restaurant Jacques Cagna, where he met and worked with Dan Barber. In 1995, Restaurant Daniel brought Michael back to the United States, and two years later he became sous-chef, and then chef de cuisine. He joined Blue Hill in September 2001.

JEFFREY BANK AND CHRIS METZ are co-owners of Artie's New York Delicatessen, named in honor of the late restaurateur Arthur Cutler, an original planner of the venture. They also collaborated on Abigael's Grill and the King David Delicatessen.

Jeffrey, who has a degree in political science from the State University of New York at Albany, had planned to study law but happily discovered his calling the summer after he graduated from college. Chris, a graduate of Syracuse University, worked with chefs Anne Rosenzweig and Phil McGrath and went on to study at London's Cordon Bleu Cooking School. Their restaurant is a re-creation of a 1930s-style Jewish deli. They are most proud of their home-cured pastrami, created from a secret recipe.

DAN BARBER, chef-owner of Manhattan's Blue Hill Restaurant and Dan Barber Catering, Inc., is a native New Yorker and a graduate of Tufts University. He began cooking for family and friends at Blue Hill

Farm in the Berkshires, the home of his grandmother, where much of the produce for the restaurant and catering company is still grown. Dan apprenticed at Chez Panisse and Joe's, in California, and Michel Rostang and Apicus, in France. Dan opened Blue Hill in April 2000 and was named by Food & Wine magazine as one of America's Top New Chefs of 2002.

DIANA BARRIOS TREVIÑO has been a key player in her family's San Antonio restaurant, Los Barrios, since it opened in 1979. Diana is actively involved in the culinary media and has appeared on her local NBC station doing a live cooking segment, as well as on FoodNation with Bobby Flay and Good Morning America with Emeril Lagasse. She is the author of Los Barrios Family Cookbook (Villard, 2002). Diana is a member of Les Dames D'Escoffier and several local chambers of commerce. She is married to Roland Treviño and is the mother of Jordan, Evan, and Diego.

RICK BAYLESS is the chef and owner of Chicago's famous Frontera Grill and Topolobampo. Born into an Oklahoma City family of restaurateurs, he learned about Mexican cooking as an undergraduate student in Spanish and Latin American culture.

Among his many awards are Food & Wine magazine, Best New Chef of 1988; James Beard Foundation, Best American Chef: Midwest, 1991; both the Beard Foundation's National Chef of the Year and the International Association of Culinary Professionals Chef of the Year awards, 1995; and the James Beard Foundation's Humanitarian of the Year, 1998. He has been inducted into Who's Who of American Food and Drink.

Rick has appeared widely on television and radio, and has written for numerous publications, including Eating Well, Food & Wine, Vegetarian Times, Travel & Leisure, and Saveur, where he is a contributing editor. His twenty-six-part television series, Mexico One Plate at a Time, and the companion book of the same name debuted in 2000. He is chairman of Chefs' Collaborative and is active in Share Our Strength. He is a restaurant consultant, teaches Mexican cooking, and leads cooking and cultural tours to Mexico.

PHILIPPE BERTINEAU, executive chef of Payard Pâtisserie and Bistro, in Manhattan, was raised on his family's farm in the Poitou-Charentes region of France. His culinary study included several apprenticeships in the kitchens of Bordeaux, southwestern France, and the Basque region of France, including the prestigious Hôtel du Palais, in Biarritz. He traveled to London, where he spent a year at the Auberge de Provence, and then returned to France, where he spent another year at Restaurant Vanel, in Toulouse.

Moving to New York, Philippe became sous-chef for Park Bistro, and in 1993 joined Daniel Boulud for the opening of Daniel, where he was sous-chef until 1997. In August 1997, he became executive chef of Payard. In 1998, he received the White Truffle Award from the Italian Consulate in New York, and in 2001, New York magazine named him Best Unsung Chef.

JIM BOTSACOS, executive chef of Molyvos, in Manhattan, is a descendant of talented Greek-American and Italian-American chefs and is a graduate of Rhode Island's Johnson and Wales University. Starting his career at New York's "21" Club, he advanced from summer intern to saucier to sous-chef, and then became executive sous-chef. Also in New York, he was the first executive chef at the Park Avalon restaurant and was consulting chef at the Blue Water Grill. In 1997, with his move to Molyvos, he traveled to Greece to research the country's regional home cooking. The New York Times awarded Molyvos three stars in 1997, Esquire magazine's John Mariani named the restaurant among the "Best in America" that same year, and Molyvos made New York magazine's "Best of 1999" list. Chef Botsacos has appeared on network television on The Early Show, Today, and Martha Stewart Living; and on the TV Food Network on Food Today and Cooking Live. He was featured chef in Bon Appétit magazine's annual restaurant issue in September 2000.

ANTOINE BOUTERIN, executive chef and owner of Bouterin, on Manhattan's Upper East Side, was born on a historic farm in Saint-Rémy-de-Provence. Although he came from a family of farmers, he decided at the age of twelve to become a chef and soon afterward apprenticed at the two-star Riboto de Taven in Les-Baux-de-Provence. He honed his skills at the celebrated L'Escale, near Marseilles, among other fine restaurants, and moved to Paris, where, despite his youth, he became chef at the fashionable Quai d'Orsay. His next move was to Manhattan's Le Périgord, where he was executive chef from 1982 to 1995. He then opened the successful Bouterin, filling it with the art and food of his native Provence. Chef Bouterin is the author of Cooking with Antoine at Le Périgord (Putnam, 1986), Antoine Bouterin's Desserts from Le Périgord (Putnam, 1989), and Cooking Provence (Macmillan, 1994).

DAVID BURKE, executive chef and partner of the Smith and Wollensky Restaurant Group, created the cuisine at New York's Park Avenue Cafe, Maloney & Porcelli, and ONEc.p.s., as well as at Chicago's Park Avenue Cafe and Mrs. Park's Tavern.

A graduate of the Culinary Institute of America, Chef Burke studied pastry arts at the École Lenôtre in Plasir, France, and worked as a stagiaire at a number of renowned French restaurants before returning to the United States. He served as executive chef at the River Café from 1987 to 1991; he then became executive chef and partner at the Park Avenue Cafe.

Among his many honors, Chef Burke was named Chef of the Year by both the Vatel Club and Chef magazine in 1998, and won the American Academy of Hospitality Sciences Five-Diamond Award of Excellence. He received the Robert Mondavi Culinary Award of Excellence in 1996 and 1997, and in 1996 he won the CIA's first Auggie Award (named for August Escoffier). In 1991, Chef Burke was named to the National Advisory Committee of Chefs in America and was voted Chef of the Year. In 1988 he won the Meilleurs Ouvriers de France diploma, as well as the Nippon Award of Excellence, in Tokyo.

He is the author of Cooking with David Burke of the Park Avenue Cafe.

SCOTT CAMPBELL, executive chef and owner of Avenue, on New York City's Upper West Side, began his career at Detroit's famed London Chop House. Moving to New York, he became sous-chef at the Plaza Hotel's Oak Room, and then studied and taught at Peter Kump's Cooking School. He is a graduate of the first class of the Beringer School of American Chefs in Napa Valley, directed by his longtime mentor, Madeleine Kamman.

He cooked at many high-profile New York restaurants, including Windows on the World, Union Square Café, Le Cirque (with Daniel Boulud), QV (with Joachim Splichal), and Hubert's, and he was the opening chef at Sfuzzi, Lincon Center.

Chef Campbell is a James Beard Foundation Rising Star of American Cuisine and co-chair of its Chefs' Round Table. He is well known for his many charitable activities and was awarded the 1996 Mayor's Certificate for Outstanding Volunteer Services by Mayor Rudolph Giuliani.

ANDREW CARMELLINI, executive chef of New York's Café Boulud, is a graduate of the Culinary Institute of America. During his time at the CIA, he completed stagiaires in a series of top Manhattan restaurants and spent his weekends cooking for then governor Mario Cuomo and his family in the governor's mansion in Albany. When Andrew cooked at the three-star San Domenico, owner Tony May sent him to study with Chef Valentino Mercatelli at San Domenico in Italy. Upon his return to the United States, he spent three years at New York's San Domenico and then moved to Gray Kunz's Lespinasse. In 1996, he began a six-month European tour, working in the kitchens of a host of top restaurants. Back home again, he became sous-chef at Le Cirque 2000, and then moved to the new Café Boulud, working under Daniel Boulud. Andrew was named one of America's Ten Best New Chefs of 2000 by Food & Wine magazine and received the James Beard Foundation's Perrier-Jouët Rising Star Chef of the Year Award in 2000.

FRANK COE is the chef-owner of the Wild Goose, in Cutchogue, Long Island, which he runs with his wife, Barbara Sweeney. A native of Cork, Ireland, Frank has cooked in France, England, Australia, and several Asian nations. In London, he owned two private dining clubs, Le Chasse and the Funny Farm. In Manhattan, he worked at Daniel, Le Bernardin, and Can, and he owned and operated the award-winning Druids in Manhattan's Hell's Kitchen neighborhood.

Frank's mother, Elizabeth Mellerick, was a pastry chef in France and Switzerland, and his love of cooking began in her kitchen when he was only six years old. At seventeen, he traveled to Lyons, France, to study cooking, and almost ten years later, he went to Singapore, where he cooked for six months. His cuisine is based on the finest of seasonal foods, which have inspired him since he picked herbs and vegetables in his family's garden as a child. His inspiration comes from the market and from the various cultures he has explored as a chef.

RON CRISMON, chef-owner of the Tribeca restaurant Bubby's Pie Company, is a native New Yorker. He trained in a traditional apprenticeship program, held restaurant jobs in Atlanta, and was sous-chef for the Hyatt Corporation. Ron had been working as a catering chef in Manhattan when he decided to open Bubby's in 1990, at age twenty-eight.

The restaurant's combination of homey warmth and downtown funkiness has, from the start, attracted high-profile diners from the worlds of entertainment and politics. It is acclaimed for its home-cooked American food, especially its pies, breakfast, brunch, meat loaf, and barbecue. Ron says, "I've been cooking meat and potatoes since I started to crawl." Ron is the creator of Loco Soda, a fruit juice–based soft drink with a surprise kick: fresh chili peppers. The electrifying drink is available in lime, mango, blackberry, and raspberry flavors.

CRAIG CUPANI, a 1988 graduate of the Culinary Institute of America, has most recently been executive chef at Manhattan's Patroon restaurant. Also in Manhattan, he served as chef de cuisine at the Brasserie, sous-chef at Tabla, executive chef/general manager at Butterfield 81, executive sous-chef (under Chef Michael Lomonoco) at the "21" Club, and roundsman (under Chef John Doherty) at the Waldorf-Astoria. His food is "creative American," based on the highest-quality ingredients available, prepared with skill and imagination.

ANDREA CURTO, chef at Wish restaurant in Miami's South Beach, was born in Vero Beach, Florida, and is a graduate of the Culinary Institute of America. Her love of cooking was nurtured by her Italian grandmother. Before Wish, she cooked at Manhattan's Tribeca Grill and The Heights in Coral Gables, Florida. One of Food & Wine magazine's Ten Best New Chefs of 2000, Andrea was cited for creating dishes that are bold yet perfectly balanced. The New York Times called Wish "one of SoBe's best restaurants."

MITCHELL DAVIS has been the director of publications for the James Beard Foundation since December 1993. During that time, he has moonlighted as a freelance writer, restaurant critic, and cookbook author. Whenever he is feeling overwhelmed by all of his work, or lonely, he makes his favorite Mac and Cheese for himself and tries to finish it all. His books include Cook Something and Foie Gras: A Passion (co-authored with Michael Ginor), and his latest book will be published in 2002.

His restaurant reviews have appeared in a number of national magazines, including Food & Wine, GQ, and Time Out New York. Mitchell is also working toward a Ph.D. in the Department of Food Studies at New York University. His scholarly work has appeared in the journal Gastronomica and has been presented at international food conferences.

JOHN DELUCIE, executive chef of Manhattan's Soho Grand Hotel, is in charge of the celebrated food at Upstairs, Grand Bar & Lounge, catering, and room service. A 1985 graduate of the Gallatin Division of New York University and the master chef program at the New School for the Culinary Arts, John has worked with Andy D'Amico and David Walzog at Arizona 206, Rick Laakonen at Luxe, Rick Moonen at Oceana, and Jonathan Waxman at Colina, among others. He has been a featured chef at the James Beard House and has appeared on television. His cooking has been praised in The New York Times, The New York Observer, and USA Today.

ANDREW DICATALDO, executive chef of Manhattan's celebrated Patria, is a graduate of Johnson & Wales University. He cooked at the Hyatt Regency Hotel in Miami and at South Beach's ultrahip Scratch Restaurant, where he was introduced to local Florida produce and Latino ingredients. In 1990, Andrew became executive sous-chef at Yuca, Miami's famous Nuevo Cubano restaurant, and from there moved to Manhattan's Patria, first as chef de cuisine and then, in 1999, as executive chef. He is tenacious about finding the finest, freshest ingredients, and has been praised for his deft handling of spices and flavors. William Grimes, the New York Times restaurant critic, found him deserving of "a double round of applause" as well as a three-star rating, and Patria has been voted best pan-Latino restaurant for three consecutive years by Time Out New York magazine.

ROCCO DiSPIRITO, executive chef of Manhattan's innovative Union Pacific restaurant, has been called "America's most exciting young chef" by Gourmet magazine. Rocco entered the Culinary Institute of

America at age sixteen and, after graduating in 1986, studied classical technique at the prestigious Jardin de Cygne in Paris with Dominique Cécillón. He returned to New York in 1988 to work at Adrienne, at what is now the Peninsula Hotel. He earned a B.A. in business from Boston University in 1990, and later cooked at Aujourd'hui in Boston. Returning to Manhattan, he embarked upon a series of stagiaires with the city's leading chefs: David Bouley, Charlie Palmer, Gilbert LeCoze, and Gray Kunz. He then became part of Lespinasse's opening team, and in 1995 opened Dava Restaurant in Manhattan as executive chef. He was named a Best New Chef of 1999 by Food & Wine magazine and was nominated for a 1999 James Beard Foundation Award. Chef DiSpirito has been praised for his unique outlook on modern cuisine and his "unbridled chutzpah."

KEITH DRESSER is currently a test cook and member of the editorial staff at Cook's Illustrated magazine, and has been cooking on New England's coast for his entire career. He has been sous-chef at Boston's Red Clay and executive chef of the Regatta of Falmouth, in Massachusetts. He has cooked at Hamersley's Bistro in Boston's South End and at Eat, in Somerville. Keith studied at the New England Culinary Institute in Montpelier, Vermont, and at Harvard University.

WYLIE DuFRESNE, chef-owner of 71 Clinton Fresh Food, in the heart of New York's Lower East Side, received his B.A. in philosophy from Colby College in Waterville, Maine, and graduated from the French Culinary Institute. As a student, he worked at Al Forno in Providence, Rhode Island, and the Gotham Bar and Grill in New York. After a stagiaire in L'Esperance restaurant in Burgundy, France, he joined Jean-Georges Vongerichten for six years at Jo Jo, as chef at Prime in the Bellagio, Las Vegas, and as sous-chef at Restaurant Jean-Georges in New York.

Wylie was a finalist in the Perrier-Jouët Rising Star Chef of the Year Award for 2000 for the James Beard Foundation; has been honored by New York magazine as one of ten individuals who have positively affected life in the city in the past year; and was named the French Culinary Institute's graduate of the year. The New Yorker, The New York Observer, The New York Times, and Esquire magazine all have praised his work enthusiastically.

LOREN FALSONE AND ERIC MOSHIER, executive chefs and owners of Empire, in Providence, Rhode Island, are graduates of Johnson and Wales University, where they met. This husband-and-wife team was chosen by Food & Wine magazine to be among America's Ten Best New Chefs of 2000, and they have been praised for their inventive interpretations of Italian home cooking. Before opening Empire, Eric and Loren cooked at Al Forno, in Providence, under Johanne Killeen and George Germon.

BOBBY FLAY, chef and partner of Manhattan's popular Mesa Grill and Bolo, began working at the Joe Allen Restaurant at age seventeen, where he so impressed the management that Joe Allen paid his tuition to the prestigious French Culinary Institute. After working with restaurateur Jonathan Waxman, Bobby moved to Manhattan's Miracle Grill and raised it to near-cult status with his colorful southwestern creations. Bobby's own Mesa Grill opened in 1991, followed by Bolo, dedicated to exploring Spanish cuisine, in 1993.

In 1993, Bobby was voted the James Beard Foundation's Rising Star Chef of the Year, and the French Culinary Institute honored him with its first Outstanding Graduate Award. He is the author of Bobby Flay's Bold American Food (Warner Books, 1994), Bobby Flay's From My Kitchen to Your Table (Crown, 1998), Bobby Flay's Boy Meets Grill (Hyperion, 1999), and Bobby Flay Cooks American (Hyperion, 2001). He is well known to television viewers for his popular shows Grillin' and Chillin', The Main Ingredient, Hot Off the Grill, Boy Meets Grill, and FoodNation.

LAURA FRANKEL, owner and executive chef of Shallots gourmet kosher restaurants in Manhattan and Chicago, is a graduate of Northwestern University, the Cooking Hospitality Institute of Chicago, and the French Pastry School at City Colleges of Chicago. Her restaurants have been enthusiastically reviewed in the Chicago press.

After extensive professional kitchen experience, Chef Frankel took a respite to have a family (she is the mother of three) and then returned and opened Shallots in Chicago. One year later, she opened Shallots NY. She is now working on a cookbook and contemplating the production of a packaged-food product.

MARK FRANZ, executive chef and co-owner of Farallon in San Francisco, is a graduate of the California Culinary Academy and a third-generation restaurateur. He has cooked at Jeremiah Tower's Stars Restaurant and Balboa Café, and Ernie's, in San Francisco, and the Santa Fe Bar and Grill, in Berkeley. Under Mark's stewardship, Farallon has been nominated by the James Beard Foundation as one of the best restaurants in the United States, has been chosen one of the best newcomers by Esquire, Bon Appétit, and Food & Wine magazines, and was the highest-rated newcomer in the 1999 Zagat Survey.

IRA FREEHOF, founder and owner of New York's two Comfort Diners, is a diner historian and aficionado. He has been part of the New York restaurant scene for many years as manager and director of operations for several well-known and highly successful ventures, including Steak Frites, Chat n' Chew, and Isabella's. Ira and the Comfort Diners have been featured in Woman's Day, Bon Appétit, Chocolatier, New York, Newsday, and The New York Times, as well as on television and radio.

MARK GAIER and CLARK FRASIER, chef-owners of Arrows Restaurant in Ogunquit, Maine, have created a classic country restaurant that has garnered enthusiastic reviews in USA Today, Wine Spectator, Town & Country, Bon Appétit, and Boston Magazine, among others, and was named one of America's Fifty Best Restaurants of 2001 by Gourmet magazine.

Clark grew up in Carmel, California—fresh-produce heaven, where vegetables and fruit are available all year round. When he went to China to study Chinese, he developed expertise in the cuisine of China and learned "why food tastes so good when it is in season." He moved to San Francisco to set up an import-export business but instead went to work at Jeremiah Tower's Stars Restaurant, where he became chef tournant. There he met Mark Gaier, who was to become his partner in Arrows in 1988.

Mark, who grew up near Dayton, Ohio, was inspired by his mother, a wonderful cook. He worked in publishing in Blue Hill, Maine, and then studied culinary arts under Jean Wallach in Boston. Later, working at the Whistling Oyster, under Mark Allen, he developed many of his skills as a chef. In the mid-eighties, he joined the staff at Stars Restaurant, as chef tournant.

SANDRO GAMBA, chef de cuisine for the Park Hyatt Hotel in Chicago and its restaurant, NoMI, was previously executive chef at Lespinasse, in Washington, D.C., where he was selected as one of the World's Best Chefs by the American Academy of Hospitality Sciences. Named by Food & Wine magazine as one of America's Top New Chefs of 2001, he has worked extensively in both France and the United States and has trained under Alain Ducasse, at Le Louis XV; Joel Robouchon, at Le Jamin; and Roger Verge, at Le Moulin de Mougins. His grandmother Jeannette, the chef-owner of Les Cinq Ponts, in Neufcha^teau, France, was a strong influence on his cuisine, teaching him that simplicity and authenticity should be his goals in cooking.

JEAN-LOUIS GERIN, chef-owner of Restaurant Jean-Louis, in Greenwich, Connecticut, has been widely praised for his fresher, lighter, more intensely flavored versions of classic cuisine, "La Nouvelle Classique." He was born in Annecy in the French Alps, and both his father and his grandfather were talented amateur chefs.

When his family moved to Talloires, thirteen-year-old Jean-Louis took a summer job at the Michelin three-star Auberge du Père Bis. He later received formal restaurant training and a degree in business from l'École Hôteliere de Thonon les Bains, and then returned to Auberge du Père Bise to continue his apprenticeship.

Jean-Louis later worked at the three-star Oustau de Beaumanière and, along with his friend Chef Guy Savoy, at La Barriere de Clichy, in Paris. The two opened Guy Savoy in Paris, where Jean-Louis became Savoy's assistant in charge of purchasing and staff. In 1984, Jean-Louis joined Savoy's chic French restaurant in Greenwich, and by 1985 had agreed to purchase the restaurant, renaming it Restaurant Jean-Louis. In 1986, Jean-Louis married Linda Chardain, daughter of restaurateur Rene Chardain.

TIM GOODELL is executive chef and owner of Aubergine, in Newport Beach, Troquet, in Costa Mesa, and Red Pearl Kitchen, in Huntington Beach, California. After graduating from the California Culinary Academy in San Francisco, he honed his skills at the Ritz-Carlton Dining Room in San Francisco and Pascal's in Newport Beach. Tim was voted one of America's Ten Best New Chefs of 2000 by Food & Wine magazine, and his cooking was praised for successfully combining French technique with California ingredients.

LAURENT GRAS, executive chef at San Francisco's renowned Fifth Floor, at the Hotel Palomar, is a native of France's Côte d'Azur, where he grew up with fruit orchards, the freshest fish from the Mediterranean, and a family olive grove where oil was pressed every December.

Beginning at age eighteen, he spent seven years in French Michelin-starred kitchens and then became chef de cuisine at Restaurant Guy Savoy in Paris for two years. Next, he spent five years as chef de cuisine for Alain Ducasse at Restaurant Alain Ducasse and Hôtel de Paris, where he achieved three Michelin stars. In 1997, Gras headed for New York and the executive chef position at the Waldorf-Astoria's Peacock Alley, where he quickly earned three stars from New York Times critic Ruth Reichl.

In November 2001, Chef Gras moved to California and immediately researched the area's best producers, explored its restaurants, and immersed himself in the local culture while evolving his menu. At Fifth Floor, Gras has achieved a culinary maturity based on experience, world travels, and talent. He credits the influence of his mentors—Jacques Maximin, Alain Ducasse, and Alain Senderen. He also adheres to his three personal principles: "Flavor, aesthetic, and perfection, in that order."

ALEXANDRA GUARNASCHELLI, chef at Butter, in Manhattan, has been an instructor in both professional and recreational cooking at the Institute of Culinary Education. She began her career in 1992 at Manhattan's An American Place, cooking with Larry Forgione and Richard D'Orazi. She moved to France, where she trained at La Varenne and L'Essential. In Paris, she became chef de partie at Guy Savoy, and later, sous-chef at La Butte Chaillot. Alexandra assisted Patricia Wells with her book Patricia Wells at Home in Provence and with Patricia's publication L'Atelier of Joël Robouchon.

Returning to the United States in 1997, Alexandra became chef de partie, and later, sous-chef, at Daniel Boulud's Daniel. She then worked as sous-chef at Joachim Bernard Spilchal's Patina, and finally returned to New York, with Chef Spilchal, to open Nick & Stef's Steakhouse, first as sous-chef and then as executive chef, where she remained until 2002.

GORDON HAMERSLEY, chef and owner of Boston's legendary Hamersley's Bistro, began cooking as a student at Boston University in the early 1970s and trained at various local French restaurants. In 1979, he moved to Ma Maison in Los Angeles, where Wolfgang Puck was the chef. In 1983, after spending a year in Nice, he became sous-chef to Chef Lydia Shire at the Boston Hotel.

In 1987, Chef Hamersley and his wife, Fiona, opened Hamersley's Bistro, serving traditional French-inspired bistro food as well as contemporary American dishes cooked with New England ingredients. He won the James Beard Award for Best Chef: Northeast in 1995 and was named one of Food & Wine magazine's Ten Best New Chefs for 1988. Hamersley's Bistro was named Best of Boston by Boston magazine from 1988 through 1995, and in 1996 won the magazine's Hall of Fame award. In 1997, The Boston Globe awarded Hamersley's Bistro four stars.

Gordon appeared on Julia Child's television series Cooking with Master Chefs and is included in the cookbook of the same name. He is a member of the American Institute of Food and Wine and Chefs' Collaborative 2000.

GLENN HARRIS, executive chef and partner at Jane, in Manhattan, began his lifelong interest in cooking as a child in his mother's Coney Island kitchen. By the age of twelve, he was working part-time in a local Chinese restaurant, and by the time he was seventeen, he was a partner in a small but successful local eatery. After graduation from the French Culinary Institute, Glenn worked at several popular New York restaurants, and in 1995 was hired by Jonathan Waxman (then of Ark restaurants) to take over the Museum Cafe. He later became the opening chef at Ark's acclaimed Bryant Park Grill. In April 2001, he opened Jane Restaurant with Jeffrey Lefcourt.

GERRY HAYDEN, executive chef and partner of Manhattan's Amuse restaurant, is a graduate of the Culinary Institute of America. He became sous-chef and pastry chef when Charlie Palmer opened Aureole in 1988. Gerry moved to Tribeca Grill in 1990 as Don Pintabona's sous-chef, and then to San Francisco as sous-chef under Chef George Morrone. He returned to New York to head up Drew Nieporent's East Hampton Point and was then hired as executive chef of Marguery Grill (which Esquire magazine named Best New Restaurant, under Gerry's leadership). In 1999, he returned to Aureole as chef de cuisine, and in 2003, opened Amuse.

LESLIE HOLLEY-McKEN, a caterer and graduate of the New York Restaurant School, inherited the love and skills of cooking from her mother, Pearl. A weaver and textile designer as well as an innovative chef, Leslie has a bachelor's degree in fine art. She was chef at Brooklyn's New Prospect at Home before founding In Good Taste, her catering firm in Laurelton, Queens.

THOMAS JOHN, executive chef of Mantra, in Boston, grew up in southern India with a two-acre garden behind his house, and learned early on from his parents the connection between freshness and taste. Herbs, seeds, vegetables, and fruits were plucked just minutes before use, whether for traditional holiday feasts or just for lunch on Monday. In his cooking, Chef John uses a subtle hand to introduce the cornucopia of Indian spices to the freshest foods available. Using French technique, he aims for a sophisticated palate that blends accessibility with exoticism. America's agricultural bounty provides him with an almost limitless pantry of ingredients from which to create, in his words, "like a mad Indian scientist."

A graduate of Punjab University and the Oberoi School of Hotel Management, Chef John cooked at the Oberoi Hotel in Delhi, where his recipes became the basis for the hotel's Food of India cookbook. Shortly thereafter, he was named executive chef of Le Meridien, in Pune, where he oversaw the property's four international restaurants, including Spice Island, a concept he developed to showcase India's lesser-known flavors.

Esquire magazine named Mantra one of the Top New Restaurants of 2001, and Food & Wine magazine named Chef Thomas John one of America's Top New Chefs of 2001. His cuisine has been praised by The Wall Street Journal, the Economist, InStyle, Details, Bon Appétit, Travel & Leisure, Town & Country, Architecture, and the Robb Report.

KEVIN JOHNSON, head chef and partner of The Grange Hall in Greenwich Village, has had over eighteen years of diverse cooking experience. He collaborated on the start-ups of Café Artiste and Savoy, in Louisville, Kentucky, as well as Sugar Reef, in Manhattan's East Village, and has had catering and corporate dining experience. At The Grange Hall, whose motto is "Food from the American Farm," he creates a unique style of contemporary American food with traditional heartland references.

MELISSA KELLY, executive chef and co-owner of Primo, in Rockland, Maine, was named Best Chef: Northeast by the James Beard Foundation in 1999. She won attention as executive chef of the widely praised Old Chatham Sheepherding Company Inn in Upstate New York and has been featured in The New York Times, The Boston Globe, Gourmet, Bon Appétit, Art Culinaire, New York magazine, and many other publications. Food & Wine voted her one of the Upcoming Chefs of the 1990s, and Nation's Restaurant News named her one of 2000's New Taste-Makers. She grew up on Long Island, working in the family garden, fishing, and learning about cooking from her Italian grandmother. Chef Kelly graduated first in her class from the Culinary Institute of America.

MATTHEW KENNEY has been executive chef and owner of Commissary NY in Manhattan; Commissary, in Portland, Maine; Commune Atlanta; and Nickerson Tavern, in Searsport, Maine. He is a graduate of the French Culinary Institute and in 1995 was granted its Outstanding Graduate Award, as well as being named PBS Rising Star Chef. In 1994 and 1995, he was nominated for the James Beard Foundation's Rising Star Chef Award, and he was recognized by Food & Wine magazine in 1994 as one of the Ten Best New Chefs in America. He is the author of Matthew Kenney's Mediterranean Cooking (Chronicle Books, 1997) and Matthew Kenney's Big City Cooking (Chronicle Books, 2003).

LEVANA KIRSCHENBAUM, chef and founder of Manhattan's Levana Restaurant, Tableclassics catering service, and Levana's Place gourmet kosher cooking school, was born and raised in Morocco and learned to cook and appreciate exotic cuisine at her mother's side. She earned a degree in psychology from the Sorbonne, and traveled to Spain and Israel, where she added to her extensive repertoire of multicultural dishes.

Levana has conducted master cooking classes at the Natural Gourmet Institute for Food and Health, Macy's New York, the Ninety-second Street Y, and the Sephardic Center Cooking Institute. She has appeared on the PBS television series The United Tastes of America and WOR radio's Food Talk, with Arthur Schwartz. She is the author of Levana's Table: Kosher Cooking for Everyone (Stewart, Tabori & Chang, 2002).

ANITA LO, chef and owner (with partner Jennifer Scism) of Annisa Restaurant, in Manhattan's West Village, was born in Michigan and studied French at Columbia University. In the summer of her junior year, Anita traveled to France to study cooking, and immediately after graduation, she went to work at Bouley Restaurant. Returning to France, she earned her degree in cooking at the Ritz-Escoffier School, graduating with honors. Anita then served internships at several Paris restaurants, under such noted chefs as Michel Rostang and Guy Savoy. She moved to Manhattan's Chanterelle, where she worked through all the stations, and next became the chef of Can, a French-Vietnamese restaurant in SoHo. There she met Jennifer Scism, who was the sous-chef.

Anita spent two and a half years as chef at Maxim's and then moved to Mirezi Restaurant, where she won rave reviews, followed by television appearances on NBC, CNN, and Food Network. Avenue Asia magazine named her one of the 500 Most Influential Asian-Americans. After two years, she left Mirezi and traveled with Jennifer through Southeast Asia and Mediterranean Europe, planning their future restaurant, Annisa.

MITCHEL LONDON, owner of Mitchel London Foods, a prepared foods, catering, and pastry shop with three branches in Manhattan, is a graduate of and former teacher at the Rhode Island School of Design's Culinary Arts School. He served for seven years as chef to Mayor Ed Koch and is the author of Mitchel London's Gracie Mansion Cookbook (Contemporary Books, 1989). In addition to retail and catering, Mitchel London Foods is a purveyor of pastries to fine-food emporiums such as Dean & DeLuca and Balducci's. Mitchel also acts as a consultant to the prepared foods, pastry, and café departments at Fairway Market in Manhattan.

WALDY MALOUF, chef and co-owner of the Beacon restaurants in Manhattan and Stamford, Connecticut, graduated from the Culinary Institute of America in 1975, winning first prize in the Carras Culinary Competition. His extensive professional experience includes affiliations with the Four Seasons, La Côte Basque, the St. Regis Hotel, the Hudson River Club, and the Rainbow Room, all in New York City, and La Crémaillère, in Banksville, New York.

Chef Malouf has been featured in Metropolitan Home, New York, Ladies' Home Journal, and Food & Wine, among other publications, and has made many television appearances. He is currently developing a thirteen-part travel and food series for PBS. His The Hudson River Valley Cookbook was nominated for a Julia Child Award from the International Association of Culinary Professionals (IACP) and was named one of the year's ten best cookbooks by The New York Times Book Review. He was honored at the CIA 1996 Golden Anniversary Gala and has been named a Great Chef of New York numerous times by the James Beard Foundation. In 1997 he was inducted into the Nation's Restaurant News Hall of Fame.

PHILIP MCGRATH is the chef-owner of the Iron Horse Grill in Pleasantville, New York, with his wife, Catherine Coreale, and they are also principals in Creative Culinary Consultants. Chef McGrath earned a B.S. degree from St. Francis College in Brooklyn Heights, and graduated first in his class from the Culinary Institute of America.

He has been executive chef at the Castle at Tarrytown and its award-winning Equus Restaurant. His culinary background includes positions at the Doubles Club, Prunelle, the Sign of the Dove, Glorious Foods, the Ritz Cafe, the Carlyle Hotel, and Jean-Jacques Rachou's Le Levandou and La Côte Basque, all in Manhattan. During visits to France, he worked at Restaurant Troisgros, in Roanne; L'Esperance, in St. Pere Sous Vezelay, and Restaurant Michel Rostang, in Paris.

Chef McGrath has been a lecturer at NYU's Hotel and Restaurant Management Certificate Program and has a cable television show, Cooking with the Iron Horse.

HENRY ARCHER MEER made an early career choice, and his classical training at the Culinary Institute of America led him to the legendary La Côte Basque, where he worked for over eight years. He then moved to Lutèce and cooked alongside Chef André Soltner for ten years, the last four as sous-chef. He opened SoHo's Cub Room in 1994 and in 1998 opened City Hall Restaurant—the quintessential New York eatery—in a landmark Tribeca building. Here he has re-created classic New York cuisine and added a clever, contemporary twist.

Chef Meer works with farmers in the tristate area to strengthen the important farm/restaurant relationship, and participates in Chefs Collaborative and the Council on the Environment of New York City, which operates the local greenmarkets.

JOSÉ ARTURO MOLINA, executive chef at New York's Chat n' Chew restaurant, was born and raised in Guayaquil, Ecuador, where his father was a jeweler. A self-taught cook, Chef Molina started in the restaurant business as a dishwasher and rose to the position of chef. He previously worked at Manhattan's Sporting Club. He has been praised for his creativity and unique treatment of pastas and seafood dishes.

MICHAEL O'NEILL, executive chef at Fairway Market in New York City, is a 1979 graduate of the prestigious Le Cordon Bleu cooking school in Paris. He has worked in Boston's Parker House; the Contemporary Hotel in Disney World, Orlando; and the exclusive Starlight Country Inn in Pennsylvania.

CHARLIE PALMER is chef-owner of Aureole, Alva, Métrazur, and Lenox in New York City; Astra in New York and Los Angeles; Aureole and Charlie Palmer Steak at the Four Seasons in Las Vegas; and Hotel Healdsburg and Dry Creek Kitchen in Sonoma, California. Chef Palmer was raised on a farm in Upstate New York. A graduate of the Culinary Institute of America, he cooked at La Côte Basque and the Waccabuc Country Club before becoming executive chef at the River Café, which he raised to three-star status. At age twenty-eight, he opened the highly praised Aureole.

A recipient of 1997 and 1998 James Beard awards and the 1996 Restaurants and Institutions Ivy Award, he is the author of Great American Food and Charlie Palmer's Casual Cooking.

CARLA PELLEGRINO is executive chef and co-owner of Baldoria, in the heart of Manhattan's theater district. Baldoria (which means "festivity" in Italian) is co-owned by her husband, Frank Pellegrino, Jr., whose family has operated Rao's, in east Harlem, since 1896. Carla was born in Brazil and moved to Liguria, in northern Italy, at the age of seventeen. She learned to cook from her mother and owned a boutique catering company in Italy before moving to New York. Her dream was to have her own restaurant, and with that goal, she graduated from New York's French Culinary Institute. Her creations for Baldoria have been highly praised in the press.

STEVEN PICKER, executive chef and owner of Good, in New York's Greenwich Village, is a master of American comfort cooking, often with a twist. His wide culinary experience includes restaurants from Woods to Le Bernardin, from the casual Quilted Giraffe to the elegant catering of Glorious Food. Steven's food combines hearty rustic flavors with a sophisticated visual edge. His dishes meld elements from a broad array of cuisines but feature a uniquely American approach.

DON PINTABONA has been executive chef of New York's Tribeca Grill since its opening in 1990. After graduating from the Culinary Institute of America in 1982, he began a worldwide odyssey that would take him to more than thirty countries and into several renowned kitchens, including Michelin three-star Georges Blanc in France, Gentille Alouete in Osaka, Japan, and the River Café and Aureole in New York City.

Don's food has been featured in Gourmet, Bon Appétit, and GQ, among many other publications, and he has appeared on numerous television programs. He is the author of The Tribeca Grill Cookbook and is one of the five members of the Continental Airlines' Congress of Chefs.

MAARTEN PINXTEREN was born in Amsterdam, Holland, and began his culinary career at age seventeen, in 1990, at Restaurant Vertigo. After completing an apprenticeship at the one-hundred-year-old Dikker en Thijs Hotel, he went on to serve as sous-chef in several popular Amsterdam restaurants, as well as in Cafe Bahia, in Portugal. Maarten became head chef of Cafe Toussaint in Amsterdam in 2000 and moved across the Atlantic in 2001 to be head chef of Restaurant NL, in Manhattan. He is currently working in the Netherlands.

DEBRA PONZEK, chef and owner of Aux Délices gourmet prepared foods shops in Greenwich, Connecticut, has received accolades for her innovative and subtle Provençal-inspired cuisine. Her early interest in cooking was nurtured by her mother and grandmother, but it wasn't until Debra was an engineering student at Boston University that she decided to pursue a career as a chef. She enrolled in the Culinary Institute of America and, after graduating in 1984, worked in top New Jersey restaurants. She was then hired by Drew Nieporent as sous-chef at Montrachet, in Manhattan, and soon was promoted to chef, a position she held for seven years. Under her stewardship, Montrachet earned three consecutive three-star reviews from The New York Times.

Debra was named a Food & Wine magazine Best New Chef of 1990 and a James Beard Foundation Rising Star Chef of the Year in 1991. She was the first American to receive the Moreau Award for culinary excellence from the Frederick Wildman and Sons Company. Debra is the author of The Summer House Cookbook (Clarkson Potter, 2003) and French Food, American Accent: Debra Ponzek's Spirited Cuisine (Clarkson Potter, 1996).

ALEX PORTER is executive chef at Norma's in New York's Le Parker Meridien Hotel. Treating breakfast as a dining experience, Alex has added new twists to old breakfast favorites. Recently he has rethought classic lunch items as well, as illustrated by his recipe for macaroni and cheese. A graduate of Colchester Avenue Catering College in Cardiff, Wales, Alex is a tireless supporter of City Harvest, working to feed the homeless of New York City.

WALTER POTENZA, chef and owner of Rhode Island's Sunflower Café, in Cranston, and La Locanda del Coccio, A Pranzo, Aquaviva, and Zucchero, all in Providence, was born in Abruzzo, Italy. He is a respected master of Italian-Jewish cuisine, as well as the art of terra-cotta cookery, a method invented by the Etruscans three hundred years before the Roman Empire.

Chef Potenza is the director of Etruria International Cooking School in Gubbio, Italy, and Providence, Rhode Island; the president of Italcuochi America; the president of Accadèmia Italiana della Cucina, New England chapter; the president of the Rhode Island Culinary Educational Center; a food master of the Italian Culinary Institute; and a member of the "Italia a Tavola" Committee, an organization dedicated to the preservation and diffusion of the Italian culture in the United States. He has appeared in national and international publications and on television and radio, and is the host of the cable television show Stir It Up.

NORA POUILLON is chef and owner of Nora—the first certified organic restaurant in the country—and Asia Nora, both in Washington, D.C. Born in Vienna, she moved to the United States in 1965 and operated a catering business and a cooking school before opening her first restaurant.

Chef Pouillon has consulted and developed products for Green Circle Organics, Fresh Fields Wholefoods Market, and Walnut Acres. She is a founding member of Chefs Collaborative, a leading spokesperson for the National Resources Defense Council (NRDC)/SeaWeb "Give North Atlantic Swordfish a Break" campaign; a member of the Organic Trade Association; a member of the advisory board of Foodfit.com; and a participant in the Harvard School of Public Health Nutrition Roundtable discussions.

Her book, Cooking with Nora (Random House, 1996), was a finalist for the Julia Child Cookbook Award for a first book. Among her many honors, Nora was given the Chef of the Year Award of Excellence by the International Association of Culinary Professionals (IACP) and was chosen as one of the dozen "power chefs" in Washington, D.C., by The Washington Post.

CYRIL RENAUD was born in a small town on the Brittany coast, where family and food were the center of life, and by the age of seven, he knew he wanted to become a chef. He began his culinary training in fine restaurants throughout Europe, and coming to the United States, he worked at Cellar in the Sky, on top of the World Trade Center, which he left in 1993. He moved on to the original Bouley, as chef de cuisine, and then became the youngest chef at La Caravelle, at age twenty-seven. In 1999, he was nominated for the James Beard Foundation's Rising Star Chef of the Year Award.

After leaving La Caravelle, he concentrated on painting—working in acrylic and watercolor, and using windowpanes from turn-of-the-century brownstones in his artistic creations. His artwork now adorns the walls of Fleur de Sel, in Manhattan. The interior structure of the restaurant, as well as the decor, was refurbished by his father, and the salt mills on each table were handpicked and brought from France by his mother.

ILENE ROSEN is a graduate of the French Culinary Institute. In her first professional job in the food industry, as savory chef of the City Bakery in Manhattan, she has established herself as a fearless new talent. Ilene is possessed by the bounty of the Union Square Greenmarket, and she routinely stalks New York's Chinatown with fervor and joy, in search of new foods to work with. She takes exotic as well as familiar ingredients and cooks clear, distinct, assured foods that have won her a loyal and growing following in downtown Manhattan.

FELINO SAMSON, partner and executive chef of Boston's Bomboa, was born in the Philippines and raised in Michigan. He is a graduate of Michigan State University and the Fashion Institute of Technology, and spent nine years working in the fashion industry. Turning his talents to the culinary world, he joined the staff of Manhattan's Sign of the Dove and subsequently became chef de cuisine at Boston's La Bettola and executive chef of Galleria Italiana.

In 1999, Samson entered Shreve, Crump, & Lowe's Edible Art Festival, and his prosciutto-covered Botero-inspired sculpture was judged as best overall entry. Several of his edible art pieces have been featured on television programs. That same year, Felino joined Bomboa, whose food has been featured in Art Culinaire, Food & Wine, Bon Appétit, and People magazines and has won the Wine Spectator Award of Excellence.

ARTHUR SCHWARTZ is a cookbook author and cooking teacher, and the host of Food Talk, a daily program heard on WOR radio in the New York City metropolitan area. His website is appropriately called www.thefoodmaven.com.

All four of his cookbooks have been nominated for national awards: Cooking in a Small Kitchen (Little Brown, 1978), What to Cook When You Think There's Nothing in the House to Eat (HarperCollins, 1992 and 2000), Soup Suppers (HarperCollins, 1994), and Naples at Table: Cooking in Campania (HarperCollins, 1998). He is working on a history of food in New York City to be published by Stewart, Tabori and Chang in 2004.

Schwartz has written for numerous magazines, including The New York Times Magazine, Saveur, Food & Wine, Gourmet, Cuisine, Vintage, Vogue, Lui, Playbill, Great Recipes, and Travel-Holiday. He has appeared on the Food Network, the Learning Channel, Discovery Channel, the Lifetime Network, New York's

MetroGuide, Good Day New York, Live with Regis, and many public television cooking programs. He has lectured and conducted seminars at New York University, Columbia University, New York City Technical College, the French Culinary Institute, and the Culinary Institute of America (CIA). He teaches and lectures at the major cooking schools in the metro New York area.

BARBARA SHINN AND DAVID PAGE, owners of Home Restaurant and Shinn Vineyard, were born and raised in the Midwest and met in California in 1988, while David was cooking at the Dakota Grill and Barbara was earning her M.F.A. In the Bay Area, David cooked at Masa's, Postrio, and Café Americain. They moved to New York City in 1990 and quickly immersed themselves in its culinary community. In 1993, they opened Home, a small West Village restaurant with a local American menu that includes many wines from the North Fork of Long Island. In 2000, they planted their own twenty-two-acre vineyard on the North Fork, specializing in Merlot, and plan to produce small lots of high-quality handcrafted wines. They are the authors of Recipes from Home.

WILLIAM SNELL is executive chef and owner, with his wife, Christine, of Cocotte, in Brooklyn's Park Slope, and of Loulou, in Fort Greene—named after their young daughter. As a child in New Jersey, William learned to hunt and fish with his father, and he decided at an early age that he wanted to be a chef. He began his formal training in New Brunswick's Frog and the Peach Restaurant, and moved to the Tribeca Grill to work with Don Pintabona. He then became chef de cuisine at City Wine & Cigar Co., where he met Christine, a native of Brittany and a graduate of l'École Parisienne d'Hôtesses et de Tourisme. William also worked at Oran Nor, on Nantucket, and consulted in New York before opening his own restaurants.

KATY SPARKS, executive chef at Quilty's, in New York City's SoHo, is the child of a Vermont professor who dabbled in cattle and chickens, and whose family vacations were planned around dining destinations. After studying linguistics, Katy graduated from Johnson and Wales University in 1986, at the top of her class.

She cooked at Campagne, in Seattle, and the Quilted Giraffe, in New York City, before moving to Mesa

Grill and Bolo, where chef Bobby Flay became her mentor. She then worked with chef Erika Gilmore at Kokachin, moved briefly to Solstice, and finally settled happily at Quilty's.

Katy has been named one of the Ten Best New Chefs of 1998 by Food & Wine magazine and a Rising Star Chef by both Wine Spectator and Restaurant Hospitality magazines. Her unique style—"Katycuisine"—is as varied as the seasons of the year and as exciting as the ethnic richness of New York.

DEBORAH STANTON is chef and owner of Deborah, in Greenwich Village, which has been praised by the New York Daily News as "over the top American, both in style and generosity." Deborah had previously been chef at Galaxy, in Manhattan, CHOW, in Miami's South Beach, and Woo Lae Oak, in SoHo, and has received rave reviews from The New York Times, Food & Wine, New York magazine, Time Out New York, Paper magazine, Metrosource, and Art Culinaire. Her career was temporarily halted when she was struck by an automobile, rendering her completely disabled. But after several surgeries and more than a year of treatment, she has returned to work with strength and determination.

JOHN SUNDSTROM, executive chef at Seattle's Earth and Ocean, was named a Food & Wine Best New Chef of 2001. Originally from Salt Lake City, John learned cooking in a Japanese restaurant and sushi bar, before graduating with honors from the New England Culinary Institute in Montpelier, Vermont. He then worked in prominent hotels, including the Ritz-Carlton Laguna Niguel, Club XIX at the Lodge at Pebble Beach, and the Stein Ericksen Lodge.

In Seattle, John began cooking at Raison d'Être Cafe, where he established contacts with local farmers. After stints at Café Sport and Campagne, John became sous-chef and then executive chef at the Dahlia Lounge.

In March 1999, John toured Japan, researching Japanese food and culture, and in October and November of that year, in New York and San Francisco, he worked with renowned chefs Daniel Boulud, Jean-George Vongerichten, Gary Danko, and Traci Des Jardins. He then ran the kitchen at Carmelita, in Seattle, before taking the top spot at Earth and Ocean.

ALLEN SUSSER established Chef Allen's Restaurant in Miami Beach in 1986. After earning degrees from New York City Technical College and Le Cordon Bleu, he worked at the Bristol Hotel in Paris and went on to other kitchens in Florida and New York, most notably that of Le Cirque. His highly praised cuisine encompasses the foods, cultures, and techniques of the Mediterranean, the Americas, Asia, and India. Among his many honors: Honorary Doctor of Culinary Arts, Johnson and Wales University; National Advisory Board, James Beard Foundation; Gourmet magazine's Top Table in South Florida, 2000; Best Chef, Southeastern Region, James Beard Foundation, 1994; number one restaurant for food and most popular in Miami, 1999 Zagat Survey; National Board of Directors, American Institute of Wine and Food. He is the author of New World Cuisine and Cookery (Doubleday, 1995) and The Great Citrus Book (Ten Speed Press, 1997).

ALAN TARDI, chef-owner of Follonico in New York City, studied music at the University of Illinois and the San Francisco Conservatory and attended the New School for Social Research in New York. He cooked at Chanterelle; Ristorante La Chiusa in Montefollonico, Italy; Restaurant Lafayette; and Le Madri (as executive chef). In 1992, he opened the critically acclaimed Follonico. Alan is a strong supporter of Chefs' Collaborative 2000, the Slow Food movement, and the American Institute of Food and Wine, and is an active member of New York City Greenmarket's Farmer-Consumer Advisory Committee. He has taught cooking classes in New York, served frequently on juries at the French Culinary Institute, and acted as guest chef-instructor at the Culinary Institute of America. Alan has written articles for the journals Fine Cooking and Wine and Spirits.

SUE TORRES is the chef of Sueño, in Chelsea. She has been the executive chef of Hell's Kitchen, in the Manhattan neighborhood of the same name, where she introduced her own "progressive Mexican" cuisine. A graduate of the Culinary Institute of America, where she was a co-founder of its Saucier Club, she served her externship at the "21" Club. She worked in the kitchens of La Grenouille, Lola, and Steve Hanson's Isabella's, where she was a sous-chef at the age of twenty-one. She then moved to Arizona 206, where she became aware of the many ingredients and possibilities of Mexican food, and later became executive chef of the Rocking Horse Cafe Mexicana. Sue traveled to Mexico to study classic Mexican fare with Diana Kennedy.

Working Woman magazine has chosen Sue as one of the "20 under 30" successful American women. She is active in Share Our Strength and the James Beard Taste Makers, and she works with inner-city children in the Days of Taste and Dinner Party programs.

JANOS WILDER, chef-owner of Janos and J Bar in Tucson, Arizona, earned a degree in political science from the University of California, Berkeley. He moved to Boulder, Colorado, and worked his way up from cook to sous-chef to chef at the city's top restaurants. He was chef at the Gold Hill Inn in Gold Hill, Colorado, and then moved to Le Mirage in Santa Fe, New Mexico, before heading to France to work in the Bordeaux restaurants La Reserve and La Duberne. In 1983, Janos and his wife, Rebecca, opened Janos on the grounds of the Tucson Museum of Art (since moved to the Westin La Paloma Resort), and in 1998, they opened the casual J Bar restaurant.

Chef Wilder was inducted into the Scottsdale Culinary Hall of Fame in 1993 and was named Best Chef: Southwest by the James Beard Foundation in May 2000. He is the author of Janos: Recipes and Tales from a Southwest Restaurant.

JOYCE WILDER is a native San Franciscan who raised her family (including her son, chef Janos Wilder) on the midpeninsula. A great host and accomplished home cook, Mrs. Wilder is inspired by cookbooks, magazines, and her extensive travels. She has created numerous recipes that have become part of her family's culinary traditions, and her recipe for macaroni and cheese was a household favorite when her children were young.

JOSEPH WREDE, a native of Phoenix, Arizona, and the chef and co-owner of Joseph's Table in Taos, New Mexico, was voted one of America's Ten Best New Chefs of 2000 by Food & Wine magazine. He is a graduate of Peter Kump's New York Cooking School and a cum laude graduate of Regis College in Colorado. Before working at Aubergine Café and Today's Gourmet, both in Denver, Colorado, he "worked in one bad restaurant after another in every conceivable capacity." Joseph's food is about adventure, availability, and mood, and he is known for his skillful combinations of ingredients.

PATRICIA YEO has been co-executive chef of the restaurants AZ and Pazo, in Manhattan. She is a native of Eugene, Oregon, and a graduate of Princeton University, where she earned her doctorate in biochemistry, and the New York Restaurant School. In 1989, during a break in her postdoctoral studies, she took a cooking class and was inspired to turn in her lab coat for chef whites.

At culinary school, Patricia met Bobby Flay, who was then at Miracle Grill and hired her upon her graduation. When Bobby opened Mesa Grill in 1991, Patricia became sous-chef. She then moved to the West Coast to work at Barbara Tropp's China Moon. Patricia returned to Manhattan in 1993, as sous-chef of Flay's restaurant Bolo, where she worked for two years. She later opened San Francisco's Hawthorne Lane, under Chef Anne Gingrass, and after three years, she set off to explore Asia.

In 2000, Patricia opened AZ, to rave reviews from New York magazine, the New York Observer, The New York Times, the New York Daily News, and the New York Post. She opened the popular Pazo in 2002, and is the author of Cooking from A to Z (St. Martin's Press, 2002).

Index

A

Acheson, Hugh, 275
  Short Rib Shepherd's Pies with
    Borlotti Beans and Chive Potato
    Crust, 160–62
acorn squash, in Moroccan-Spiced
  Cassoulet, 158–59
Adams, Jody, 275
  Baked Stuffed Pasta Spirals,
    100–101
al dente, 3
Aleppo pepper:
  Pastitsio, 61–64
  sources for, 120, 135
Alsatian Meat-and-Potato Casserole
  (Baeckeofe), 215–16
American cheese, 6
  Chat n' Chew Macaroni and Cheese,
    28–29
  City Hall Mac and Cheese,
    32–33
  Comfort Diner Mac and Cheese,
    30–31
  Mac and Cheddar Salad, 41
  Queens (N.Y.) Mac and Cheese,
    39–40
  Ten-Minute Mac and Cheese, 34
Ancho-Bourbon Sauce, 258
Angerer, Daniel, 276
  Potato-Crusted Lamb Cakes,
    231–33

Anthony, Michael, 276
  Braised Short Ribs with Pan-Roasted
    Ruby Crescent Fingerlings,
    156–57
Appenzeller, 6
appetizers and first courses:
  Potato Gnocchi with Ragù
    Bolognese, 195–97
  Short Rib–Stuffed Potatoes, Spicy,
    163–65
apple(s):
  Cider–Balsamic Sauce, 262
  Granny Smith, Slices, Grilled,
    255
  Slices, Sautéed, 201–3
Arrows' Leg of Venison with Roasted
  Yams, 248–49
Artichoke Hearts, Baked Cellentani
  with Four Cheeses, Prosciutto,
  Portobellos, and, 97–99
Artie's Deli Mac and Cheese, 92
Asiago, 6
  Baked Four-Cheese Pasta, 26–27
  Dad Page's Macaroni and Cheese,
    23–24
  Macaroni and Cheese Provençal with
    Cod, 57–58
  Macaroni and Cheese with Oysters
    and Pork Sausage, 80–81
  Wisconsin, Macaroni with,
    15–16

B

baby shells, 4
  Farfalle al Quattro Formaggi, 49–50
bacon, 130
  Dutch Stamppot, 267–68
  Joseph's Table Mac and Cheese with
    Dried Cherry Chutney and
    Roquefort Sauce, 114–16
  Lovers' Mashed Potatoes, 269–70
  pancetta, in Wish Macaroni and
    Cheese, 51–52
  Roasted New Potatoes with Chive
    Flowers, Green Tomato Dressing
    and, 273–74
  Rösti Potatoes, 151
  Tartiflette de Cocotte (Potato Gratin
    with Cheese and Bacon),
    271–72
Baeckeofe (Alsatian Meat-and-Potato
  Casserole), 215–16
baking dishes, 10
Bank, Jeffrey, 276
  Artie's Deli Mac and Cheese, 92
balsamic:
  Apple Cider Sauce, 262
  Syrup, 166
Barbecue Spice Rub, 163
Barber, Dan, 276–77
  Braised Short Ribs with Pan-Roasted
    Ruby Crescent Fingerlings,
    156–57

barley, in Moroccan-Spiced Cassoulet,
  158–59
basil:
  Macaroni and Cheese Provençal with
    Cod, 57–58
  Macaroni and Manchego, 66
  Macaroni with Duck Prosciutto,
    Chanterelles, and Mascarpone,
    95–96
  Mozzarella Mac, 53–54
Bayless, Rick, 277
  Today's Macaroni and Cheese,
    84–85
béchamel, 9–10
  Mitchel London's tips for, 17
  Yogurt Topping, 63
beef, cuts of, 128–29
beef and potatoes, 139–97
  Boeuf Bourguignon, 183–84
  Braised Beef Cheeks with Fingerling
    Potato Purée, 178–80
  Chiles Rellenos with Warm Mild
    Tomato Sauce, 192–94
  Malaysian Beef Rendang with Sweet
    Potato–Coconut Purée, 185–86
  Meat Loaf, Crispy, with Chanterelle-
    Buttermilk Gravy and Potato
    Gratin, 189–91
  Meat Loaf Stuffed with Mashed
    Potatoes and Cheddar, 187–88
  Moroccan-Spiced Cassoulet,
    158–59
  Potato Gnocchi with Ragù Bolognese,
    195–97
  Provençal Bouilli (Boiled Beef and
    Vegetables), 181–83
  Roasted Beef Shanks with Vegetables
    and Potatoes, 169–70
  see also mixed meats and potatoes;
    shepherd's pies; short rib(s);
    steaks

beef cheeks, 128
  Braised, with Fingerling Potato
    Purée, 178–80
  source for, 135
beef chuck, 128
  Malaysian Beef Rendang with
    Sweet Potato–Coconut Purée,
    185–86
  Provençal Bouilli (Boiled Beef and
    Vegetables), 181–83
beef chuck, ground:
  Chiles Rellenos with Warm Mild
    Tomato Sauce, 192–94
  Meat Loaf, Crispy, with Chanterelle-
    Buttermilk Gravy and Potato
    Gratin, 189–91
  Meat Loaf Stuffed with Mashed
    Potatoes and Cheddar, 187–88
  Potato Gnocchi with Ragù
    Bolognese, 195–97
beef, in Pastitsio, 61–64
beef rump, 128
beef shank(s):
  Roasted, with Vegetables and
    Potatoes, 169–70
  Zinfandel-Braised, Shepherd's Pie of,
    171–73
beef short rib(s), 128
  Braised, with Mashed Boniatos and
    Gingered Baby Bok Choy,
    Bomboa's, 153–55
  Braised, with Pan-Roasted Ruby
    Crescent Fingerlings, 156–57
  Hash with Sunny Eggs and Balsamic
    Syrup, 166–68
  Moroccan-Spiced Cassoulet,
    158–59
  Shepherd's Pies with Borlotti Beans
    and Chive Potato Crust,
    160–62
  -Stuffed Potatoes, Spicy, 163–65

beef shoulder, 129
  Boeuf Bourguignon, 183–84
Belgian endive, in Joseph's Table Mac
  and Cheese with Dried Cherry
  Chutney and Roquefort Sauce,
  114–16
Bel Paese, 6
  Baked Cellentani with Four Cheeses,
    Prosciutto, Artichoke Hearts, and
    Portobellos, 97–99
Bertineau, Philippe, 277–78
  Baeckeofe (Alsatian Meat-and-Potato
    Casserole), 215–16
black pepper, cracking, 149
blue cheese, 6
  Chunks of Lobster Swimming in
    Cheesy Macaroni, 112–13
  see also Gorgonzola; Roquefort
Boeuf Bourguignon, 183–84
Boiled Beef and Vegetables (Provençal
  Bouilli), 181–82
Bok Choy, Gingered Baby, 155
Bolognese Sauce (Ragù Bolognese),
  195–96
Bomboa's Braised Short Ribs with
  Mashed Boniatos and Gingered
  Baby Bok Choy, 153–55
boniatos (Cuban sweet potatoes), 133
  Mashed, 154
borlotti (cranberry) beans:
  Short Rib Shepherd's Pies with,
    160–62
  source for, 135
Botsacos, Jim, 278
  Roasted Greek Leg of Lamb with
    Rustic Potatoes and Okra, Onion,
    and Tomato Stew, 237–39
  Pastitsio, 61–64
Bouilli, Provençal (Boiled Beef and
  Vegetables), 181–82
Bourbon-Ancho Sauce, 258

Bouterin, Antoine, 278–79
  Macaroni Gratin Mas Antoine,
    55–56
  Provençal Bouilli (Boiled Beef and
    Vegetables), 181–82
braising, 127
bread crumbs, 8–9
"bridegrooms,"
  see ziti
Brie, 6
Brine-Marinated Pork Chops with
    Scallion-Smashed Potatoes and
    Grilled Granny Smith Apple Slices,
    253–55
bucatini, 4
Burke, David, 279
  ONEc.p.s. Wild Mushroom and
    Truffle Macaroni and Cheese,
    106–7
butter, 10
  clarifying, 107
Buttermilk-Chanterelle Gravy, 189–91
butternut squash, in Moroccan-Spiced
    Cassoulet, 158–59

C
cabbage, in Provençal Bouilli (Boiled
    Beef and Vegetables), 181–82
cabrales, 6
caciocavallo, 6
  Baked Cellentani with Four Cheeses,
    Prosciutto, Artichoke Hearts, and
    Portobellos, 97–99
cakes (savory):
  Lamb, Potato-Crusted, 231–33
  Lamb-Stuffed Potato Kubbeh,
    246–47
  Spicy Short Rib–Stuffed Potatoes,
    163–65
  Veal Croquettes with Dilled New
    Potatoes, 213–14

California Truffled Macaroni and Cheese,
    110–11
Camembert, 6
Campbell, Scott, 279–80
  Mac and Smoked Cheddar with Ham
    and Chipotles, 90–91
Cantal, 6
  Macaroni with Westphalian Ham
    and, 78–79
Carmellini, Andrew, 280
  Fontina and White Truffle Macaroni,
    102–3
casseroles:
  Baeckeofe (Alsatian Meat-and-Potato
    Casserole), 215–16
  Moroccan-Spiced Cassoulet,
    158–59
  see also shepherd's pies
Cassoulet, Moroccan-Spiced, 158–59
cavatappi, 4
  Mac and Cheese Soho Grand, 19–20
  Today's Macaroni and Cheese,
    84–85
cavatelli, 4
  Macaroni with Wisconsin Asiago,
    15–16
Celery Seed–Crusted Veal Roast with
    Red Pepper–Potato Pancakes,
    205–6
cellentani, 4
  Baked, with Four Cheeses,
    Prosciutto, Artichoke Hearts, and
    Portobellos, 97–99
Champvallon, Lamb Chops, 226–27
Chanterelles:
  Buttermilk Gravy, 189–91
  Macaroni with Duck Prosciutto,
    Mascarpone, and, 95–96
  and Potato Hash, 224
Chat n' Chew Macaroni and Cheese,
    28–29

Cheddar, 5, 6
  Artie's Deli Mac and Cheese, 92
  Baked Four-Cheese Pasta, 26–27
  California Truffled Macaroni and
    Cheese, 110–11
  Chat n' Chew Macaroni and Cheese,
    28–29
  Chunks of Lobster Swimming in
    Cheesy Macaroni, 112–13
  City Bakery Macaroni and Cheese,
    21–22
  Comfort Diner Mac and Cheese,
    30–31
  Dad Page's Macaroni and Cheese,
    23–24
  Fairway Market Mac and Cheese,
    25
  London Mac and Cheese, 17–18
  Mac and, Salad, 41
  Mac and Cheese Soho Grand, 19–20
  Macaroni and Cheese Croquettes,
    74–75
  Macaroni and Cheese Provençal with
    Cod, 57–58
  Macaroni and Cheese with Oysters
    and Pork Sausage, 80–81
  Macaroni with Duck Prosciutto,
    Chanterelles, and Mascarpone,
    95–96
  Macaroni with Wisconsin Asiago,
    15–16
  Meat Loaf Stuffed with Mashed
    Potatoes and, 187–88
  Mom's Mac and Cheese with
    Tomatoes, 38
  Potato Gratin, 190
  Queens (N.Y.) Mac and Cheese,
    39–40
  Simple Mac and Cheese for Two, 35
  Smoked, Mac and, with Ham and
    Chipotles, 90–91

Today's Macaroni and Cheese, 84–85

Tomatoey Mac and Cheese, 36–37

White, Baked Macaroni with Cremini Mushrooms and, 93–94

cheeses, 5–8

Cheddar, Meat Loaf Stuffed with Mashed Potatoes and, 187–88

determining amounts of, 5–6

Goat, Chorizo, and Potato Quesadillas, 264–66

Parmigiano-Reggiano, in Mashed-Potato Topping (for shepherd's pie), 172–73

Potato Gratin, 190

Raclette Potato Pancakes, 145–46

sources for, 119

Tartiflette de Cocotte (Potato Gratin with Cheese and Bacon), 271–72

see also specific cheeses

Chef Frank's Flavorful Lamb Stew, 242–43

Cherry, Dried, Chutney, Joseph's Table Mac and Cheese with Roquefort Sauce and, 114–16

chèvre, 6

see also goat cheese

chile(s):

Ancho-Bourbon Sauce, 258

Chipotles, Mac and Smoked Cheddar with Ham and, 90–91

Green, Mac and Cheese, 88–89

jalapeño, in Pesto, 261

poblanos, roasting, 264

Red, Herb Crust, Macaroni with Many Cheeses in, 86–87

Rellenos with Warm Mild Tomato Sauce, 192–94

Roasted Poblano Puree, 89

sources for, 135

chili powders and ground chili peppers, 135

chipotles:

cutting, 91

Mac and Smoked Cheddar with Ham and, 90–91

chive:

Flowers, Roasted New Potatoes with Bacon, Green Tomato Dressing and, 273–74

Potato Crust (for shepherd's pie), 161

chops, 127

Pork, Brine-Marinated, with Scallion-Smashed Potatoes and Grilled Granny Smith Apple Slices, 253–55

see also lamb chops; veal chops

chorizo, 130

Potato, and Goat Cheese Quesadillas, 264–66

chuck, see beef chuck; beef chuck, ground

Chutney, Dried Cherry, Joseph's Table Mac and Cheese with Roquefort Sauce and, 114–16

cilantro, in Green Chile Mac and Cheese, 88–89

Cilantro Pesto, 261

City Bakery Macaroni and Cheese, 21–22

City Hall Mac and Cheese, 32–33

Classic Dish, The, 12–41

Baked Four-Cheese Pasta, 26–27

Chat n' Chew, 28–29

City Bakery, 21–22

City Hall, 32–33

Comfort Diner, 30–31

Dad Page's, 23–24

Fairway Market, 25

London, 17–18

Mac and Cheddar Salad, 41

Mom's, with Tomatoes, 38

Queens (N.Y.), 39–40

Simple, for Two, 35

Soho Grand, 19–20

Ten-Minute, 34

Tomatoey, 36–37

with Wisconsin Asiago, 15–16

Coconut–Sweet Potato Purée, 186

Cod, Macaroni and Cheese Provençal with, 57–58

Coe, Frank, 280

Chef Frank's Flavorful Lamb Stew, 242–43

Comfort Diner Mac and Cheese, 30–31

Comté, 6

Fairway Market Mac and Cheese, 25

conchiglie, 4

Baked, with Roasted Garlic–Cheese Sauce, Ricotta Cheese, and White Truffle Oil, 108–9

corn bread crumbs, 9

cottage cheese, 6, 7

Sweet Noodle and Cheese Kugel, 68

Country-Style Veal Chops with Potatoes and Mushrooms, 203–4

cracker crumbs, 9

cranberry beans, see borlotti (cranberry) beans

cream cheese, in Sweet Noodle and Cheese Kugel, 68

Cremini Mushrooms, Baked Macaroni with White Cheddar Cheese and, 93–94

Crismon, Ron, 281

Crispy Meat Loaf with Chanterelle-Buttermilk Gravy and Potato Gratin, 189–91

crisp toppings, 8–9

Croquettes, Macaroni and Cheese, 74–75

Croquettes, Veal, with Dilled New Potatoes, 213–14

crumbs, for crisp toppings, 8–9

cumin, in Chat n' Chew Macaroni and Cheese, 28–29

Cupani, Craig, 281
Sliced Steak and Mushroom Salad with Caramelized Onions and Bacon-Rösti Potatoes, 150–52

Curto, Andrea, 281
Wish Macaroni and Cheese, 51–52

D

Dad Page's Macaroni and Cheese, 23–24

Davis, Mitchell, 281–82
Tomatoey Mac and Cheese, 36–37

DeLucie, John, 282
Mac and Cheese Soho Grand, 19–20

demi-glace, sources for, 135

desserts:
Sweetened Mascarpone and Noodle Pudding, 117–18
Sweet Noodle and Cheese Kugel, 68

Dicataldo, Andrew, 282
Spicy Short Rib–Stuffed Potatoes, 163–65

Dilled New Potatoes, 214

DiSpirito, Rocco, 282–83
Macaroni and Cheese Croquettes, 74–75

ditali, 4

ditali ligati, 4
Sweetened Mascarpone and Noodle Pudding, 117–18

ditalini, 4
ONEc.p.s. Wild Mushroom and Truffle Macaroni and Cheese, 106–7

Dresser, Keith, 283
Baked Four-Cheese Pasta, 26–27
Potato Gnocchi with Ragù Bolognese, 195–97

Dressing, Green Tomato, 273

Dry Jack, 7
Dad Page's Macaroni and Cheese, 23–24

duck fat, source for, 136

Duck Prosciutto, Macaroni with Chanterelles, Mascarpone, and, 95–96

DuFresne, Wylie, 283
Ten-Minute Mac and Cheese, 34

Dutch Stamppot, 267–68

E

egg(s), 10
Sunny, Beef Short Rib Hash with Balsamic Syrup and, 166–168
Sweetened Mascarpone and Noodle Pudding, 117–18
Sweet Noodle and Cheese Kugel, 68
whites, in Macaroni with Cantal Cheese and Westphalian Ham, 78–79

egg noodles, 4
Sweet Noodle and Cheese Kugel, 68

elbow macaroni, 4
California Truffled Macaroni and Cheese, 110–11
Chat n' Chew Macaroni and Cheese, 28–29
Chunks of Lobster Swimming in Cheesy Macaroni, 112–13
City Bakery Macaroni and Cheese, 21–22
Comfort Diner Mac and Cheese, 30–31
Dad Page's Macaroni and Cheese, 23–24

Fairway Market Mac and Cheese, 25
Green Chile Mac and Cheese, 88–89
Joseph's Table Mac and Cheese with Dried Cherry Chutney and Roquefort Sauce, 114–16
Mac and Cheddar Salad, 41
Mac and Smoked Cheddar with Ham and Chipotles, 90–91
Macaroni and Cheese Croquettes, 74–75
Macaroni and Feta Salad, 65
Macaroni and Manchego, 66
Macaroni Gratin Mas Antoine, 55–56
Macaroni with Cantal Cheese and Westphalian Ham, 78–79
Macaroni with Duck Prosciutto, Chanterelles, and Mascarpone, 95–96
Mom's Mac and Cheese with Tomatoes, 38
Queens (N.Y.) Mac and Cheese, 39–40
Swiss Mac with Potatoes, 67
Today's Macaroni and Cheese, 84–85

elbow twists, 4

Emmentaler, 7

escarole, in Dutch Stamppot, 267–68

F

Fairway Market Mac and Cheese, 25

Falsone, Loren, 284
Baked Cellentani with Four Cheeses, Prosciutto, Artichoke Hearts, and Portobellos, 97–99
Sweetened Mascarpone and Noodle Pudding, 117–18

farfalle, 4
    Artie's Deli Mac and Cheese, 92
    with Fontina, Tasso Ham, and Baby
        Spinach, 76–77
    Macaroni with Many Cheeses in Red
        Chile–Herb Crust, 86–87
    al Quattro Formaggi, 49–50
farfalline, 4
    Sweetened Mascarpone and Noodle
        Pudding, 117–18
fennel:
    Macaroni and Cheese Provençal
        with Cod, 57–58
    Macaroni and Manchego, 66
feta, 7
    Greek (and Organic) Macaroni and
        Cheese, 59–60
    and Macaroni Salad, 65
figs, in Baked Stuffed Pasta Spirals,
    100–101
filet mignon, 129
    Grilled, with Tarragon Potato Salad,
        Beefsteak Tomatoes, and Mustard
        Vinaigrette, 143–44
fingerling potato(es), 133
    Purée, 179–80
    Ruby Crescent, 134
    Ruby Crescent, Pan-Roasted,
        157
first courses, see appetizers and first
    courses
Flay, Bobby, 284
    Baked Conchiglie with Roasted
        Garlic–Cheese Sauce, Ricotta
        Cheese, and White Truffle Oil,
        108–9
    New Mexican Rubbed Pork
        Tenderloin with Bourbon-Ancho
        Sauce and Roasted Garlic–Sweet
        Onion Potato Gratin, 256–59
flour, 10

foie gras:
    sources for, 120
    Terrine of Macaroni, Goat Cheese,
        and, 82–83
fonduta:
    Orecchiette con, 47–48
    Pasta with Fresh Truffles and, 104–5
fontina, 7
    Baked Conchiglie with Roasted
        Garlic–Cheese Sauce, Ricotta
        Cheese, and White Truffle Oil,
        108–9
    Baked Four-Cheese Pasta, 26–27
    Comfort Diner Mac and Cheese,
        30–31
    Farfalle al Quattro Formaggi, 49–50
    Farfalle with Tasso Ham, Baby
        Spinach, and, 76–77
    Orecchiette con Fonduta, 47–48
    Pasta with Fonduta and Fresh
        Truffles, 104–5
    Rigatoni al Forno, 45–46
    and White Truffle Macaroni, 102–3
    Wish Macaroni and Cheese, 51–52
four-cheese Mac:
    Baked Cellentani with Four Cheeses,
        Prosciutto, Artichoke Hearts, and
        Portobellos, 97–99
    Baked Four-Cheese Pasta,
        26–27
    Farfalle al Quattro Formaggi,
        49–50
Frankel, Laura, 284
    Moroccan-Spiced Cassoulet,
        158–59
Franz, Mark, 285
    Pasta with Fonduta and Fresh
        Truffles, 104–5
    Slow-Roasted Lamb Shoulder with
        Potatoes, Garlic, and Rosemary,
        240–41

Frasier, Clark, 285
    Arrows' Leg of Venison with Roasted
        Yams, 248–49
Freehof, Ira, 285
    Comfort Diner Mac and Cheese,
        30–31
fusilli, 4
    Pasta with Fonduta and Fresh
        Truffles, 104–5
    Today's Macaroni and Cheese,
        84–85

G
Gaier, Mark, 285
    Arrows' Leg of Venison with Roasted
        Yams, 248–49
galangal, source for, 136
Gamba, Sandro, 286
    Roasted Leg of Lamb with
        Grandmother Jeannette's Truffled
        Mashed Potatoes, 234–36
garganelli, 4
garlic:
    Dad Page's Macaroni and Cheese,
        23–24
    Macaroni and Cheese Provençal with
        Cod, 57–58
    Pastitsio, 61–64
    Roasted, Cheese Sauce, Baked
        Conchiglie with Ricotta Cheese,
        White Truffle Oil, and, 108–9
    Roasted, Sweet Onion Potato Gratin,
        257
    roasting head of, 259
    roasting and pureeing, 79
Gerin, Jean-Louis, 286
    Lamb Chops Champvallon,
        226–27
German Butterball potatoes, 133
    Creamy, 200–1
Gingered Baby Bok Choy, 155

gnocchi, potato:
    with Ragù Bolognese, 195–97
    Veal Stew Baked with, 207–9
goat cheese:
    chévre, 6
Goat Cheese, Chorizo, and Potato
        Quesadillas, 264–66
    Terrine of Macaroni, Foie Gras, and,
        82–83
Goodell, Tim, 286
    California Truffled Macaroni and
        Cheese, 110–11
Gorgonzola, 7
    Baked Stuffed Pasta Spirals,
        100–101
    California Truffled Macaroni and
        Cheese, 110–11
    Farfalle al Quattro Formaggi,
        49–50
Gorgonzola Dolce (or Dolcelatte), 7
    Rigatoni al Forno, 45–46
Gouda, 7
Grana Padano, 7
    Baked Macaroni with White Cheddar
        Cheese and Cremini Mushrooms,
        93–94
    City Bakery Macaroni and Cheese,
        21–22
    London Mac and Cheese, 17–18
    Rigatoni al Forno, 45–46
Gras, Laurent, 287
    Veal Tournedos with Caramelized and
        Creamy Potatoes and Sautéed
        Apple Slices, 200–2
gratins:
    Potato (Crismon), 190
    Potato (Pouillon), 142
    Roasted Garlic–Sweet Onion Potato,
        257
    Tartiflette de Cocotte (Potato Gratin
        with Cheese and Bacon), 271–72

Gravy, Chanterelle-Buttermilk,
        189–91
Greek:
    Macaroni and Feta Salad, 65
    (and Organic) Macaroni and Cheese,
        59–60
    Pastitsio, 61–64
Greek Roasted Leg of Lamb with Rustic
        Potatoes and Okra, Onion, and
        Tomato Stew, 237–39
Green Chile Mac and Cheese, 88–89
Green Tomato Dressing, 273
grilled:
    Filet Mignon with Tarragon Potato
        Salad, Beefsteak Tomatoes, and
        Mustard Vinaigrette, 143–44
    Lamb Chops, Herb-, with
        Chanterelle and Potato Hash,
        223–25
    New York Strip Steak, Rosemary-
        Marinated, with Potato Gratin,
        141–42
    Pork Chops, Brine-Marinated,
        with Scallion-Smashed
        Potatoes and Grilled Granny
        Smith Apple Slices,
        253–55
    Shell Steak with Raclette Potato
        Pancakes, 145–47
grilling, 127
ground meat, 127
    Lamb-Stuffed Potato Kubbeh,
        246–47
    Old-Fashioned Shepherd's Pie,
        244–46
    La Svizzera (Italian-Style
        Hamburgers) with Prosciutto
        Mashed Potatoes, 217–19
    Veal Croquettes with Dilled New
        Potatoes, 213–14
    see also beef chuck, ground

Gruyère, 7
    Chunks of Lobster Swimming in
        Cheesy Macaroni, 112–13
    City Bakery Macaroni and Cheese,
        21–22
    Macaroni and Cheese Croquettes,
        74–75
    Macaroni and Cheese with Oysters
        and Pork Sausage, 80–81
Guarnaschelli, Alexandra, 287
    Bacon Lovers' Mashed Potatoes,
        269–70

H
ham, 130
    Mac and Smoked Cheddar with
        Chipotles and, 90–91
    Split Pea, and Potato Soup, 263
    Tasso, Farfalle with Fontina, Baby
        Spinach, and, 76–77
    Westphalian, Macaroni with Cantal
        cheese and, 78–79
    see also prosciutto
Hamburgers, Italian-Style
        (La Svizzera) with Prosciutto
        Mashed Potatoes, 217–19
Hamersley, Gordon, 287–88
    Macaroni and Cheese Provençal
        with Cod, 57–58
    Macaroni and Cheese with Oysters
        and Pork Sausage, 80–81
    Terrine of Macaroni, Goat Cheese,
        and Foie Gras, 82–83
Harris, Glenn, 288
    Sweet Potato–Stuffed Roulade of
        Pork, 260
hash:
    Beef Short Rib, with Sunny Eggs
        and Balsamic Syrup,
        166–68
    Chanterelle and Potato, 224

Hayden, Gerry, 288
    Slow-Braised Veal and Vanilla Sweet
        Potato Shepherd's Pie, 210–12
Herb-Grilled Lamb Chops with
    Chanterelle and Potato Hash,
    223–25
hickory smoke powder, sources for, 136
Holley-McKen, Leslie, 289
    Queens (N.Y.) Mac and Cheese,
    39–40

I
Idaho (russet) potatoes, 134
Indian-Spiced Rack of Lamb with Potato
    Tikki and Mint Yogurt, 228–30
ingredients, 10
    cheeses, 5–8
    crisp toppings, 8–9
    meats, 127–31
    pasta, 3–5
    potatoes, 132–34
    sources for, 135–37
International Mac, 42–68
    Farfalle al Quattro Formaggi, 49–50
    Greek (and Organic) Macaroni and
        Cheese, 59–60
    Macaroni and Cheese Provençal with
        Cod, 57–58
    Macaroni and Feta Salad, 65
    Macaroni and Manchego, 66
    Macaroni Gratin Mas Antoine, 55–56
    Mozzarella Mac, 53–54
    Orecchiette con Fonduta, 47–48
    Pastitsio, 61–64
    Rigatoni al Forno, 45–46
    Sweet Noodle and Cheese Kugel, 68
    Swiss Mac with Potatoes, 67
    Wish Macaroni and Cheese, 51–52
Italian:
    Farfalle al Quattro Formaggi, 49–50
    Mozzarella Mac, 53–54

    Orecchiette con Fonduta, 47–48
    Rigatoni al Forno, 45–46
    Wish Macaroni and Cheese, 51–52

J
jalapeños, in Pesto, 261
John, Thomas, 289
    Indian-Spiced Rack of Lamb with
        Potato Tikki and Mint Yogurt,
        228–30
Johnson, Kevin, 289
    Baked Macaroni with White Cheddar
        Cheese and Cremini Mushrooms,
        93–94
Joseph's Table Mac and Cheese with
    Dried Cherry Chutney and
    Roquefort Sauce, 114–16

K
kaffir lime leaves, source for, 136
kashkaval, 7
kasseri, 7
kefalotyri, 7
    Pastitsio, 61–64
Kelly, Melissa, 290
    Orecchiette con Fonduta, 47–48
Kenney, Matthew, 290
    Macaroni with Wisconsin Asiago,
        15–16
    Meat Loaf Stuffed with Mashed
        Potatoes and Cheddar, 187–88
kielbasa, 130
    Dutch Stamppot, 267–68
Kirschenbaum, Levana, 290
    Boeuf Bourguignon, 183–84
Kubbeh, Lamb-Stuffed Potato, 246–47
Kugel, Sweet Noodle and Cheese, 68

L
lamb, cuts of, 129–30
lamb, in Pastitsio, 61–64

lamb and potatoes, 221–47
    Herb-Grilled Lamb Chops with
        Chanterelle and Potato Hash,
        223–25
    Indian-Spiced Rack of Lamb with
        Potato Tikki and Mint Yogurt,
        228–30
    Lamb Chops Champvallon,
        226–27
    Lamb Stew, Chef Frank's Flavorful,
        242–43
    Lamb-Stuffed Potato Kubbeh,
        246–47
    Potato-Crusted Lamb Cakes, 231–33
    Roasted Greek Leg of Lamb with
        Rustic Potatoes and Okra, Onion,
        and Tomato Stew, 237–39
    Roasted Leg of Lamb with
        Grandmother Jeannette's Truffled
        Mashed Potatoes, 234–36
    Shepherd's Pie, Old-Fashioned,
        244–45
    Slow-Roasted Lamb Shoulder with
        Potatoes, Garlic, and Rosemary,
        240–41
    see also mixed meats and potatoes
lamb chops, 129
    Champvallon, 226–27
    Herb-Grilled, with Chanterelle and
        Potato Hash, 223–26
lamb shanks, 129
    Potato-Crusted Lamb Cakes,
        231–33
lamb shoulder, 130
    Chef Frank's Flavorful Lamb Stew,
        242–43
    Slow-Roasted, with Potatoes, Garlic,
        and Rosemary, 240–41
Leek Garnish, 254
leeks, in Terrine of Macaroni, Goat
    Cheese, and Foie Gras, 82–83

leg of lamb, 129
    Roasted, with Grandmother
      Jeannette's Truffled Mashed
      Potatoes, 234–36
    Roasted Greek, with Rustic Potatoes
      and Okra, Onion, and Tomato
      Stew, 237–39
lemongrass, source for, 136
Lo, Anita, 291
    Grilled Shell Steak with Raclette
      Potato Pancakes, 145–47
Lobster, Chunks of, Swimming in Cheesy
    Macaroni, 112–13
London, Mitchel, 291
    Mac and Cheese, 17–18
    Seared Rib-Eye Steak with Crisp and
      Creamy Potatoes, 148–49

M
Mac and Cheese Today, 70–118
    Artie's Deli Mac and Cheese, 92
    Baked Cellentani with Four Cheeses,
      Prosciutto, Artichoke Hearts, and
      Portobellos, 97–99
    Baked Conchiglie with Roasted
      Garlic–Cheese Sauce, Ricotta
      Cheese, and White Truffle Oil,
      108–9
    Baked Macaroni with White Cheddar
      Cheese and Cremini Mushrooms,
      93–94
    Baked Stuffed Pasta Spirals,
      100–101
    California Truffled Macaroni and
      Cheese, 110–11
    Chunks of Lobster Swimming in
      Cheesy Macaroni, 112–13
    Farfalle with Fontina, Tasso Ham,
      and Baby Spinach, 76–77
    Fontina and White Truffle Macaroni,
      102–3

Green Chile Mac and Cheese, 88–89
Joseph's Table Mac and Cheese with
    Dried Cherry Chutney and
    Roquefort Sauce, 114–16
Mac and Smoked Cheddar with Ham
    and Chipotles, 90–91
Macaroni and Cheese Croquettes,
    74–75
Macaroni and Cheese with Oysters
    and Pork Sausage, 80–81
Macaroni with Cantal Cheese and
    Westphalian Ham, 78–79
Macaroni with Duck Prosciutto,
    Chanterelles, and Mascarpone,
    95–96
Macaroni with Many Cheeses
    in Red Chile–Herb Crust, 86–87
ONEc.p.s. Wild Mushroom and
    Truffle Macaroni and Cheese,
    106–7
Pasta with Fonduta and Fresh
    Truffles, 104–5
Penne with Roquefort, 73
Sweetened Mascarpone and Noodle
    Pudding, 117–18
Terrine of Macaroni, Goat Cheese,
    and Foie Gras, 82–83
Today's Macaroni and Cheese,
    84–85s
macaroni and cheese:
    baking dishes for, 10
    béchamel for, 9–10
    cheeses for, 5–8
    crisp toppings for, 8–9
    history of, 2
    ingredient notes for, 10
    pasta for, 3–5
    two basic rules for, 2
    see also The Classic Dish;
      International Mac; Mac and
      Cheese Today

Malaysian Beef Rendang with Sweet
    Potato–Coconut Purée, 185–86
Malouf, Waldy, 291–92
    Penne with Roquefort, 73
Manchego, 7
    Macaroni and, 66
mascarpone, 7
    Macaroni with Duck Prosciutto,
      Chanterelles and, 95–96
    Sweetened, and Noodle Pudding,
      117–18
    ONEc.p.s. Wild Mushroom and
      Truffle Macaroni and Cheese,
      106–7
mashed potatoes:
    Bacon Lovers', 269–70
    Boniatos, 154
    Meat Loaf Stuffed with Cheddar and,
      187–88
    Prosciutto, 217–18
    Truffled, 235–36
    see also potato toppings for
      shepherd's pie
McGrath, Philip, 292
    Grilled Filet Mignon with Tarragon
      Potato Salad, Beefsteak
      Tomatoes, and Mustard
      Vinaigrette, 143–44
meat, 127–31
    buying, 127
    cooking methods for, 127–28
    ground, 127
    and potatoes, 125–26 (see also
      beef and potatoes; lamb and
      potatoes; mixed meats and
      potatoes; pork and potatoes;
      veal and potatoes)
    types and cuts of, 128–31
meat loaf:
    Crispy, with Chanterelle-Buttermilk
      Gravy and Potato Gratin, 189–91

Stuffed with Mashed Potatoes and
Cheddar, 187–88
Meer, Henry Archer, 292–93
City Hall Mac and Cheese, 32–33
Shepherd's Pie of Beef Shank
Braised in Zinfandel, 171–73
Merlot-Braised Oxtail, Shepherd's Pie of,
174–77
Metz, Chris, 276
Artie's Deli Mac and Cheese, 92
mezzani, 4
Ten-Minute Mac and Cheese, 34
mezza rigatoni, 5
Farfalle al Quattro Formaggi,
49–50
Middle Eastern flavors:
Lamb-Stuffed Potato Kubbeh,
246–47
Moroccan-Spiced Cassoulet, 158–59
Mint Yogurt, 228
mixed meats and potatoes, 199,
215–219
Baeckeofe (Alsatian Meat-and-Potato
Casserole), 215–16
La Svizzera (Italian-Style
Hamburgers) with Prosciutto
Mashed Potatoes, 217–19
Molina, José Arturo, 293
Chat n' Chew Macaroni and Cheese,
28–29
Mom's Mac and Cheese with Tomatoes,
38
Monterey Jack, 7
Chunks of Lobster Swimming in
Cheesy Macaroni, 112–13
City Hall Mac and Cheese, 32–33
Green Chile Mac and Cheese,
88–89
morels, in Orecchiette con Fonduta,
47–48
Moroccan-Spiced Cassoulet, 158–59

Moshier, Eric, 284
Baked Cellentani with Four Cheeses,
Prosciutto, Artichoke Hearts, and
Portobellos, 97–99
Sweetened Mascarpone and Noodle
Pudding, 117–18
mozzarella, 7
Baked Cellentani with Four Cheeses,
Prosciutto, Artichoke Hearts, and
Portobellos, 97–99
Baked Conchiglie with Roasted Garlic–
Cheese Sauce, Ricotta Cheese, and
White Truffle Oil, 108–9
Mac, 53–54
Rigatoni al Forno, 45–46
mushroom(s):
Chanterelle and Potato Hash, 224
Chanterelle-Buttermilk Gravy, 189–91
Chanterelles, Macaroni with Duck
Prosciutto, Mascarpone, and,
95–96
Country-Style Veal Chops with
Potatoes and, 203–4
Cremini, Baked Macaroni with White
Cheddar Cheese and, 93–94
morels, in Orecchiette con Fonduta,
47–48
Portobellos, Baked Cellentani with
Four Cheeses, Prosciutto, Artichoke
Hearts, and, 97–99
portobellos, in Baked Stuffed Pasta
Spirals, 100–101
shiitake, in Macaroni with Many
Cheeses in Red Chile–Herb Crust,
86–87
shiitake, in Slow-Braised Veal and
Vanilla Sweet Potato Shepherd's
Pie, 210–12
shiitake, in Tartiflette de Cocotte
(Potato Gratin with Cheese and
Bacon), 271–72

and Sliced Steak Salad, 150–52
Wild, and Truffle Macaroni and
Cheese, ONEc.p.s., 106–7
wild, in Shepherd's Pie of Merlot-
Braised Oxtail, 174–77
wild, sources for, 120
mustard:
Baked Macaroni with White Cheddar
Cheese and Cremini Mushrooms,
93–94
Comfort Diner Mac and Cheese,
30–31
Queens (N.Y.) Mac and Cheese,
39–40
Sauce, 146
Vinaigrette, 143

N
New Mexican Rubbed Pork Tenderloin
with Bourbon-Ancho Sauce
and Roasted Garlic–Sweet
Onion Potato Gratin, 256–59
new potato(es), 132, 134
Dilled, 214
Roasted, 274
Roasted, with Bacon, Chive Flowers,
and Green Tomato Dressing,
273–74
New York Strip Steak, Grilled Rosemary-
Marinated, with Potato Gratin,
141–42
noodle(s):
and Cheese Kugel, Sweet, 68
egg, 4
and Mascarpone Pudding,
Sweetened, 117–18

O
Okra, Onion, and Tomato Stew, 239
Old-Fashioned Shepherd's Pie, 244–
45

olives:
  Greek (and Organic) Macaroni and
    Cheese, 59–60
  Macaroni and Cheese Provençal with
    Cod, 57–58
  Macaroni and Feta Salad, 65
O'Neill, Michael, 293
  Fairway Market Mac and Cheese, 25
onion(s):
  Caramelized, and Bacon-Rösti
    Potatoes, 150–51
  Dad Page's Macaroni and Cheese,
    23–24
  Mac and Cheese Soho Grand, 19
  Macaroni with Cantal Cheese and
    Westphalian Ham, 78–79
  Okra, and Tomato Stew, 239
  Pastitsio, 61–64
  red, in Macaroni and Feta Salad, 65
  Sweet, Roasted Garlic Potato Gratin,
    257
  Terrine of Macaroni, Goat Cheese,
    and Foie Gras, 82–83
orange zest, in Sweetened Mascarpone
    and Noodle Pudding, 117–18
orecchiette, 4
  Farfalle al Quattro Formaggi, 49–50
  con Fonduta, 47–48
  Macaroni with Cantal Cheese and
    Westphalian Ham, 78–79
oregano, source for, 136
oxtail, 128
  Merlot-Braised, Shepherd's Pie of,
    174–77
Oysters, Macaroni and Cheese with Pork
    Sausage and, 80–81

P
Page, David, 298
  Dad Page's Macaroni and Cheese,
    23–24

Palmer, Charlie, 293
  Macaroni with Cantal Cheese and
    Westphalian Ham, 78–79
pancakes:
  Bacon-Rösti Potatoes, 151
  Raclette Potato, 145–46
  Red Pepper–Potato, 206
pancetta, 130
  in Wish Macaroni and Cheese, 51–52
panko (Japanese bread crumbs), 9
Parmesan, 5, 7
  Baked Four-Cheese Pasta, 26–27
  Chat n' Chew Macaroni and Cheese,
    28–29
  City Bakery Macaroni and Cheese,
    21–22
  Greek (and Organic) Macaroni and
    Cheese, 59–60
  Macaroni and Cheese Provençal with
    Cod, 57–58
  Mashed-Potato Topping (for
    shepherd's pie), 172–73
  Potato Gratin, 190
Parmigiano-Reggiano, 5, 8
  Baked Cellentani with Four Cheeses,
    Prosciutto, Artichoke Hearts, and
    Portobellos, 97–99
  Baked Conchiglie with Roasted
    Garlic–Cheese Sauce, Ricotta
    Cheese, and White Truffle Oil,
    108–9
  Baked Macaroni with White Cheddar
    Cheese and Cremini Mushrooms,
    93–94
  California Truffled Macaroni and
    Cheese, 110–11
  Green Chile Mac and Cheese, 88–89
  London Mac and Cheese, 17–18
  Macaroni with Duck Prosciutto,
    Chanterelles, and Mascarpone,
    95–96

Macaroni with Wisconsin Asiago,
    15–16
Mozzarella Mac, 53–54
ONEc.p.s. Wild Mushroom and Truffle
    Macaroni and Cheese, 106–7
Rigatoni al Forno, 45–46
Wish Macaroni and Cheese, 51–52
parsnips:
  Provençal Bouilli (Boiled Beef and
    Vegetables), 181–182
  Roasted Beef Shanks with Vegetables
    and Potatoes, 169–70
pasta, 3–5
  al dente, 3
  artisanal, sources for, 119
  cooking, 4
  dried, shapes, 4–5
  dried, yields, 4
  Gnocchi, Veal Stew Baked with,
    207–9
  Potato Gnocchi with Ragù Bolognese,
    195–97
pastina, 4
  Sweetened Mascarpone and Noodle
    Pudding, 117–18
Pastitsio, 61–64
pastrami, in Artie's Deli Mac and
    Cheese, 92
Pea (Split), Ham, and Potato Soup, 263
pecorino, 8
  London Mac and Cheese, 17–18
  Macaroni and Cheese Provençal with
    Cod, 57–58
Pellegrino, Carla, 293
  La Svizzera (Italian-Style
    Hamburgers) with Prosciutto
    Mashed Potatoes, 217–19
penne, 4
  Baked Four-Cheese Pasta, 26–27
  with Fontina, Tasso Ham, and Baby
    Spinach, 76–77

Fontina and White Truffle Macaroni, 102–3

London Mac and Cheese, 17–18

Macaroni and Cheese Provençal with Cod, 57–58

Macaroni and Cheese with Oysters and Pork Sausage, 80–81

Pasta with Fonduta and Fresh Truffles, 104–5

Pastitsio, 61–64

with Roquefort, 73

Simple Mac and Cheese for Two, 35

Ten-Minute Mac and Cheese, 34

Terrine of Macaroni, Goat Cheese, and Foie Gras, 82–83

Tomatoey Mac and Cheese, 36–37

penne rigate, 5

City Hall Mac and Cheese, 32–33

Mozzarella Mac, 53–54

pepper, 10

pepper, red:

Mac and Cheddar Salad, 41

Macaroni and Cheese Provençal with Cod, 57–58

peppers, see chile(s); red pepper(s)

Peruvian Blue or Purple potatoes, 133

Pesto, 261

Picker, Steven, 294

Green Chile Mac and Cheese, 88–89

pies, savory, see shepherd's pies

Pintabona, Don, 294

Farfalle al Quattro Formaggi, 49–50

Pinxteren, Maarten, 294

Dutch Stamppot, 267–68

poblano chile(s):

Chiles Rellenos with Warm Mild Tomato Sauce, 192–94

Green Chile Mac and Cheese, 88–89

Roasted, Puree, 89

roasting, 264

pomegranate molasses, sources for, 136

Ponzek, Debra, 294–95

Farfalle with Fontina, Tasso Ham, and Baby Spinach, 76–77

Split Pea, Ham, and Potato Soup, 263

porcini, in ONEc.p.s. Wild Mushroom and Truffle Macaroni and Cheese, 106–7

pork, forms of, 130

pork and potatoes, 251–74

Bacon Lovers' Mashed Potatoes, 269–70

Brine-Marinated Pork Chops with Scallion-Smashed Potatoes and Grilled Granny Smith Apple Slices, 253–55

Chorizo, Potato, and Goat Cheese Quesadillas, 264–66

Dutch Stamppot, 267–68

New Mexican Rubbed Pork Tenderloin with Bourbon-Ancho Sauce and Roasted Garlic–Sweet Onion Potato Gratin, 256–59

Roasted New Potatoes with Bacon, Chive Flowers, and Green Tomato Dressing, 273–74

Split Pea, Ham, and Potato Soup, 263

Sweet Potato–Stuffed Roulade of Pork, 260–62

Tartiflette de Cocotte (Potato Gratin with Cheese and Bacon), 271–72

see also mixed meats and potatoes

Pork Chops, Brine-Marinated, with Scallion-Smashed Potatoes and Grilled Granny Smith Apple Slices, 253–55

pork loin, 130

Sweet Potato–Stuffed Roulade of Pork, 260–62

pork sausage

Sausage, Macaroni and Cheese with Oysters and, 80–81

see also bacon; ham; prosciutto

pork tenderloin, 130

New Mexican Rubbed, with Bourbon-Ancho Sauce and Roasted Garlic–Sweet Onion Potato Gratin, 256–59

Porter, Alex, 295

Chunks of Lobster Swimming in Cheesy Macaroni, 112–13

portobellos:

and Sliced Steak Salad, 150–52

Baked Cellentani with Four Cheeses, Prosciutto, Artichoke Hearts, and, 97–99

Baked Stuffed Pasta Spirals, 100–101

potato(es), 132–34

buying, 133

sources for, 136

starch classifications of, 132–33

storing, 133

Swiss Mac with, 67

varieties of, 133–34

see also beef and potatoes; lamb and potatoes; mixed meats and potatoes; pork and potatoes; veal and potatoes; specific varieties of potatoes

potato gnocchi:

with Ragù Bolognese, 195–97

Veal Stew Baked with, 207–9

potato side dishes:

Bacon Lovers' Mashed Potatoes, 269–70

Bacon-Rösti Potatoes, 151

Caramelized Potatoes, 201

Chanterelle and Potato Hash, 224

Creamy Potatoes, 200–1

Crisp and Creamy Potatoes, 148–49
Dilled New Potatoes, 214
Fingerling Potato Purée, 179–80
Pan-Roasted Ruby Crescent
    Fingerlings, 157
Potato Gratin (Crismon), 190
Potato Gratin (Pouillon), 142
Potato Tikki, 229–30
Prosciutto Mashed Potatoes,
    217–18
Raclette Potato Pancakes, 145–46
Red Pepper–Potato Pancakes, 206
Roasted Garlic–Sweet Onion Potato
    Gratin, 257
Scallion-Smashed Potatoes, 254
Tarragon Potato Salad, 143–44
Truffled Mashed Potatoes, 235–36
see also sweet potato(es)
potato toppings for shepherd's pie,
    172–73, 244
Chive, 161
Truffled, 176
Potenza, Walter, 295
Veal Stew Baked with Gnocchi,
    207–9
Pouillon, Nora, 296
Greek (and Organic) Macaroni and
    Cheese, 59–60
Grilled Rosemary-Marinated New
    York Strip Steak with Potato Gratin,
    141–42
prosciutto, 130
Baked Cellentani with Four Cheeses,
    Artichoke Hearts, Portobellos, and,
    97–99
Duck, Macaroni with Chanterelles,
    Mascarpone, and, 95–96
Mashed Potatoes, 217–18
Provençal:
Bouilli (Boiled Beef and Vegetables),
    181–82

Macaroni and Cheese with Cod,
    57–58
Macaroni Gratin Mas Antoine, 55–56
puddings:
    Sweetened Mascarpone and Noodle,
        117–18
    Sweet Noodle and Cheese Kugel, 68
purées:
    Fingerling Potato, 179–80
    Sweet Potato–Coconut, 186

Q
Queens (N.Y.) Mac and Cheese,
    39–40
Quesadillas, Chorizo, Potato, and Goat
    Cheese, 264–66

R
rack of lamb, 129
    Indian-Spiced, with Potato Tikki and
        Mint Yogurt, 228–30
rack of veal, 131
    Celery Seed–Crusted Roast, with Red
        Pepper–Potato Pancakes,
        205–6
raclette, 8
    ONEc.p.s. Wild Mushroom and
        Truffle Macaroni and Cheese,
        106–7
    Potato Pancakes, 145–46
radiatore, 5
radishes:
    Mac and Cheddar Salad, 41
    Macaroni and Feta Salad, 65
raisins, in Sweet Noodle and Cheese
    Kugel, 68
ramps:
    Orecchiette con Fonduta, 47–48
    source for, 120
ras el hanout:
    Pastitsio, 61–64

source for, 120
Red Chile–Herb Crust, Macaroni with
    Many Cheeses in, 86–87
Reblochon cheese, in Tartiflette de
    Cocotte (Potato Gratin with Cheese
    and Bacon), 271–72
Red Bliss potatoes, 134
    Bacon Lovers' Mashed Potatoes,
        269–70
Red Devil Sauce, in Queens (N.Y.) Mac
    and Cheese, 39–40
red pepper(s):
    Potato Pancakes, 206
    roasting, 264
Renaud, Cyril, 296
    Braised Beef Cheeks with Fingerling
        Potato Purée, 56–58
Rendang, Beef, with Sweet
        Potato–Coconut Purée, Malaysian,
        185–86
rib-eye steak, 129
    Seared, with Crisp and Creamy
        Potatoes, 148–49
ricotta, 6, 8
    Baked Conchiglie with Roasted
        Garlic–Cheese Sauce, White Truffle
        Oil, and, 108–9
rigatoni, 5
    al Forno, 45–46
    Macaroni with Cantal Cheese and
        Westphalian Ham, 78–79
    Mozzarella Mac, 53–54
roasting, 128
robiola, 8
    Farfalle al Quattro Formaggi,
        49–50
Roquefort, 6, 8
    Penne with, 73
    Sauce, Joseph's Table Mac and
        Cheese with Dried Cherry Chutney
        and, 114–16

Rosemary-Marinated New York Strip
    Steak, Grilled, with Potato Gratin,
    141–142
Rosen, Ilene, 296-97
    City Bakery Macaroni and Cheese,
        21–22
    Roasted New Potatoes with Bacon,
        Chive Flowers, and Green Tomato
        Dressing, 273–74
Rösti Potatoes, Bacon, 151
rotelle, 5
    Wish Macaroni and Cheese, 51–52
rotini, 5
    Today's Macaroni and Cheese,
        84–85
Roulade of Pork, Sweet Potato–Stuffed,
    260–62
rubs, see spice rubs
Ruby Crescent fingerling potatoes,
    134
    Pan-Roasted, 157
russet (Idaho) potatoes, 134

S
salads:
    Mac and Cheddar, 41
    Macaroni and Feta, 65
    Potato, Tarragon, 143–44
    Sliced Steak and Mushroom, with
        Caramelized Onions and Bacon-
        Rösti Potatoes, 150–52
salsa, in Today's Macaroni and Cheese,
    84–85
salt, 10
Samson, Felino, 297
    Bomboa's Braised Short Ribs with
        Mashed Boniatos and Gingered
        Baby Bok Choy, 153–55
sauces:
    Balsamic–Apple Cider, 262
    Balsamic Syrup, 166

Bourbon-Ancho, 258
Chanterelle-Buttermilk Gravy,
    189–91
Green Tomato Dressing, 273
Mint Yogurt, 228
Mustard, 146
Pesto, 261
Ragù Bolognese, 195–96
Tomato, Warm Mild, 192
see also vinaigrettes
sausage:
    Chorizo, Potato, and Goat Cheese
        Quesadillas, 264–66
    chorizo and kielbasa, 130
    kielbasa, in Dutch Stamppot,
        267–68
    Pork, Macaroni and Cheese with
        Oysters and, 80–81
sautéeing, 128
scallions, in Mac and Cheddar Salad,
    41
Scallion-Smashed Potatoes, 254
Schwartz, Arthur, 297–98
    Roasted Beef Shanks with Vegetables
        and Potatoes, 169–70
Schwartz, Joan:
    Lamb-Stuffed Potato Kubbeh,
        246–47
    Mac and Cheddar Salad, 41
    Macaroni and Feta Salad, 65
    Mozzarella Mac, 53–54
    Old-Fashioned Shepherd's Pie,
        244–45
    Simple Mac and Cheese for Two,
        35
    Sweet Noodle and Cheese Kugel,
        68
    Swiss Mac with Potatoes, 67
    Veal Chops, Country-Style, with
        Potatoes and Mushrooms,
        203–4

Veal Croquettes with Dilled New
    Potatoes, 213–14
seafood:
    Cod, Macaroni and Cheese Provençal
        with, 57–58
    Lobster, Chunks of, Swimming in
        Cheesy Macaroni, 112–13
    Oysters, Macaroni and Cheese with
        Pork Sausage and, 80–81
shells, 4
    Ten-Minute Mac and Cheese, 34
    see also baby shells; conchiglie
shell, or strip loin, steak, 129
    Grilled, with Raclette Potato
        Pancakes, 145–47
    New York, Grilled Rosemary-
        Marinated, with Potato Gratin,
        141–42
shepherd's pies:
    of Beef Shank Braised in Zinfandel,
        171–73
    of Merlot-Braised Oxtail, 174–77
    Old-Fashioned, 244–45
    Short Rib, with Borlotti Beans and
        Chive Potato Crust, 160–62
    Slow-Braised Veal and Vanilla Sweet
        Potato, 210–12
shiitake mushrooms:
    in Macaroni with Many Cheeses in
        Red Chile–Herb Crust, 86–87
    Slow-Braised Veal and Vanilla Sweet
        Potato Shepherd's Pie, 210–12
    Tartiflette de Cocotte (Potato Gratin
        with Cheese and Bacon),
        271–72
Shinn, Barbara, 298
    Dad Page's Macaroni and Cheese,
        23–24
short macaroni, 4
    London Mac and Cheese, 17–18
short rib(s), see beef short rib(s)

side dishes:
    Apple Slices, Sautéed, 201–2
    Bok Choy, Gingered Baby, 155
    Granny Smith Apple Slices, Grilled,
        255
    Leek Garnish, 254
    Okra, Onion, and Tomato Stew, 239
    see also potato side dishes; sweet
        potato(es)
Simple Mac and Cheese for Two, 35
skirt steak, 129
    Sliced, and Mushroom Salad with
        Caramelized Onions and Bacon-
        Rösti Potatoes, 150–152
Smashed Potatoes, Scallion, 254
Smoked Cheddar, Mac and, with Ham
    and Chipotles, 90–91
Snell, William, 298
    Tartiflette de Cocotte (Potato Gratin
        with Cheese and Bacon), 271–72
Soho Grand, Mac and Cheese,
    19–20
Soup, Split Pea, Ham, and Potato, 263
sources, 135–37
Sparks, Katy, 298-99
    Macaroni with Many Cheeses in Red
        Chile–Herb Crust, 86–87
spice rubs:
    Barbecue, 163
    New Mexican, 256
Spicy Short Rib–Stuffed Potatoes,
    163–65
Spilchal, Joachim Bernard, 269
Split Pea, Ham, and Potato Soup, 263
spinach:
    Baby, Farfalle with Fontina, Tasso
        Ham, and, 76–77
    Baked Stuffed Pasta Spirals,
        100–101
    Greek (and Organic) Macaroni and
        Cheese, 59–60

Terrine of Macaroni, Goat Cheese,
    and Foie Gras, 82–83
squash (winter), in Moroccan-Spiced
    Cassoulet, 158–59
Stamppot, Dutch, 267–68
Stanton, Deborah, 299
    Beef Short Rib Hash with Sunny
        Eggs and Balsamic Syrup,
        166–68
    Brine-Marinated Pork Chops with
        Scallion-Smashed Potatoes and
        Grilled Granny Smith Apple Slices,
        253–55
steaks, 127,129
    Filet Mignon, Grilled, with Tarragon
        Potato Salad, Beefsteak Tomatoes,
        and Mustard Vinaigrette,
        143–44
    New York Strip, Grilled Rosemary-
        Marinated, with Potato Gratin,
        141–42
    Rib-Eye, Seared, with Crisp and
        Creamy Potatoes, 148–49
    Shell, Grilled, with Raclette Potato
        Pancakes, 145–47
    Sliced, and Mushroom Salad with
        Caramelized Onions and Bacon-
        Rösti Potatoes, 150–52
stewing, 128
stews:
    Boeuf Bourguignon, 183–84
    Lamb, Chef Frank's Flavorful,
        142–43
    Okra, Onion, and Tomato, 239
    Provençal Bouilli (Boiled Beef and
        Vegetables), 181–82
    Veal, Baked with Gnocchi, 207–9
strip loin steak, see shell, or strip loin,
    steak
Stuffed Pasta Spirals, Baked,
    100–101

Sundstrom, John, 299
    Herb-Grilled Lamb Chops with
        Chanterelle and Potato Hash,
        223–25
    Shepherd's Pie of Merlot-Braised
        Oxtail, 174–77
Susser, Allen, 300
    Celery Seed–Crusted Veal Roast with
        Red Pepper–Potato Pancakes,
        205–6
    Macaroni and Manchego, 66
Svizzera, La (Italian-Style Hamburgers)
    with Prosciutto Mashed Potatoes,
    217–19
Sweetened Mascarpone and Noodle
    Pudding, 117–18
Sweet Noodle and Cheese Kugel, 68
Sweet potato(es), 134
    Coconut Purée, 186
    Cuban (boniatos), 133
    Mashed Boniatos, 154
    Moroccan-Spiced Cassoulet,
        158–59
    Roasted Yams, 249
    –Stuffed Roulade of Pork, 260–62
    Vanilla, and Slow-Braised Veal
        Shepherd's Pie, 210–12
Swiss cheese, 5–6, 8
    Macaroni Gratin Mas Antoine,
        55–56
    Swiss Mac with Potatoes, 67
Swiss Mac with Potatoes, 67
Syrup, Balsamic, 166

T
Taleggio, 8
    Farfalle al Quattro Formaggi,
        49–50
Tardi, Alan, 3, 300
    Rigatoni al Forno, 45–46
Tarragon Potato Salad, 143–44

Tartiflette de Cocotte (Potato Gratin with Cheese and Bacon), 271–72
Ten-Minute Mac and Cheese, 34
Terrine of Macaroni, Goat Cheese, and Foie Gras, 82–83
"thimbles," see ditali
Tikki, Potato, 229–30
"tiny dough," see pastina
tomato(es):
　　Concasse, 115–16
　　Dad Page's Macaroni and Cheese, 23–24
　　Greek (and Organic) Macaroni and Cheese, 59–60
　　Green Chile Mac and Cheese, 88–89
　　Green, Dressing, 273
　　London Mac and Cheese, 17–18
　　Macaroni and Cheese Provençal with Cod, 57–58
　　Macaroni and Feta Salad, 65
　　Macaroni with Duck Prosciutto, Chanterelles, and Mascarpone, 95–96
　　Mom's Mac and Cheese with, 38
　　Mozzarella Mac, 53–54
　　Okra, and Onion Stew, 239
　　oven-roasting, 18
　　Pastitsio, 61–64
　　Sauce, 62
　　Sauce, Warm Mild, 192
　　Tomatoey Mac and Cheese, 36–37
toppings, crisp, 8–9
Torres, Sue, 300–1
　　Chorizo, Potato, and Goat Cheese Quesadillas, 264–66
tortillas, in Chorizo, Potato, and Goat Cheese Quesadillas, 264–66
tortilla crumbs, 9
　　Green Chile Mac and Cheese, 88–89

Treviño, Diana Barrios, 277
　　Chiles Rellenos with Warm Mild Tomato Sauce, 192–94
truffle(d)(s) and truffle oil:
　　black, source for, 137
　　butter, source for, 136
　　Fresh, Pasta with Fonduta and, 104–5
　　Macaroni and Cheese, California, 110–11
　　Mashed Potatoes, 235–36
　　Mashed-Potato Topping (for shepherd's pie), 176
　　oil, source for, 137
　　Potato Gratin, 142
　　sources for, 120
　　White, and Fontina Macaroni, 102–3
　　White, Oil, Baked Conchiglie with Roasted Garlic–Cheese Sauce, Ricotta Cheese and, 108–9
　　white, oil, in Orecchiette con Fonduta, 47–48
　　and Wild Mushroom Macaroni and Cheese, ONEc.p.s., 106–7
turnips, in Provençal Bouilli (Boiled Beef and Vegetables), 59–60

V
vanilla, in Sweet Noodle and Cheese Kugel, 68
Vanilla Sweet Potato and Slow-Braised Veal Shepherd's Pie, 210–12
veal, cuts of, 131
veal and potatoes, 199–214
　　Celery Seed–Crusted Veal Roast with Red Pepper–Potato Pancakes, 205–6
　　Country-Style Veal Chops with Potatoes and Mushrooms, 203–4

Slow-Braised Veal and Vanilla Sweet Potato Shepherd's Pie, 210–12
Veal Croquettes with Dilled New Potatoes, 213–14
Veal Stew Baked with Gnocchi, 207–9
Veal Tournedos with Caramelized and Creamy Potatoes and Sautéed Apple Slices, 200–2
veal chops, 131
　　Country-Style, with Potatoes and Mushrooms, 203–5
　　Veal Tournedos with Caramelized and Creamy Potatoes and Sautéed Apple Slices, 200–2
Velveeta, 8
　　Queens (N.Y.) Mac and Cheese, 39–40
venison:
　　Arrows' Leg of, with Roasted Yams, 248–49
　　sources for, 137
Vinaigrette, Mustard, 143

W
"wagon wheels," see rotelle
　　walnuts, in Baked Stuffed Pasta Spirals, 100–101
Wilder, Janos, 301
　　Macaroni with Duck Prosciutto, Chanterelles, and Mascarpone, 95–96
Wilder, Joyce, 301
　　Mom's Mac and Cheese with Tomatoes, 38
wine:
　　Merlot-Braised Oxtail, Shepherd's Pie of, 174–77
　　Zinfandel-Braised Beef Shank, Shepherd's Pie of, 171–73

Wish Macaroni and Cheese, 51–52
Wrede, Joseph, 301
    Joseph's Table Mac and Cheese with
        Dried Cherry Chutney and
        Roquefort Sauce, 114–16

Y
Yams, Roasted, 249
Yeo, Patricia, 302
    Malaysian Beef Rendang with Sweet
        Potato–Coconut Purée,
        185–86
Yogurt–Béchamel Topping, 63
Yogurt, Mint, 228
Yukon Gold potato(es), 134
    Bacon Lovers' Mashed Potatoes,
        269–70

Baeckoefe (Alsatian Meat-and-Potato
    Casserole), 215–16
Beef Short Rib Hash with Sunny
    Eggs and Balsamic Syrup,
    166–68
Caramelized, 201
and Chanterelle Hash, 224
Chive Crust (for shepherd's pie), 161
Country-Style Veal Chops with
    Mushrooms and, 203–4
Mashed, Topping (for shepherd's
    pie), 172–73
Moroccan-Spiced Cassoulet, 158–59
Salad, Tarragon, 143–44
Scallion-Smashed, 254
Tartiflette de Cocotte (Potato Gratin
    with Cheese and Bacon), 271–72

Truffled Mashed, 235–36
Truffled-Mashed-, Topping (for
    shepherd's pie), 176

Z
Zinfandel-Braised Beef Shank,
    Shepherd's Pie of, 171–73
ziti, 5
    Baked Macaroni with White Cheddar
        Cheese and Cremini Mushrooms,
        93–94
    London Mac and Cheese,
        17–18
    Pasta with Fonduta and Fresh
        Truffles, 104–5
    Terrine of Macaroni, Goat Cheese,
        and Foie Gras, 82–83